teach yourself...

Paradox 5.0

for Windows

Douglas J. Wolf

MIS:
PRESS

A Subsidiary of
Henry Holt and Co., Inc.

Copyright 1994 by MIS:Press
a subsidiary of Henry Holt and Company, Inc.
115 West 18th Street
New York, New York, 10011

First Edition—1994

Wolf, Douglas J., 1956–
  Teach yourself--Paradox 5.0 for Windows / Douglas J. Wolf.
    p. cm.
  Includes index.
  ISBN 1-55828-359-5 : $21.95
  1. Data base management. 2. Paradox for Windows (Computer file)
  I. Title.
  QA76.9.D3W655 1994
  005.75'65--dc20   94-22466
                     CIP

Printed in the United States of America.

10 9 8 7 6 5 4 3 2 1

MIS:Press books are available at special discounts for bulk purchases for sales promotions, premiums, fund-raising, or educational use. Special editions or book excerpts can also be created to specification.

For details contact: Special Sales Director
              MIS:Press
              a subsidiary of Henry Holt and Company, Inc.
              115 West 18th Street
              New York, New York 10011

Trademarks

Publisher: Brenda McLaughlin
Managing Editor: Cary Sullivan
Development Editor: Laura Lewin
Production Editor: Stephanie Doyle
Production Assistant: Joseph McPartland

Dedication

I hereby dedicate this book to members of the Concord Coalition. The Concord Coalition was founded by Senators Paul Tsongas and Warren Rudman for the single purpose of eliminating the deficit and paying off the debt of the United States.

At the time of this writing, the debt is over 4.5 trillion dollars. Or, equal to 17,000 dollars for every person in the U.S. We are borrowing at the rate of 500 million dollars per day. Literally, we are borrowing to pay interest on our old debt. No nation can survive this indefinitely. We are close to collapse.

The *paradox* of huge amounts of government spending, which should give us prosperity, full employment and a utopian social situation, is that our debt and deficit is producing the opposite.

The members are determined to keep the pressure on Congress to make the hard choices to stave off bankruptcy. If you are so inclined, call 1-800-231-6800 to join.

Contents

Chapter 3: Viewing and Locating Records in Tables.................................... 69

Chapter 4: Creating Tables 97

Chapter 5: Table Fine-Tuning........................ 135

Chapter 6: Retrieving Information by Query.. 179

Chapter 7: Paradox Reports 215

Chapter 8: Working with the Form Screen ... 245

Acknowledgments

Special thanks to Laura Lewin, and Stephanie Doyle at MIS:Press, and Nan Borreson at Borland International.

Introduction

Teach yourself...Paradox 5.0 for Windows, contains 9 chapters designed to take you through the intricacies of Paradox for Windows. What may seem like complicated processes are broken down into manageable units. The sequence of chapters is designed to help you build skills from one chapter to the next so that you can expand your ability to work with Paradox for Windows.

You may examine the chapters in order to build on your skills. At the same time, the book is designed so you are able to look up the specific task you need to accomplish after you know the basics. The most important basic is learning to create and edit a table, which takes you through *Chapter 4*.

The sample tables that can be installed with Paradox are used in this book to illustrate procedures. If you did not install those sample tables, go back to your original set of disks and start the install process so that you can add the sample tables.

1

What Paradox for Windows Is

Borland continues to publish software programs that combine power with simplicity. The name *Paradox*, a contradictory statement, represents the conundrum of power combined with simplicity. The consistent and clear menu system, along with the Paradox for Windows SpeedBar, allows you to use just what you need to get the job done. But, when you need additional power, Paradox for Windows can handle that too. Described briefly, Paradox for Windows is a full-featured relational database management system for use by itself or with a network. From beginner to experienced database user, the tool enhances database productivity.

Who This Book Is For

The beginning to intermediate Paradox for Windows user will get the most from this book. It is full of details, explanations, and tips that will enhance their understanding of a database in general and a relational database specifically. The beginning computer user will find this book a welcome place to start learning about databases.

This is an introductory book, not a reference book. Therefore, you will not know everything there is to know about Paradox for Windows when you complete this book. You will learn the fundamentals about creating and editing tables, doing a query, searching and sorting data, and creating reports and graphs. Once you have completed this book, you will have a greater understanding of the Paradox for Windows documentation.

What This Book Teaches You

This book covers the ideas you need to understand in order to get the most out of Paradox. The chapters cover the following topics:

Chapter 1 discusses databases and the manner in which Paradox is used to create databases. The terms used to describe the Paradox tools and objects are explained.

Chapter 2 covers the fundamentals of the Paradox screen and how to access the menus. The Paradox desktop is illustrated. A sample database table is opened, and each of its components is described and examined.

Chapter 3 covers viewing and locating records in tables. The use of the locate and Navigation button are explained.

Chapter 4 shows you how to begin creating Paradox tables. A sample example table takes you through the basics of building your own table.

Chapter 5 expands your knowledge of table creation by adding validity checks, a lookup, and a picture entry.

Chapter 6 covers queries. A query is a question; you can ask questions of your database using Query by Example techniques. We begin with a simple query and build into a multitable, multiquery example.

Chapter 7 examines reports. After entering data into a table and creating a query, you then can print the answers to your query in the form of a report. Or, you can print mailing labels.

Chapter 8 covers the means to create form entry screens. Paradox tables can be created by entering data into a table or into a form. A form is closer to the paper world of data entry.

Chapter 9 delves into using the graphing abilities of Paradox to select the specific data you want and then represent it graphically on the screen. Printing graphs and linking is covered too.

System Requirements

You must have an IBM or IBM compatible personal computer that is 80386 or higher, with a minimum of 4 megabytes of RAM. I recommend that you have 8 megabytes of RAM. Also, you need a hard disk drive with at least 25 megabytes of free space plus one disk drive for 5.25-inch or 3.5-inch disks. You must have Microsoft Windows 3.0 or higher. While CGA monitors are not supported by Paradox for Windows, a variety of EGA and VGA monitors are supported. A mouse is required for design elements, but not for data entry.

Paradox for Windows Installation

Installing Paradox for Windows creates a directory on your hard disk for the application and sample files. The program is copied to the directory and added to the Windows Program Manager. The installation program modifies the **WIN.INI** initialization file so that Paradox is compatible with Windows.

Install Paradox for Windows by following these steps:

1. Start Windows.

2. Place the Paradox for Windows Program Disk #1 in drive A.

3. Click on **File/Run** from the Program Manager menu.

4. Type **A:\INSTALL** in the command line text box.

5. Click on **OK**.

A status window displays a list of the files the installation program is copying to the Windows directory. The Paradox for Windows Installation dialog box displays. At this point you choose whether or not to install the sample files. Be aware that the sample files require about 300K of disk space.

When the Paradox for Windows icon displays on the Windows Program Manager, Paradox for Windows is installed.

Chapter Formats and Conventions

Each chapter begins with an introduction and a list of the main headings found in the chapter. At the end of every chapter you find a summary that lists the keystrokes covered in the chapter in more detail.

The tasks included in each chapter are listed step by step. You will be able to accomplish any one of them. These practice sessions will build your confidence even further as your understanding of Paradox for Windows grows.

The conventions used in this book follow the format here:

Selecting a menu sequence such as the File menu and then the Print menu are recorded as: File/Print.

The characters and/or symbols you enter display as: **Victor**.

When using combination command keys, press the first key and hold it; then press the second key. This action is represented with a plus sign, such as: **Ctrl+R**.

A Windows Primer

If you are totally new to Windows, take a few moments to read and try the examples given in the next few paragraphs to become more comfortable with the Windows environment. If you are comfortable with Windows, jump ahead to the first chapter.

Every program that runs in Windows, runs in a *window*. A window is a box on the computer screen with a border. Paradox for Windows runs in an *application window*, while the other components, such as a report is in a window contained by the application window, called the *document window*. Paradox uses the terms *parent window* to describe the application window, and any other Paradox window is called a *child window*.

When you start Windows, the default window is the Program Manager. In it, are the main and accessories windows and the windows of any application that you have installed. If you are running Windows version 3.1, you can move the program icon for Paradox into the startup window. Doing so causes Windows to open Paradox automatically every time you start Windows.

You start any application (like Paradox) by double-clicking the icon that represents the program. After that, the program appears in its application window. The exercises that follow are general in that they apply to any Windows application.

Maximizing or Minimizing a Document Window

The document maximize and minimize buttons are located in the upper-right corner of the document window. They appear as upward- and downward-pointing triangles.

1. Move the mouse pointer to the upward-pointing arrow in the document window and click. The document window fills the entire screen. In place of the up and down triangles, a single button appears to the far right of the menu names. This is the restore button.

2. Click on the restore button. The document window resizes to less than full screen.

3. Click on the minimize button. Now the document window is reduced to an icon in the lower-left corner of the screen.

4. Click on the document icon. The Document Control menu appears.

5. Click on the restore button. The document is restored to the size it was prior to minimizing.

Keyboard Steps

You may also effect the same steps with your keyboard.

1. Press **Alt+Minus**. This opens the Document Control menu at the upper-left side of the screen.

2. Press **N** (the underlined letter in the word). The document window is minimized.

3. Press **Alt+Minus** again. The Document Control menu reappears.

4. Because **Restore** is the highlighted command, press **Enter**.

Moving a Dialog Box

To move a dialog box that appears inside a document window:

1. Click and hold on the title bar at the top of the dialog box and drag the box to where you want it to be displayed.

2. Release the mouse button. You cannot resize a dialog box.

Changing the Document Window Border Position

To resize any window on display by physically moving the border:

1. Move the mouse pointer to the left edge of the window, directly on the border. The pointer should change shape to a two-headed arrow, pointing left and right.

2. Click and hold the left mouse button.

3. Move the mouse pointer to the right. As you do, a translucent gray line moves with the pointer. The original border remains in place.

4. Release the mouse button. Immediately, the left border of the window shifts to the right.

Resizing the Document Window

One final manipulation of the window size is possible.

1. Move the mouse pointer to the lower-right corner of the window. The pointer should assume the shape of a two-headed arrow pointing diagonally, northwest to southeast.

2. Click and hold the left mouse button.

3. Move the mouse in any direction. The upper-left corner of the NoteBook window remains anchored, allowing you to move the translucent gray lines representing the right side and bottom borders to any position you choose.

4. Release the mouse button. The window assumes the new size.

Keyboard

Follow the keyboard steps above using the **Size** command on the Document Control menu.

Task Manager

The Task Manager in Windows is the fastest way to switch from one application to another. Unlike DOS, where you must close one application before opening another, with Windows you can open several applications in their respective windows, and access them at any time. The Task Manager keeps track of which application windows are open, listing them for your choosing.

To open the Task Manager and select an application:

1. Click on the application control button in the upper-left corner of the Window.

2. Click on the switch to button. The Task List dialog box appears with a list of all open applications.

3. Double-click on the application you wish to switch to, or click on the application name and then click on the switch to button.

You can also use this dialog box to close an application.

Moving the Mouse Pointer

Other mouse instructions used in this book include the following:

Instruction	Action
Point	Move the mouse pointer to a specific area on the screen.
Click	Quickly press and release the left mouse button. (You lefties can reset the mouse buttons so that the right button is the primary button.)
Double-click	Quickly press and release the left mouse button twice.
Click and Hold	Press the left mouse button and hold it down.
Click and Drag	Press and hold the left mouse button while moving the mouse pointer to extend the cell selection.

Moving the mouse pointer to a menu name and clicking opens that menu. With a menu open, you can move the mouse pointer to a menu selection and click to activate the item. As you can see, the use of the mouse is very intuitive. Once you begin using it to open menus and make selections, it becomes natural.

Chapter ▶ 1

Introducing Paradox
for Windows

You are ready to use your computer to collect and maintain information on a full-featured, relational database. But, just as important as the process of getting information into a database is the process of getting information out of the database in a useful format. In this chapter, you will learn about:

▼ Databases and how they work

▼ The difference between a flat-file database and a relational database

▼ Paradox for Windows terms

▼ The keyboard

9

What Is a Database?

Databases are tables of information. Your phone book is a *database table*. The categories of information in this table are the first and last name, the address, and the phone number. Your address book is a table of information with each entry having the category of name, address, and phone number. Though you may not think of these everyday items as databases, that is what they are. Even your desk blotter with the scribbled names and phone numbers is a database. The most important database table on your desk is probably your Rolodex. The term *table* is introduced here because Paradox for Windows is based on the concept of tables of information.

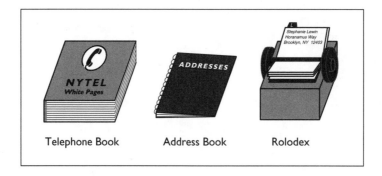

Figure 1.1 *Several familiar databases—a phone book, an address book, and a Rolodex. These are flat-file database tables*

All of these table examples have several things in common. First, they have individual records that are arranged in a particular order, usually alphabetical. A *record* is the several pieces of information that belong together. In the case of the phone book, the name, address, and phone number are the pieces of information that make up one record. Second, each record has its own line listing, in the case of the phone book, or its own Rolodex card. Third, the records are combined into a unit in the form of a phone or address book. Last, each individual piece of information, the phone number for instance, is located in the same position in every record.

By having each piece of information of a record in the same position, a *column* is created and at the top of that column is the column name. Figure 1.2 shows how information is arranged in a database table, with callouts to each of the components.

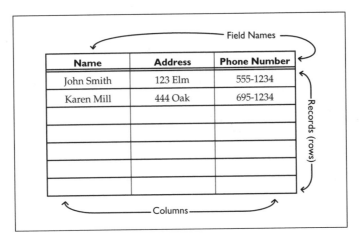

Figure 1.2 *A phone book database*

Here is one more definition; the intersection of the column with an individual record's piece of information is called a *field*. Each field contains a single piece of information. But, every record does not necessarily need to have information in each field.

The phone book works pretty well if you just need to look up phone numbers, assuming you know the name of the person you want to call. You use the alphabetical listing as your index, to find the name and then the phone number. The same is true with the Rolodex. But, what if you wanted to find a group of names that are in the same zip code. You could go through your Rolodex one card at a time and locate each card that matched the correct zip code. If you had only 50 cards, it would be easy. But, if you had several thousand, the task would be enormous. A database on a computer makes the same task a snap. A database management program can quickly scan thousands of records to find the matching zip code.

Any computer database can easily find records that have specific field entries. Remember that the zip code is entered into a field in each record. If all you want to do with Paradox is to find specific records and then print them or edit them, this is fine. However, any flat-file database can do that for you. What makes Paradox special is that it is a relational database.

A *relational database* can best be explained by the following example. Suppose that you have a business in which the same customer buys items from you many times. You begin with two tables of data, the customer information, and another table with product information. When a purchase occurs, a third table is created which combines the customer information with the products ordered. The third table is an invoice. It would make no sense for you to have to enter, by hand, all of the customer data and all of the product data in order to create the invoice. Instead, we use Paradox to assign a customer number to each customer record. Similarly, each product has a product number. Then, when we create the invoice, we simply type in the customer number and the product number and Paradox creates the third table automatically! The customer number and the product number, relate to a specific record in a different table. This relationship joins the information into an invoice. Figure 1.3 shows the relationship.

If you understand the idea of tables and how they can be related, you are well on your way to building your own tables of information.

Paradox for Windows Terms and Concepts

To work with Paradox for Windows effectively, review the terms that follow.

Tables

Tables are organized into *rows* and *columns*. A row of information is called one record. Each column holds one type of information. A column is called a field.

CUSTOMER

Customer Number	Name	Address
123	Bill Wolf	1 Palm St.

PRODUCT

Product Name	Product Number
Widget	620

INVOICE

Customer Number	Product Number	Cost	Quantity
123	620	$40–	2

Customer	Product	Amount
Bill Wolf	Widget	$80–

Figure 1.3 Two tables joined by the related numbers, create a third table

Records

A *record* holds information that is closely related to one person, place, or thing in one row. You can add as many records of information to your database as you need. In an address database, the name, address, and phone number of one person would appear on the same row.

Fields

A table holds a fixed number of columns, each of which holds a specific type of data. The information held in a column is called a *field* of data. Each column can hold numbers and letters that represent the information you want to maintain. You can view the information in a field in a list format, where the field columns are displayed vertically down the page. Once you define the fields necessary in a table of information, you will rarely add or delete a field.

After a table is created, there are a fixed number of fields, but no records. You add the records after the table is created. If you change the entry in a row, it does not affect the remainder of the database. However, if you add, delete, or change a field, the entire table is affected. For example, if you delete the phone number column, the phone number would be deleted for every record. On the other hand, deleting the phone number for a single record affects only that particular record. The other records are not affected.

Field Types

A database usually contains several types of information. Some of the information consists of alphabetic characters. The name of a product might consist of alphabetic and numeric characters. The field that holds the product's price holds only numeric characters.

When you design a Paradox for Windows database, you designate the type of information that can be entered in each field. You have nine *field types* from which to choose.

Alphanumeric

An *alphanumeric field* can contain letters, numbers, and symbols, such as $, &, %, +, and -. An address is an example of something you would put in an alphanumeric field because very often it consists of both letters and numbers.

Number

A *number field* can hold up to 15 digits, including decimal places. Paradox for Windows uses scientific notation to store numbers that are greater than 15 digits. Later you will be introduced to different ways of formatting numbers. Decimal places are not displayed in a number unless necessary and negative numbers appear with a minus sign (-) in front of them.

Remember that the way a number is formatted affects only the way it is displayed on screen, not the original number. For example, you have the number 1234.560007 and choose to format all numbers in a field with two decimal places. The number is stored as 1234.560007 but displays on the screen as 1234.56.

Money

Money fields are displayed with numbers rounded to two decimal places. In this format, negative numbers appear in parentheses and whole number separators are included. For example, the number 1234.560007 displays as $1,234.56. The number -1234.560007 displays as ($1,234.56). The number 1234 displays as $1,234.00.

Date

The *date field* type can refer to any date ranging from January 1, 100 to December 31, 9999, based on the Gregorian calendar. You can format dates in the standard format, such as MM/DD/YY. Other options are available, as in dd-Mon-yy,DD.MM.YY, or you can use YYY or YYYY as dates beyond the 20th century. Paradox for Windows does not let you enter invalid dates like **3/35/95**. Paradox for Windows allows you to sort and do arithmetic with the dates you enter in fields.

Time

This field will hold a value that indicates a time of day, noted in milliseconds. Two time formats can be used. One is the Windows time format, as defined in the Windows Control Panel International dialog box, and the second is the following format: hh:mm:ss am.

Time Stamp

A Time stamp field contains both a date and time value. The data is entered by pressing the Spacebar repeatedly until the correct data is entered.

Short Number

The *short number fields* are designed for use by advanced Paradox for Windows users. Short number fields contain only whole numbers and have a limited range. They are used in very large tables because they take less disk space than other numeric field types.

Memo

Memo fields hold text strings that are too long to place in alphanumeric fields. Use memo fields when you have more than 255 characters of text.

Formatted Memo

The formatted memo field allows you to enter text which includes formatting such as different typefaces, style, colors and sizes. The entire memo is not held in the field, but up to 45 characters are stored there. When you scroll the records, the entire memo is retrieved from your hard disk.

Graphic

Graphic fields hold graphic pictures. You can paint, draw, or scan pictures to be held as a value in a graphic field.

Object Linking and Embedding (OLE)

The *OLE fields* contain objects imported to Paradox for Windows from other Windows applications that also support OLE. Use OLE to place graphic fields when you want to be able to make changes to the graphic with Paradox for Windows.

Logical

Logical fields contain values that indicate a True or False condition. So, the field entry can indicate whether or not the record has a certain status.

Autoincrement

An autoincrement field contains long integer read-only values. Paradox inserts values automatically, beginning with the first record entered as 1, the second record 2 and so on. These values cannot be edited.

Binary

Used by Paradox for Windows application developers and advanced users, *binary fields* must be accessed through *ObjectPAL.* (ObjectPal is the Paradox tool used by programmers to design Paradox applications.) Use binary fields when working with data that Paradox for Windows is unable to interpret.

Bytes

This field type is used by ObjectPal applications and therefore is used by individuals for developing specific Paradox applications.

Paradox for Windows Objects

Paradox for Windows has a set of terms to describe the different components of the program. The different components are called *objects*. A table is an object. Similarly, when you ask a Paradox question (a *query*), Paradox creates another table with the answer. The answer table is another object. Let's go back to the example of the customer table and the product table. Both of these tables are objects, which can produce a third object, an invoice.

Tables

As discussed earlier, when you work with Paradox for Windows, you work with tables of information. You view tables, create tables, query (ask questions about) tables, and relate one table to another. So far in this chapter you have seen several examples of tables. Remember that tables are organized with columns of information, called fields, and that each row in the table contains one record of information.

Forms

When you view information from a table one record at a time, you are looking at the *form view*. The form view is similar to the Rolodex card in appearance. A form is a map that shows how one record displays on the screen. When you change information in a table, the corresponding information changes on the form. Forms can be simple, showing one record from a table, or complex, showing several records from one table or records from more than one table. An example of a Paradox for Windows form is shown in Figure 1.4.

Reports

A *report* is another object you design to represent one of your tables. Reports are printed to paper or to the screen and contain data that is sorted and grouped so that it is meaningful. Reports can be a simple listing of data or a complex arrangement of data from several tables linked together, including groupings and calculations. Figure 1.5 shows a simple report.

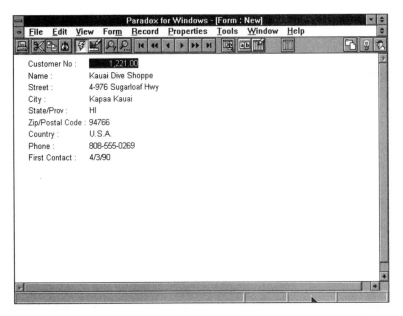

Figure 1.4 *A Record in form view*

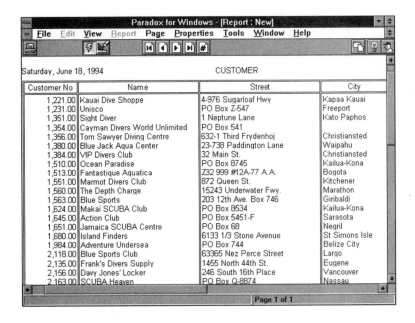

Figure 1.5 *A simple report*

Queries

A *query table* asks specific questions of the data in tables. As with other Paradox for Windows objects, you can combine tables in a query. Use a query to find or select information from a database table. The result of a query table is an answer table.

Scripts

You can create a *script* to record keystrokes, either simple or complex, that you use repeatedly. Once the keystrokes are recorded, you can replay the series of keystrokes by running a script.

Display Objects

Display objects are created using the design window SpeedBar. The display objects can be placed in the objects listed in the previous section to emphasize, highlight, feature, outline, or circle. Figure 1.6 shows the SpeedBar tools used to create display objects.

Boxes, Lines, Ellipses

Add visual emphasis using *boxes*, *lines*, and *ellipses*. Place boxes or ellipses around data you would like to feature. Lines can be used to point out specific items. These display objects make your documents more functional.

Text

With the *text tool*, create a container, then type text into the container. The text can be as long as you want it to be and formatted to your liking. The most frequent use of text is to add titles to tables, forms, and reports.

Graphics

Pictures can be placed in a graphic field as a piece of data. *Graphic images* can be placed in Paradox for Windows from a variety of formats. Cut and paste graphic images from the Windows clipboard, and they will be accepted regardless of the original format the graphic was saved in.

OLE Objects

Object Linking and Embedding lets you create a container for a file from another application. You select what you want the container to hold by inserting the source file. When you make changes to the source file, changes are also made in the *OLE object.* The object is linked to the source and embedded in your design.

Buttons

Place *buttons* in forms and attach ObjectPAL methods to them. By selecting the button, you can perform the operation defined in ObjectPAL.

Fields

Draw a *field object,* define it, and then place the field by itself in a design. Create calculated or summary fields to perform operations on table data.

Tables

Table objects that represent actual data tables can be placed in a document. This option allows you to mix single field tables and tables in the same document.

Multirecord Objects

Paradox for Windows can lay out data in a repeating pattern that you specify, using multirecord objects. Using *multirecord objects* allows you to see more than one record at a time in form view.

Graphs

Graphs can be the most advantageous way to present data. Click on the instant graph button to create a picture of your data. A graph can be customized by graph type, layout, and design.

Crosstabs

A *crosstab* converts a database table based on a relational model to a database similar to what you would find in a spreadsheet. A crosstab lets you analyze data by two factors, for example, finding salaries by education and gender. The two factors you use to analyze data in a crosstab are selected from fields in a table.

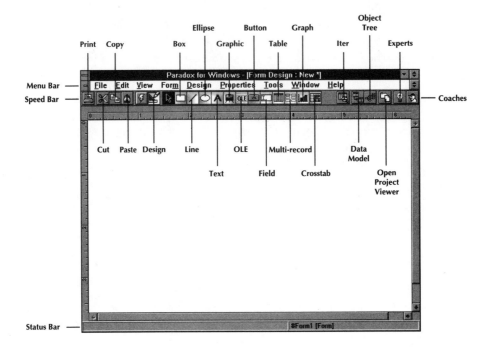

Figure 1.6 *SpeedBar tools for display objects*

Workspace

Think of an enormous table where you can display all of your data tables. This is the Paradox for Windows *workspace*. Paradox for Windows holds the table electronically and allows you to see only parts of it at one time. The screen is your window to this enormous workspace. Different tables can be brought into the workspace and moved around. When you are designing a new report, the workspace occupies the entire screen. When you are working with other objects, the SpeedBar options adjust across the top of the screen.

A Tour of the Keyboard

The computer keyboard consists of three main work areas. The *alphanumeric area* is in the center, where you will do most of your typing. This includes the **Shift**, **Ctrl**, **Alt**, and **Enter** keys.

A group of function keys appears either at the left of the alphanumeric area or across the top of the keyboard. The function keys, as the name implies, allow you to perform various functions in Paradox for Windows. A function key can be used by itself or in combination with the **Shift**, **Ctrl**, or **Alt** keys.

Most of the functions you will perform are done with the mouse, but at times, using the keyboard to perform certain functions is quicker. When this is the case, the keyboard function keys are included in this book.

To the right of the alphanumeric area, either alone or with a numeric keyboard, are the arrow keys. The number keys along with the **Enter** key and **Backspace** key are the most frequently used keys when using Paradox for Windows.

Although it is much quicker to use the mouse, you can use the **Tab** key to move between rows and columns in a table. The **Enter** key is used to select a menu option, end a task, move to another field, and insert extra lines in a report or script function. Clicking the mouse also accomplishes most of these tasks.

While in the Edit mode, delete data from fields using the **Backspace** key. Press the **Backspace** key, and the character to the left of the blinking insertion point is deleted. Hold down the **Ctrl** key and the **Backspace** key at the same time, and you delete all the data in the field.

Mouse Actions

Clicking the left mouse button accomplishes all kinds of activities in Paradox for Windows. Double-clicking icons opens files in Paradox for Windows. Clicking and dragging objects moves them to a new location. Clicking and dragging is used mostly with Display Objects. To make a selection with the mouse, put the mouse pointer on the selection you wish to make, click the mouse, and your selection is made.

Using Property Inspection

Every object in Paradox for Windows has *properties*. Properties are the visual characteristics of an object, such as the colors that display on screen or the font used for text. Right-click the mouse to display the properties for that object. The Property menu is shown. A sample Property menu is shown in Figure 1.7. From the Property menu, you can select **new properties**, to change the visual characteristics shown.

 **Shift+F2**

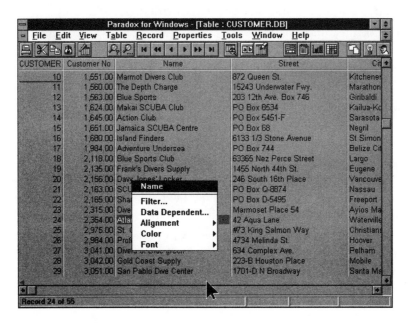

Figure 1.7 *The Property menu*

Command Summary

Command:	Mouse Click:	Keyboard Press:
Property Inspection	Right mouse button	Shift+F

Summary

In *Chapter 2*, we start Paradox for Windows and learn about the Paradox work-space components and the Paradox menus.

Chapter 2

Starting Paradox for Windows

In *Chapter 2*, we will look at the many aspects of the desktop that Paradox presents when you begin working. In addition, we will open one of the sample database tables and examine its structure.

Keep in mind that, in most cases, the first thing you will undertake with Paradox is either to open an existing table of data or to create a table structure in which to enter data. Before we can do either of those things, we must examine the Paradox desktop and the tools thereon. Take time to understand each of the tools. By doing so, you will progress much faster in your understanding of Paradox. In this chapter, you will learn how to:

▼ Start Paradox for Windows

▼ Select menu items

▼ Get Help from Paradox for Windows

▼ Look at a table

▼ Use the SpeedBar

▼ Leave Paradox for Windows

Starting Paradox

At this point, Paradox for Windows should be installed on your computer. The steps for installing Paradox for Windows can be found in the *Introduction* to this book. If you have not installed Paradox, do so now and make sure that the sample tables are installed at the same time.

To start Paradox for Windows, you access the Windows **Program Manager** by following the steps listed here:

1. At the C:> prompt, type **CD\WINDOWS**.

2. Press **Enter**.

3. Type **WIN**.

4. Press **Enter**.

The Windows Program Manager screen displays as shown in Figure 2.1.

In the Windows Program Manager screen, double-click on the Paradox for Windows icon. If you cannot see the Paradox for Windows icon, click on the Window menu at the top of the screen. A menu appears as shown in Figure 2.2.

In the pull-down menu, a list of installed Windows appears. A check mark is next to the window that is currently selected. On your screen, if Paradox does not appear, click on the **More Windows** item at the bottom of the menu. The menu now contains more installed windows. If you still do not see Paradox, click on **More Windows** again. If it is still not there, Paradox has not been properly installed. The Paradox icon looks like a picture of a check mark on a piece of paper. When you see the Paradox icon, double-click on it. In a few moments, the Paradox desktop appears.

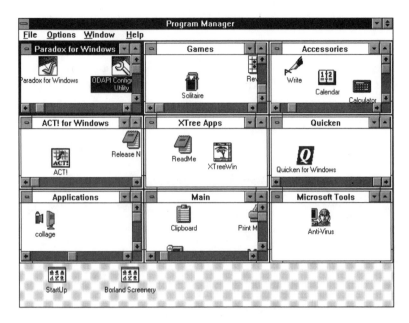

Figure 2.1 *The Windows Program Manager screen*

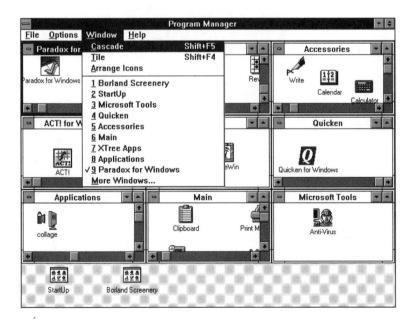

Figure 2.2 *Window menu*

The Desktop

The *desktop* is the command center for creating tables entering data, and creating reports. The desktop is shown in Figure 2.3 with the components noted.

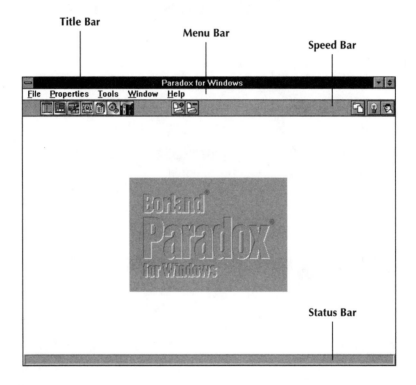

Figure 2.3 Paradox for Windows desktop

The Screen Components

Across the top of the screen, in the Title Bar, is the name of the application, Paradox for Windows. At the extreme top left corner of the screen is the control menu button, shown in Figure 2.4, which is common to all Windows applications and was discussed in the *Introduction*.

The second section down on the screen is the list of menus, beginning with File and ending with Help. This is called the *menu bar*.

The next section down is the *SpeedBar*. On the SpeedBar are icons (pictures) that can be clicked on to execute Paradox functions.

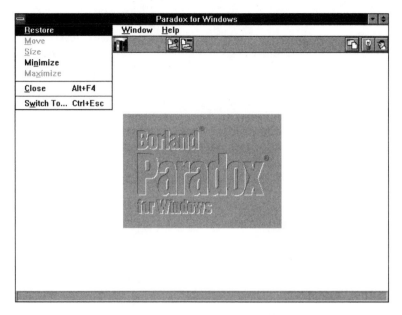

Figure 2.4 *Control menu opened*

The icons on the SpeedBar are also called *tools* or *buttons.* Don't be confused if you see these terms used interchangeably, such as "click on the open table button" or "click the open form tool."

N O T E

For example, the first icon is open table. When you click on this icon, Paradox opens the list of tables that have been created previously. The next icon is the open form icon, which opens forms that you have created. The third icon is the Open Query icon. Next you have the Open SQL Script, followed by the Open Report, Open Script and Open Library icons. Next are the Add Reference and Remove Reference icons. The Open Project Viewer icon appears at the far right of the Speedbar, next to the Expert and Coaches buttons. The Expert and Coaches are interactive Help buttons, that can guide you in the process of building tables and other Paradox objects. Each will be discussed later.

A helpful feature of Paradox is that if you move the mouse pointer over an icon—without clicking—the name of the button appears at the lower-left corner of the screen. For example, if the pointer is on the open table icon, the words *Open Table* appear in the lower-left corner of the status line.

N O T E

At the bottom of the application window is the *status line*. As mentioned in the previous paragraph, this is where you see a variety of messages. Not only are the names of the buttons displayed, but several other messages appear. We will discuss these messages as they appear. For example, with a table open on-screen, the record number and the total number of records in the table is noted.

As you use Paradox, four areas are always visible. The title bar, the menu bar functions, the SpeedBar, plus the status line. What you will see in each of those areas is dependent upon the type of object you are working with at the time. A table is one kind of object, while a report is a different type of object.

Working with the Paradox Menu System

From the opening screen or desktop, you move objects, open and close files, and access other Windows applications. The Desktop menu, which includes the File and Help menu options, is the main menu in Paradox for Windows. As objects in Paradox are created, the menu changes depend on the object in the window.

Escaping a Menu Sequence

If you select a menu item or a submenu item and then decide you do not want to take any action, how do you get out? Using the mouse, you simply click on the workspace. The menus you have selected no longer display on the screen.

If you prefer, use the keyboard method to escape out of menus. With menus and submenus open, press **Escape** until the menus are cleared from the screen.

Changing the Paradox Window Size

When you start Paradox, its windows should automatically be Maximized. If so, then you will only see the Restore and Minimize buttons. If it is not maximized, you will also see an up pointing arrow, the Maximize button.

> **1.** Click the *Restore button*. Paradox is reduced to either an icon at the bottom of the screen or one of several windows on the desktop, depending on your screen layout. This concept is confusing when first encountered. The idea behind Windows is that it tries to resemble your physical desk-

top as closely as possible. So, you can open Paradox, a word processor or any other number of applications and switch to each as needed.

In Figure 2.5, Paradox appears as one of the windows, just as it did when we first started Windows. One difference is important. Paradox is still running; it has not been closed—only its window has been reduced.

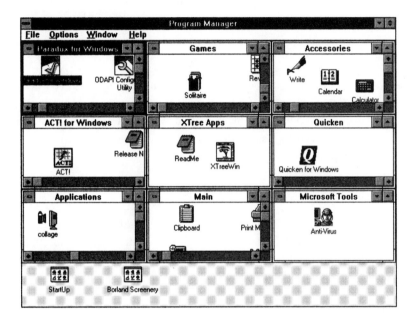

Figure 2.5 *Paradox window reduced*

2. Clicking on the maximize button makes Paradox full-screen again.

The essential idea in the previous exercise is this: With Windows as your environment, you can minimize the application that is currently on the screen and easily switch to another application without having to close the first application completely. If you have used DOS based programs, you know how time consuming switching from one program to another can be.

Parent and Child Windows

The desktop is another name for the Paradox window. This is the *parent window* in Paradox for Windows. Other windows that you open in Paradox for Windows are *child windows* to the parent. For example, when you access the

Help window, a new window opens. The Help window is a child window to the desktop parent window.

The Help window holds its own Control menu, minimize and maximize buttons, and menu and title bars. In the same way, forms display in a form window, and queries display in a query window. The child windows can be acted upon independently but cannot exist without the parent window. The commands of the desktop or parent window remain available in a child window.

The Mouse

Use the keyboard for data entry, but use the mouse for other functions in Paradox for Windows. Already you have used the mouse to select a menu item. Point the mouse arrow on the menu item you wish to select and click, and the menu displays. Take advantage of the mouse when performing other Paradox for Windows functions.

Direct Manipulation

Things that appear on the Paradox for Windows desktop are objects. Use the mouse to manipulate objects on the desktop. This includes such things as clicking and dragging an object to move it. There are many other ways to manipulate objects directly. Some of them are listed here:

▼ Move the mouse pointer to the edge of the object window. A two-headed arrow displays. Click and drag the two-headed arrow to resize the object window.

▼ Move the mouse pointer to the edge of a field column. Click and drag the two-headed arrow to resize the column.

▼ Point the mouse pointer at the title bar in the object window. Click and drag to move the object window on the desktop.

▼ Click and drag a column, moving it to a new location in a database table.

From these examples, you can see that direct manipulation is used to change the size, shape, and position of objects on the desktop.

The Menus

On the Paradox for Windows opening screen you see several menu items, File, Properties, Window, and Help. As you create objects, more menu items display on the menu bar as do more icons. A *menu* is simply a list of options that you can select for purposes of creating tables, editing records, printing reports or a number of different actions in Paradox. Let's take a look at the File menu.

Click on the File menu name. The File menu displays as you see in Figure 2.6. From the File menu you create new tables and open tables, print files, and access directories, information, and network features.

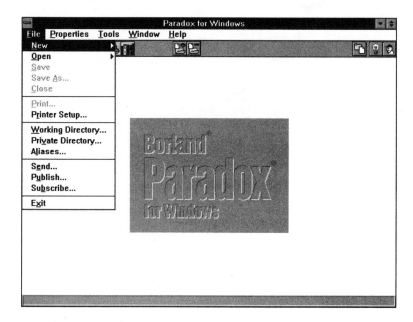

Figure 2.6 *The File menu*

File Menu Options

The list of menu *options* appears as in Figure 2.6. The first thing you may notice is that some of the options are followed by three periods (called ellipses by the cognoscente), which means that if that option is selected, a *dialog box* appears. Some of the other options have a right-pointing triangle at the far right. This triangle indicates that selecting that option causes Paradox to open a *submenu*, which lists more menu options. Last, several of the options are gray colored, and if you click on them, nothing happens. This is due to the fact that at the present moment, that option cannot be used. For example, if you have not created any object, there is nothing to save, and so the Save menu option is not usable.

File/New

Click on **New** on the File menu. A submenu displays (Figure 2.7) from which you select the new object you wish to create. From this menu, create a new form, library, query, report, script, table, or SQL file.

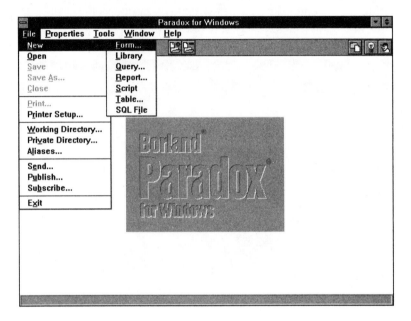

Figure 2.7 *File/New submenu*

Notice that some of the options that you can create have the ellipses following the option. This means that a dialog box opens if you select that option. Let's take a look at a dialog box.

1. Click on the **Form** option. The dialog box appears as shown in Figure 2.8.

You are presented with a dialog box that offers three choices. First, you can start with a completely blank form and design from scratch. Second, you can use the help provided by the Form Expert. The Form Export is the interactive guide to building a form. Last, you can select the Data Model/Layout Design Diagram option. To use this option, Paradox needs to know which table to use to create a form, so it lists the currently available tables in the Data Model dialog box. All dialog boxes have the same characteristics. They run in a child window. Each dialog box has Cancel and Help buttons.

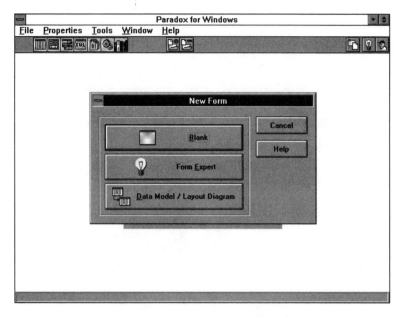

Figure 2.8 *File/New Form Data Model dialog box*

2. Click the Data Model/Layout Diagram button. The Data Model dialog appears as in Figure 2.9.

3. Click Cancel to close the dialog.

File/Open

Click on the File menu again to look at the other options. Click on the **Open** option. Paradox opens a submenu with seven more options. Normally, you cannot open any of these options unless you have first created them. However, because you have installed the Sample tables along with Paradox, you will be able to look at some objects right away. Before opening a table, let's continue to examine the remaining options on the File menu.

File/Printer Setup

Click on the **Printer Setup** option. Figure 2.10 shows a typical printer setup.

As you can see, two printers are currently available. Printers must be installed via Windows, not Paradox. If you have connected a printer that Windows does not know about, Paradox will be unable to use it. However, Paradox does allow you to modify the settings for a particular printer. For instance, if you want to change the print resolution of a laser printer, you can do so by selecting the printer and clicking on the **Modify Printer Setup** option. Click on the cancel button to close the dialog box.

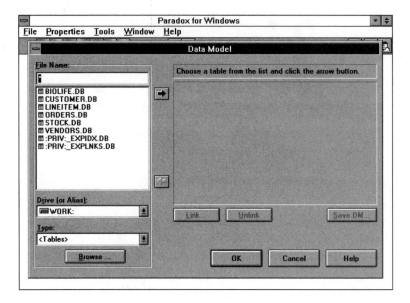

Figure 2.9 *Data Model dialog box*

These settings are not something that you need to be concerned with. To change them, you must exit Paradox and use the Configuration Utility, and this is a process for advanced users only.

▼ **Experts.** The Experts option opens the Expert control Panel. From here, you can start the Form, Mailing Labels or Report Expert assistant.

▼ **SQL Tools.** This option allows you to create aliases, new tables, delete a table, copy a table, manage indices, create Ad Hoc queries or examine the structure of a table, all in the SQL environment.

▼ **OBEX Address Book.** If you are using the EMAIL capabilities of Paradox, you will need a place to store the addresses of those people to which you want to send tables, reports and so on. Paradox provides a handy address book for that purpose. You can enter the person's name and then identify which EMAIL service to which they are connected.

▼ **OBEX Poll.** The Poll option logs onto the service to which you are connected and sends messages/objects to the recipients as you designated.

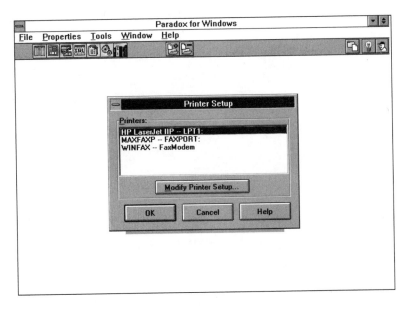

Figure 2.10 *Printer Setup dialog box*

File/Working Directory

This option determines where Paradox tries to find the tables you have created or where it saves newly created tables. This menu is important when you have several distinct tables and their supporting objects, such as reports, forms, and scripts, and each of those distinct tables should be in a separate DOS directory. Setting up new DOS directories may not be within you range of knowledge at this point, but at the end of the chapter a step-by-step example is given.

Upon installation, Paradox creates a subdirectory called WORKING, and this is the automatic (*default*) location for your tables. Another subdirectory that is created is SAMPLE, which contains several tables that we will be looking at shortly. In Figure 2.11, the Set Working Directory dialog box is displayed.

When you begin a Paradox work session, you can select the **Set Working Directory** option to determine which files you want to appear in the File/Open dialog box. If you do have several distinct subdirectories, you can tell Paradox which of the subdirectories you want to access when performing file activities.

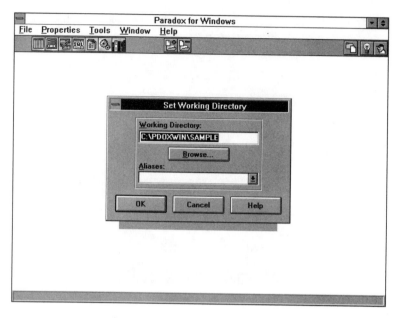

Figure 2.11 *Set Working Directory dialog box*

File/Private Directory

When you perform certain Paradox functions, such as Query, the result or answer to the query must be stored somewhere temporarily. When Paradox is installed, it creates as subdirectory called PRIVATE in order to store those tables.

File/Aliases

In the real world, an alias is a name that stands for another name. So it is with Paradox. DOS has created a logical, but complicated way of finding locations on a hard disk. For example, the location on your hard disk for Paradox file is in the PDOXWIN directory. Under that directory are the subdirectories, WORK-ING, SAMPLE, and PRIVATE. To enter the location for files, you may have to type **C:\PDOXWIN\WORKING\ACCOUNTING** as the path for Paradox to follow to find your files. The idea behind an alias is to substitute a short word for that long series of keystrokes. In this chapter, we create a subdirectory and assign an alias to it.

Send, Publish and Subscribe

These options are for sharing files or data on a network such as Windows for WorkGroups, or using EMAIL systems or an outside service such as MCI mail. In

Paradox, a program called OBEX connects Paradox to a wide variety of mail services, either on a network or to an outside service. In the past, setting up Paradox to work with all the different forms of EMAIL was very difficult. OBEX is designed to eliminate that hassle.

File/Exit

Click on this option, and you are out of Paradox. If you do it accidentally, do not worry—Paradox automatically saves your tables so nothing is lost, except any temporary tables. More on this later.

Properties Menu

The items on the Properties menu reflect what object you are working with at the time you open the menu. This feature makes sense in that Paradox does not overwhelm you with choices that cannot be used. The choices on the Properties menu when you have no objects open on the desktop are shown in Figure 2.12, the dialog box for Desktop Properties.

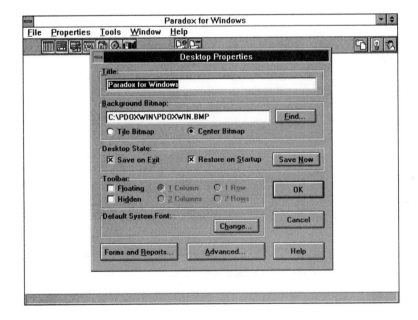

Figure 2.12 *Desktop Properties dialog box*

In this dialog box, Paradox allows you to change the Title that appears at the top of the Application window, change the Background Bitmap, change the position of the Speedbar (if you would prefer it not to be at the top of the window) and several other advanced features. At this juncture, you do not need to change anything. Note that there are two Desktop State settings that are set to on. The Save on Exit and Restore on Startup. As was mentioned previously, if you accidentally exit Paradox, the Save on exit setting saves your changes automatically. If you turn this off, changes will be lost if you exit Paradox by mistake. The second setting, is a nice feature in that when you start a Paradox session, you are returned to the workspace exactly as you left it.

You can also customize what appears on screen when selecting forms and reports. Clicking the Forms and Reports button opens a dialog box that gives you options on how you want to work. For example, if you want to create a new Form, you can bypass the New Form dialog box and go directly to a blank form screen.

ObjectPAL Preferences

The ObjectPAL preferences are for those of you who go on to be advanced Paradox applications designers and need control of the desktop environment.

Tools Menu

The Tools menu has options that are just that, tools to use for building applications and working in Paradox. A brief description of each the options on the Tools menu is given below:

▼   **Project Viewer.** The Project viewer is a simplified way of visually locating the files in your projects. Figure 2.13 shows the Project Viewer dialog box for the directory PDOXWIN\SAMPLE. In this figure, the ALL option has been clicked, so that every file in the directory is visible. With the viewer, you can click the icon on the left side of the dialog box and select the types of files you want listed.

The viewer can run on the desktop in a minimized state, so that you can click on it and take a look at the list of files at any time.

▼   **Data Model Designer.** This tool aids you in the modification of a data model. It has the same function as the Data Model dialog box, found on the File/New submenu.

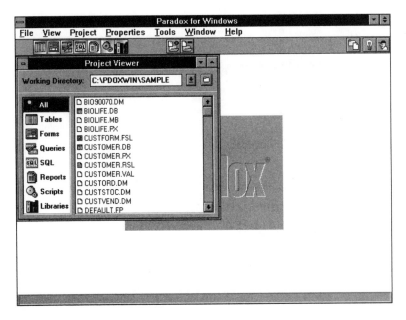

Figure 2.13 *Project Viewer*

Tools/Utilities

Click on the File menu again and then click on **Utilities**. The submenu appears as in Figure 2.14.

▼ **Add.** This option is used when you want to take records from one table and add them to another table. A good example of this is when you use a query to locate a group of records in one table that you want to move to a different table. Paradox has several ways of adding records from one table to another: The records can simply be added to the other table (appended), they can replace similar records in the other table, or both actions can take place.

▼ **Copy.** This option allows you to copy a table, query, form, report, script, or library file.

▼ **Delete.** This option allows you to delete a table, query, form, report, script, or library file.

▼ **Empty.** This option is unusual. Suppose that you have created a table that has the exact structure you want, but the wrong records. You can delete each record individually, or you can use this option to delete all records in the table with one push of a button.

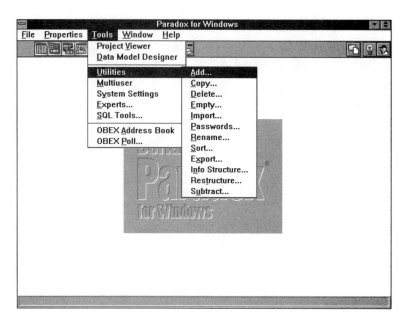

Figure 2.14   *Tools/Utilities submenu*

▼   **Import.** This option is used quite frequently when you begin working with records from other software applications. For example, if you have been saving names and addresses in a WordPerfect file, you can export the data (the names and addresses) to a comma-delimited file, which Paradox can import into a table. The **Import** option is particularly useful if you work in a business where several different types of databases are being used. Almost all databases can export an ASCII file, which is another name for a comma-delimited file.

▼   **Passwords.** This option allows you to change the status of passwords in tables. If you created a table with a password, you can use this option to shut off the password. A password keeps other Paradox users from accessing your Paradox tables. Most often, this feature is used when you are running Paradox on a network.

▼   **Rename.** Suppose that you have created a table and later decided that the name that you originally gave the table is for some reason incorrect or not appropriate. This options allows you to change the name very easily.

▼   **Sort.** As with many Paradox actions, you can sort a table of information in either of two ways. You can open the table on screen and use Table/Sort commands to effect a sort. You can also sort a table that is not open using this option. Paradox lists the table saved on disk, and you click on the table you wish to sort.

▼ **Export.** The opposite of importing a file is to export a Paradox file. *Exporting* means that the data in the Paradox table is converted to the file format you need. Again, in an situation where several types of databases are in use, this feature allows for the easy exchange of data.

▼ **Info Structure.** The **Info Structure** option displays a dialog box from which you can select a table. After selecting a table, the structure of the table is displayed. The purpose of this option is to enable you to look at the design of the table without opening the table itself.

▼ **Restructure.** After viewing the Info Structure of a particular table, you may decide to make a change. The **Restructure** option allows you to make changes to the fields without opening the entire database.

▼ **Subtract.** The **Subtract** option is used when you have duplicate records in two tables. Paradox compares the two tables you have selected and deletes the records in the table that you specified.

Tools/Multiuser

The next option on the File menu is labeled **Multiuser**. Selecting this option opens the submenu as seen in Figure 2.15.

The submenu lists several options specific to using Paradox on a network, which you may be doing. If you are not using Paradox on a network, skip ahead to the next section.

▼ **Display Locks.** Paradox tables can be locked so that other users on the network cannot access the records. The table that opens when you select this item includes the current locks on the table, the type of lock, the user who initiated the lock, and when the lock was set. When you access this option, Paradox momentarily has to set a lock on the table you are inspecting. The display lock automatically releases.

▼ **Set Locks.** This option allows you to set a lock on a file. There are several types of locks. You can lock a single record or even a whole table.

N O T E

If you lock a table, the lock remains in effect until you exit Paradox, unless you explicitly use the Set Locks option to remove the lock. Unless you want nasty messages from other network users, remember to unlock a table as soon as possible.

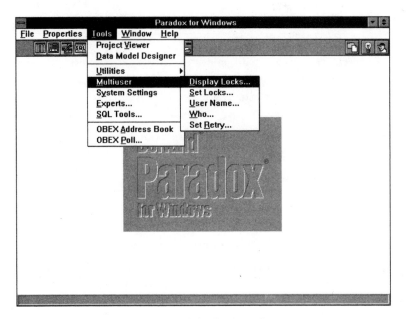

Figure 2.15 *Tools/Multiuser submenu*

▼ **User Name.** This option allows you to enter your name, which identifies you to the network. If you are not on a network, selecting this option opens the dialog box seen in Figure 2.16.

▼ **Who.** This option displays the list of users on the network.

▼ **Set Retry.** If you attempt to open a record on a network, it is possible that someone else is working on the record too. You may be locked out. Paradox will retry accessing the record by the value in seconds that you specify. The default is 0 seconds. If you select **Set Retry**, you cannot do anything else while you are waiting.

Tools/System Settings

Paradox can be customized to fit your particular needs. The list of custom features is described below.

▼ **Auto Refresh.** When you are working on a network installation of Paradox, Paradox automatically rereads the entire table at specified intervals. That way, changes made by other users on the network are available as you make your changes. The automatic interval is 5 seconds. That may be too fast, particularly if you are working on a large database. Why? Reading the data takes time, and you may want to complete all of your edits to a table before you are interrupted by a refresh. The updates *you make* are always available on-screen.

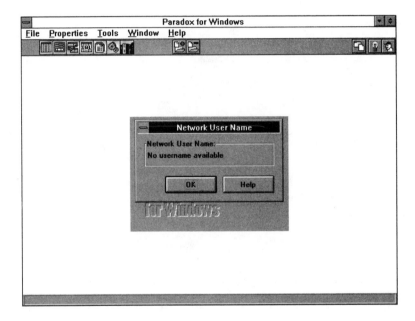

Figure 2.16 *Network User Name dialog box*

▼ **Blank as Zero.** As you become more sophisticated with your tables, you may want to perform mathematical analysis on the data in a field. An example is averaging the size of each transaction in an invoice database. If a field is blank, it will affect the outcome of the average. Instead of a blank, this setting will make Paradox count the blank as a zero, thereby making the math analysis accurate.

▼ **Drivers.** A driver is the program that makes Paradox able to work directly with a database format different from its own. Installed with Paradox are drivers for Paradox (no surprise there) and for DBASE. Borland plans to develop other drivers that will allow you to work directly with programs such as FoxPro and Access. When you select this option, a dialog box displays the installed drivers.

▼ **IDAPI.** IDAPI is the acronym for Independent Database Application Programming Interface. The settings in this dialog box determines how Paradox works with your data. Figure 2.17 shows the IDAPI dialog box. These settings are not something that you need to be concerned with. To change them, you must exit Paradox and use the Configuration Utility. This process is for advanced users only.

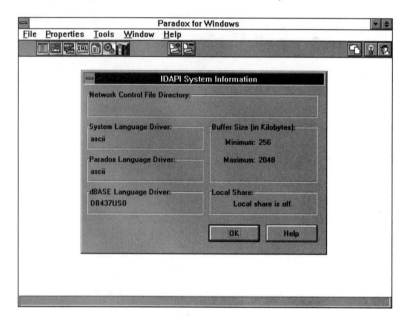

Figure 2.17 *IDAPI dialog box*

Window Menu

Remember that Paradox is the parent window and that the objects created—tables, forms, and so on—are contained in child windows. Figure 2.18 shows the Window menu. Because no child Windows are open at the present, none of the options on the Window menu are accessible.

The purpose of the Window menu items are to manipulate the child windows. The **Tile** option arranges all open child windows so that they appear in a tiled fashion, meaning a portion of each is visible on the screen. The **Cascade** option overlays open windows so that the tile bar of each window is visible. Figure 2.19 shows a series of open tables arranged as tiled windows. Figure 2.20 shows the same windows cascaded. The **Arrange Icons** options moves all minimized icons on the Desktop so that they are not hidden by overlaying each other. Use this option when you have many objects opened and minimized.

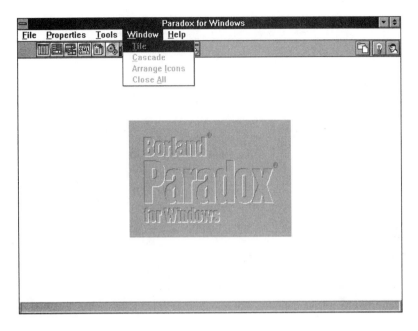

Figure 2.18 *Window menu, no options accessible*

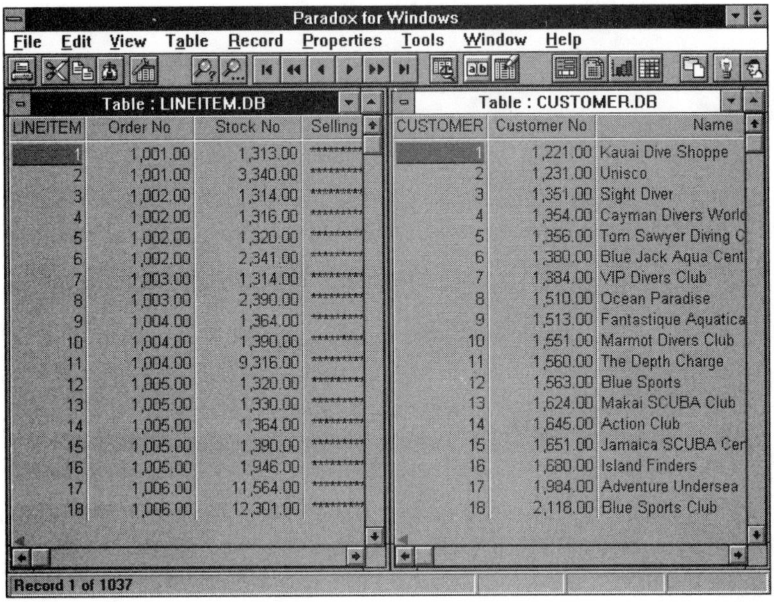

Figure 2.19 *Windows tiled*

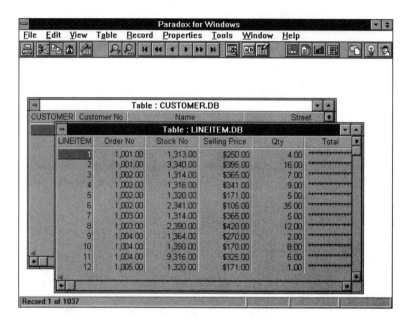

Figure 2.20 *Windows cascaded*

The last item on the menu is **Close All**, which does exactly that, closes all open windows on the desktop. It does not close Paradox, however.

Help Menu

Click open the Help menu. The Help system is context-sensitive. If you are working on a particular task, get stuck, and then access the Help menu, Paradox for Windows displays help on the task on which you are working. The initial Help menu gives you the options of **Contents**, **SpeedBar**, **Keyboard**, **Using Help**, **Support Info**, and **About**. The Paradox for Windows Help menu displays as shown in Figure 2.21.

Help/Contents

The **Contents** option is the most versatile. It is the index to all the help information that is available. Clicking on the **Contents** option opens the Help window as shown in Figure 2.22.

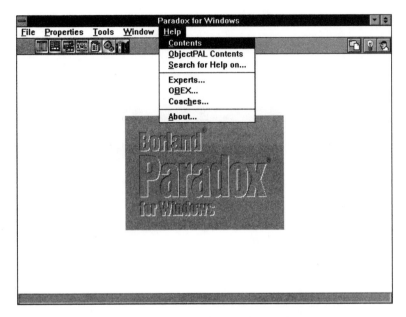

Figure 2.21 *Paradox for Windows Help menu*

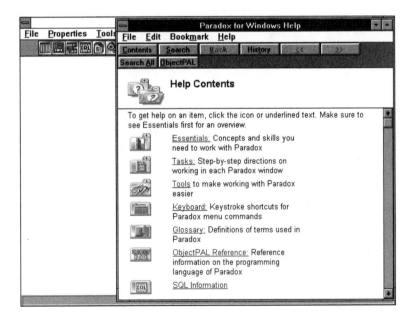

Figure 2.22 *Help Contents*

The main sections of the Help system are available here. For example, to read the information provided by the Essentials heading, you double-click on the word **Essentials**. Figure 2.23 shows the Essentials window. Notice that a further list of topics from which you can select is provided.

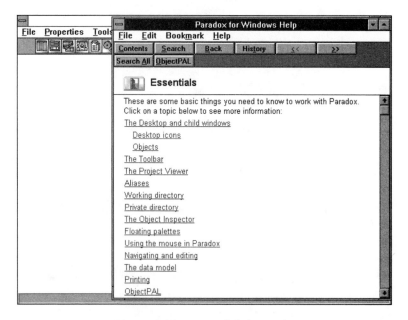

Figure 2.23 *Essentials help window*

Since we have already discussed the parent and child windows concepts, let's look at the Paradox explanation by clicking on the item **The Desktop and child Windows**. The resulting help window is shown in Figure 2.24.

A further aspect of the help screens is that terms such as *Desktop* are defined right within the text. If you do not understand a word, and it is underlined or in a different color, a definition is readily available. The pointer also changes to a hand shape if a definition is available. In Figure 2.25, the word *Desktop* has been selected and the definition is now on-screen.

If you click on the contents button again, you are returned to the original Help Contents window.

Help/Search

The search button provides a different way of finding information. Clicking on it opens the Search dialog box as shown in Figure 2.26.

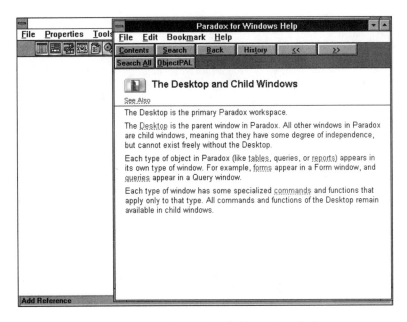

Figure 2.24 *Desktop and Child Windows help*

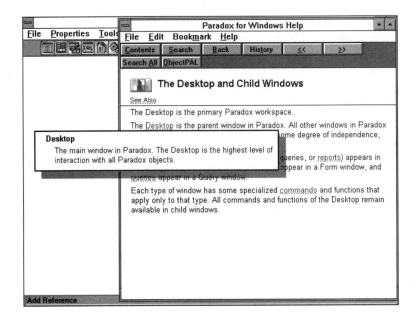

Figure 2.25 *Desktop defined in the Help*

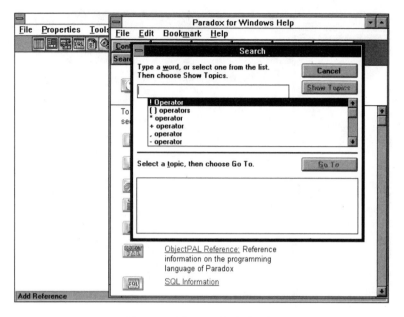

Figure 2.26 *Search dialog box*

If you know what topic you need help on, type the word or phrase in the box and then click on the show topics button. Paradox lists the topics related to the word you entered. In Figure 2.27, the word *Design* was entered as a topic. Paradox lists several possible help screens under that topic. The next step is to decide which of the topics listed is appropriate. Click on the topic and then click on the go to button.

Help/Back

The back button, when clicked, retraces the route you have taken to get to the current help window. For example, if you have selected a topic and then jumped to several more topics off of that original help screen, you can go back to the previous help screens. Paradox keeps a record of your journey.

Help/History

To further aid your navigation of the Help system, Paradox provides a list of the help windows you have viewed. Clicking on the history button opens a dialog box with the topics you have viewed, starting with the current topic at the top. The dialog box in Figure 2.28 shows a typical route.

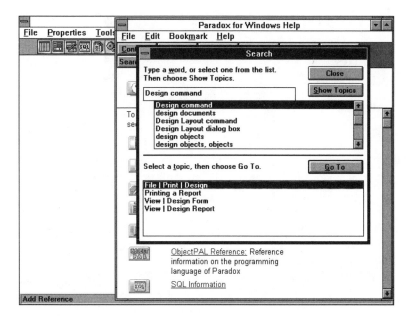

Figure 2.27 *Search dialog box, design topics*

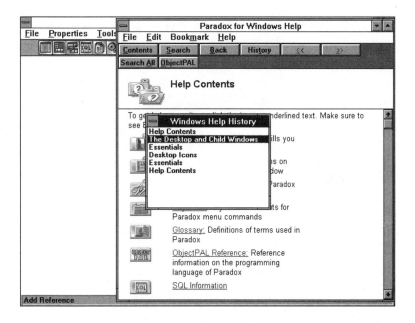

Figure 2.28 *Windows Help History dialog box*

Close the History dialog box by clicking anywhere in the Help window.

Help/Menus

The Help system has a series of menus that offer other options. Each of the menus is discussed below.

Help/File

The File menu enables you to open help files other than the Paradox help file. For example, if you want to see or print the information in the help file regarding workgroups, you can do so with this menu. Figure 2.29 shows the opened File menu.

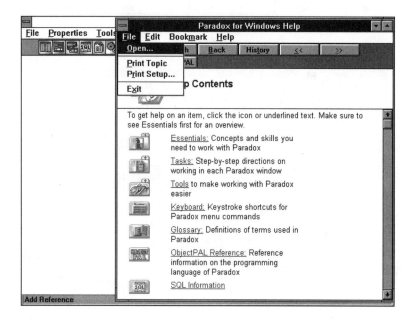

Figure 2.29 *Help/File menu*

▼ **Open.** Click on the **Open** option to access the dialog box with the list of help files, as shown in Figure 2.30.

Six possible choices are presented. The default help file is the **pdoxwin.hlp** file. The file that contains help on workgroups is named **pworkgrp.hlp**, and double-clicking that name opens the Workgroups Desktop help window as shown in Figure 2.31.

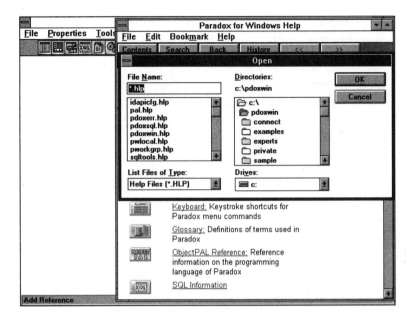

Figure 2.30 *Help/File/Open dialog box*

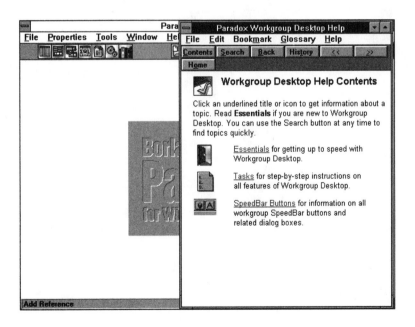

Figure 2.31 *Workgroup Desktop help window*

▼ **Print Topic.** Printing any of the help windows is a snap provided you have a printer attached and setup in Windows. Find the topic you want and click on the **Print Topic** item.

▼ **Print Setup.** If you do have problems printing, click on the **Print Setup** option to check the current printer settings. All printing in Paradox is handled by the Windows Print Manager. If you have trouble printing, check the Windows Print Manager in the main window of Windows.

Help/Edit

The Edit menu has two options, **Copy** and **Annotate**. The **Copy** option is used to select text in the Help window, which you can then copy to the Windows Clipboard. The **Annotate** option enables you to add your own help information to a help window. Suppose that you had discovered a solution to a problem in the way Paradox works on your network. To make sure the information is never lost, you can add that information to the appropriate screen using the **Annotate** option. The Annotate dialog box is shown in Figure 2.32.

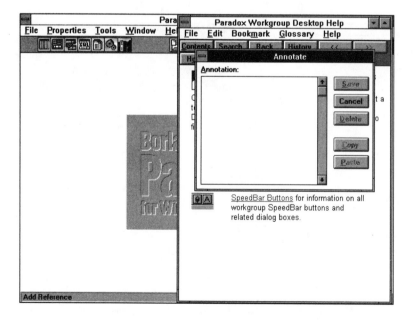

Figure 2.32 *Annotate dialog box*

If you have cut text from another location in windows, the paste button will be active. Clicking on it pastes the text from the Windows clipboard to the Annotation dialog.box.

N O T E

Remember to click on the Save button before exiting the Annotate dialog box to retain your changes.

Help/Bookmark

The Bookmark menu enables you to designate one or a series of place marks in the Help system. If you frequently turn to Help for a particular topic, rather than wading through the Contents or Search dialog boxes to find the topic, create a Bookmark. The Bookmark function is limited in that it can take you to the topic window only, not to the exact spot of your information. To define a bookmark:

1. Locate the help window for which you want a bookmark.
2. Click on the Bookmark menu. There is only one option.
3. Click on **Define**. The Bookmark Define dialog box appears as shown in Figure 2.33.

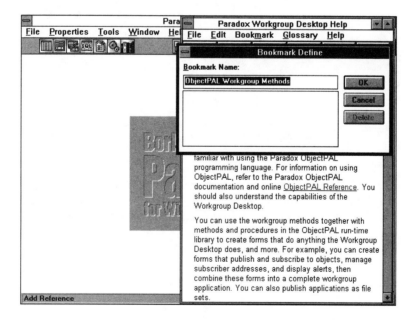

Figure 2.33 *Bookmark Define dialog box*

The name of the help window is inserted automatically in the Bookmark name field. You can change the name if needed to make it more descriptive.

4. Click on OK. The bookmark now is part of the Bookmark menu as shown in Figure 2.34.

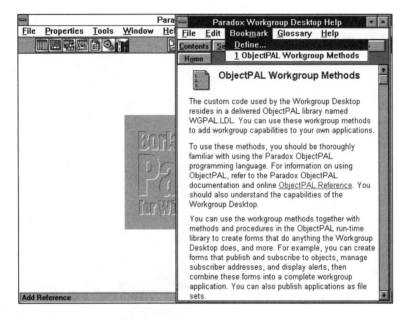

Figure 2.34 *Bookmark menu with new bookmark*

To delete a bookmark, click on the Bookmark menu and select the **Define** option. The list of defined bookmarks appears. Click on the bookmark you want to delete and click on the delete button.

Leave Help by clicking on the window control button. Click on the close button, and the help screen no longer displays. You can leave the help window by clicking on the File menu in help and then clicking on **Exit**. Use either method to return to your activity in Paradox for Windows.

Opening a Table

Now that we have covered the basics of the Paradox desktop, let's open a table to see how it appears on the desktop.

1. Click the File menu.

2. Click **Open**.

3. From the submenu, select the **Table** option. Paradox displays the Open Table dialog box as shown in Figure 2.35.

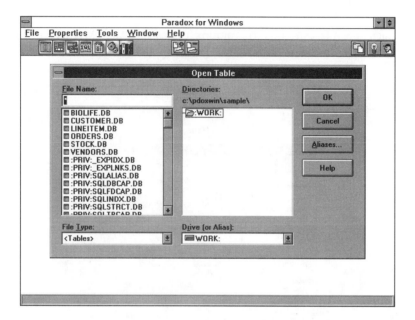

Figure 2.35 *Open Table dialog box*

N O T E

Your list of tables will not resemble the one in Figure 2.35. Remember we discussed that when Paradox is installed, several subdirectories are also created. One of those subdirectories is named EXAMPLES. In the EXAMPLES subdirectory, several tables are stored. Before we switch to the EXAMPLE subdirectory, let's examine the dialog box.

At the top of the dialog box is a field labeled File Name. In that field is an asterisk. By default, Paradox lists files that have a DB extension as in BORLAND.DB.

Underneath the File Name field, is the list of files. Each of these files is a table. This is important for you to grasp. When you use the File menu and the Open/Table options, you are shown a list of files, each of which is a Table.

The next field down is the File Type field. The indicator in this field tells you the files named above are tables.

At the top of the dialog box, to the right, is the Directories information. This is what is used in DOS to locate files. Currently, the path Paradox is using is the WORKING subdirectory, shortened to WORK.

Below the Directories information is the Drive (or Alias) field. Again, notice that WORK is the Alias where the tables are stored.

4. Click the Aliases… button. Paradox opens the Alias Manager dialog box. From this window click New. The Directory Browser opens as in Figure 2.36.

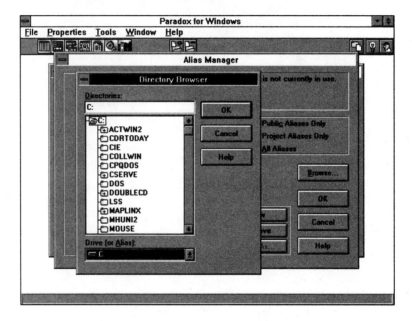

Figure 2.36 *Directory Browser dialog box*

In this example, Paradox has been installed on drive C. So, on the left side of the dialog box, the Directory Browser lists Directories on drive C.

If Paradox is installed on the D drive in your computer, click the letter D. If you are on a network, click the letter of the File Server.

N O T E

5. Double-click the directory labeled PDOXWIN. Paradox displays the sub-directories under PDOXWIN, as in Figure 2.37.

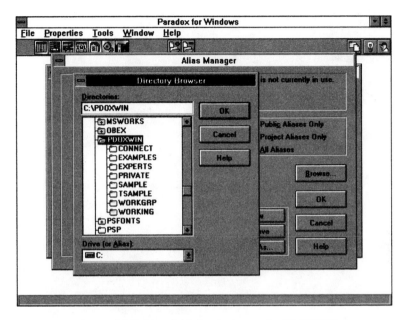

Figure 2.37 *List of subdirectories under PDOXWIN*

In the left half of the dialog box is the list of subdirectories including the EXAM-PLES subdirectory.

7. Click the EXAMPLES subdirectory.

8. Click OK. You are returned to the Alias Manager dialog box.

9. Type: BOOK in the Database Aliases field.

10. Click the Keep New button. (This was the New button but it changes identity in this process.)

11. Click OK. Paradox asks you if it is OK to save the new Aliases.

12. Click Yes. You are returned to the Open Table dialog box.

Now, you can open the CUST.DB table.

1. Click the down arrow in the Drive (or Alias) field. The list of tables in the EXAMPLES subdirectory appear.

2. Click the CUST.DB table.

3. Click OK. The table opens as in Figure 2.38.

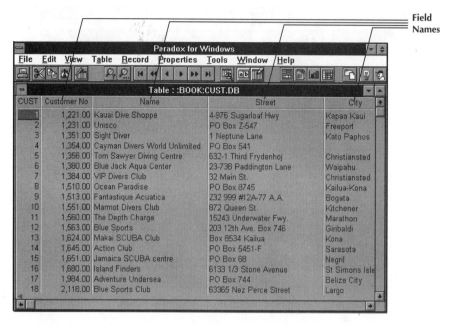

Figure 2.38 *CUST.DB table*

The entire desktop takes on a new appearance entirely! Before we consider the changes in the desktop, let's look at the table itself.

Across the top of the table, are the field names, beginning with *CUST*. Paradox automatically creates a column that numbers the records, and this is called CUST to match the table name. The next column is entitled *Customer No*, which stands for customer number. The next column is entitled *Name*, followed by *Street* and *City*. The remaining field names are not visible. To see them, you need to use the *scroll bar* at the bottom of the window.

1. Position the arrow pointer over the right-pointing arrow in the lower-right corner of the window.

2. Click the button four times, or until the *City* column has moved to the far left of the window and the *Phone* column appears. Your screen should match the one shown in Figure 2.39.

Notice that the *scroll box* is now positioned at the middle of the scroll bar. When the table was opened, the scroll box was at the far left of the scroll box.

3. Click on the right-pointing arrow until the right edge of the table appears. The *First Contact* column is the last column in the table.

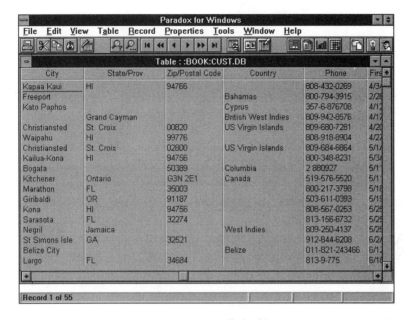

Figure 2.39 *Scrolled table*

4. Click on the scroll bar just to the right of the left-pointing arrow. This produces a large jump in the table display, so that you can once again see the *CUST* column. Look at the status line. It indicates that the table has 55 records in it.

5. Click and hold down the mouse button while the mouse pointer is positioned on the down-pointing arrow in the vertical scroll bar at the far right of the window. By holding the button down, the table scrolls continuously. Eventually, the bottom of the table will be reached.

6. Click on the scroll box just beneath the up-pointing arrow. If you hit the right spot, you should be back where you began.

Looking at the Speedbar

A new Speedbar displays below the menu bar. As with the menu items in the menu bar, the SpeedBar buttons change with each object. When a table displays, the SpeedBar looks like the one in Figure 2.39.

The first button on the left is the Print button. Click this button to print the table just as it displays on screen. The next three buttons on the left of the Table

SpeedBar are used to cut, copy and paste items in the table. Next you see the Restructure button.

The two navigation buttons on the SpeedBar allow you to search the table. Click the magnifying glass with a question mark and a dialog box displays. From the dialog box, you define the value for what you want to search. Click OK and Paradox for Windows finds the value in the database. Click the magnifying glass with the ellipses and Paradox finds the next matching value.

The next six buttons are used in table navigation. Click the button with the left-facing-facing arrow and a vertical line, and you instantly move to the first record in the table. Click the button with two left-facing arrows and you move up one page in the table. Click the button with one left-facing arrow and you move to the previous record.

The next three buttons result in the opposite action. You are able to move to the next record, the next page, or the last record in the table.

The Filter button has a picture of a table with a small magnifying glass. Use the filter button to look at a subset of the data in the table. For example, with the Filter button you can look at only the records where the shop location is the West Indies.

The SpeedBar button with the small ab is a filed view toggle button. Click this button and you toggle from *Form View* back to *Field View*.

Click the button with the writing pen and toggle between the view mode and the Edit mode. In edit mode, you can change the data entered into the table. To toggle means you click one time and you are in view mode. Click the same button again and you are in edit mode. You toggle back and forth between two modes.

Seven more buttons appear on the SpeedBar. In order, you can display a *Quick Form*, print a *Quick Report*, display *Quick Graph*, and display a *Quick Crosstab*.

The next group of three buttons on the far right side of the SpeedBar are used to pen a *Project Folder*, access Paradox for Windows Experts, and access the Paradox Coach. The Paradox Coach is like having your own Paradox personal trainer.

To perform a task when a button displays on the SpeedBar, you either click the button and the task is performed, or you click the button and a dialog box displays from which you make selections in order to perform the task. Let's put all this introductory knowledge to use.

Changing from Field View to Form View

Let's change the view of the CUST table from field view to form view using the Table SpeedBar. Click on the Quick Form button. The table is modified and appears as shown in Figure 2.40.

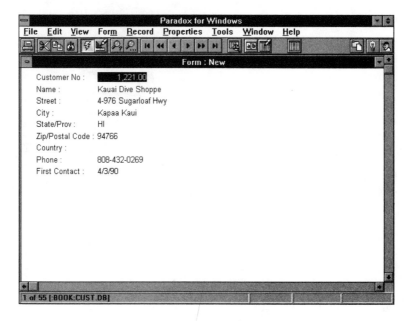

Figure 2.40 *Form View of CUST.DB table*

As you can see, Paradox creates a new window in which to display the form view of the CUST.DB table. In form view, Paradox displays a single record from the table at a time. Because this table has only nine fields (or columns) all of the fields can be seen at once in the form view. You do not have use the scroll bar to see the other data.

A key aspect of Paradox in Windows is that you can look at the table view and the form view at the same time. Remember the **Tile** option on the Window menu? Let's use it now to look at the two views in juxtaposition.

1. Click on the Window menu.

2. Click on the **Tile** option. Paradox rearranges the child windows as shown in Figure 2.41.

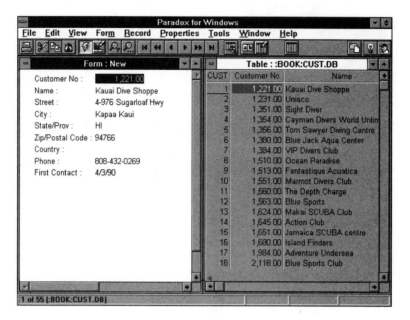

Figure 2.41 *Windows Tiled*

Because the mouse pointer was on the first record in the CUST.DB table, Paradox displays that record in form view. If the pointer had been on a different record, that record is the one Paradox would have selected for the form view.

N O T E

With the windows tiled, you can easily shift back and forth, by simply clicking on the table you want to work in.

1. Click on the CUST.DB table view. If you have a color screen, notice the change in color in the title bar of the window.

2. Click on the Window menu.

3. Click on **Cascade**. Now the windows are overlaid with the title bar of the underlying window visible at the top of the screen.

If you click on the title bar of a window below the top one, it moves to the top.

Accessing a Child Window with the Window Menu

Besides manipulating the way open windows are displayed, you can find and bring to the top of the desktop a specific window from a series of windows that are cascaded. Click on the Window menu. It is shown in Figure 2.42.

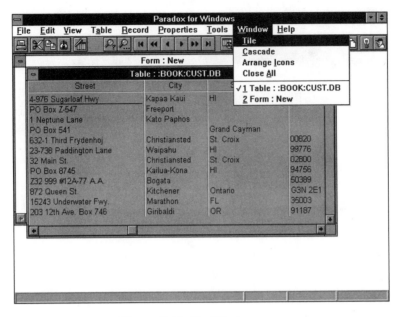

Figure 2.42 *The Window menu*

As you can see, the window menu now includes the two child windows that are open. If more windows were open, each would be listed on the Window menu. To select a window, click on the window you want to work with.

Closing a Window

Before we close this chapter, let's look at the steps to close a window. These instructions are valid for any child window open on the desktop. In this exercise, you will first *minimize* the Form window and then close it.

1. Click on the Form:New window, or use the Window menu to access the window.

2. Click on the window control button. It is located in the upper-left corner of the window frame. Figure 2.43 shows the opened control box.

The Control menu is common to all Windows programs. Each of the items on the menu is described below:

Restore—This option restores the window to its former size. If the window had been enlarged using the **Maximize** menu item, it shrinks to its smaller size. If you had used the **Minimize** item to shrink the window, click on **Restore**, and it is enlarged.

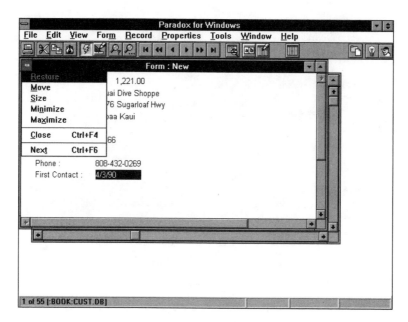

Figure 2.43 *Window Control menu*

Move—This option allows you to move the window to a different position on the desktop. If the Paradox window is full-screen, it cannot be moved.

Size—This option allows you to change the size of the window. The mouse pointer becomes a four-headed arrow. Pressing the arrow-pointing keys moves the corresponding window border. If the Paradox window is full screen-size, this item is not available.

Minimize—This option shrinks the window to an icon.

Maximize—This option enlarges the window to its maximum size. The window is at maximum size when Paradox is opened.

Close—This option closes the window. If the window is an application, such as Paradox, it terminates the program.

Next—This option accesses the next open child window on the desktop.

3. Minimize the window by clicking on the **Minimize** option. Figure 2.44 shows the Paradox desktop with the CUST.DB table open and the Form window minimized at the bottom of the desktop.

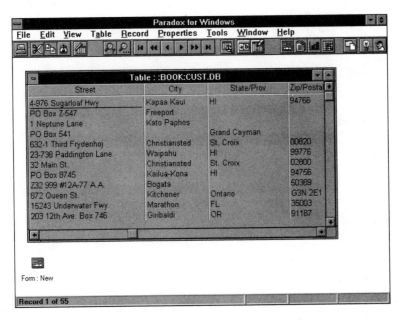

Figure 2.44 *Form window minimized*

4. Click on the Form:New icon. The Window Control menu reappears.

5. Click on the **Restore** option. The Form:Menu window is redisplayed on the desktop.

6. To close the Form:New window, click on the control menu button.

7. Click on the **Close** option. Paradox does not allow you to close an object that has been newly created with a warning message; an example of which is shown in Figure 2.45.

8. Because we do not need to keep the form view, click on the no button.

The CUST.DB table has been reduced to less than a full window because the **Tile** option was used. To maximize the window, click on the up-pointing arrow in the upper-right corner of the window frame.

Leaving Paradox

Paradox for Windows offers several methods to exit the program. The methods are listed here:

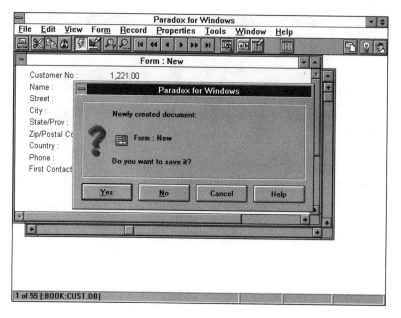

Figure 2.45 *Paradox warning dialog box*

▼ Click on the Window Control menu. Click on **Close**.

▼ Select File/Exit from the menu.

▼ Double-click on the minimize button.

▼ Press **Alt+F4**.

Summary

When you exit Paradox, you are returned to the Program Manager main screen. In the next chapter, we will examine the structure of a table and how you can begin making tables of your own.

Chapter 3

Viewing and Locating Records in Tables

In *Chapter 2*, you opened an existing database table and learned to use the scroll bars to move around the set of records. In this chapter, you will look at the structure of the database table and then consider the rules for building your own table. In this chapter, you will learn about:

- ▼ Planning a database table
- ▼ Viewing a table structure
- ▼ Locating records
- ▼ Using property inspection
- ▼ Printing a quick report

Planning a Database

You do not want to create a huge database to hold all of the information you will ever need about a database item in one record. Remember that Paradox for Windows is based on a relational model and can handle multiple tables. This means that you can link tables by using common *elements* in every table.

Steven Covey, the author of *The Seven Habits of Highly Effective People*, lists one of the seven habits as "Begin With the End in Mind." That is to say, know your goals before you begin the journey. The same is true for databases. When designing a database, you must first decide what the goals are for the database. Start by deciding what information you need to have in your database. If you have a business, some of the categories of information you might need are customer information, invoices, order information, sales records, and inventory data.

Think of everything you need in each of the three categories listed below. List them on a piece of paper so that you can organize your database. Here are some examples:

Customer Info	Invoice Info	Sales Records
First Name	Invoice Number	Salesperson
Last Name	Sale Date	Available Customers
Address	Product Number	Number of Customers
City	Quantity	Monthly Sales
State	Customer Number	Products Sold
Phone Number	Tax	Total Sales
Customer Number	Shipping	Commissions Earned
	Total Sale	

NOTE — The real value of a database is the value of the output to the end user. In a business ask the sales manager, the vice president of product development, and the financial manager what information they need. What do they get now? How do they use it? How could it be more useful? If they could design the report, what would they want to know?

The foregoing lists are not meant to be a complete list of what you might need in each of these three categories. While planning your database, you can see how useful it is to write everything down first. As we stated earlier, you might be tempted to put all the information in the lists above into one table. With Paradox for Windows, you can create three separate tables, one table for each set of information.

Take another look at the list of items under the heading Invoice Info. The customer name and address is not necessary here. If you put the customer name and address in this database, the customer who places ten orders in a month will have their name in this database ten times. Minimizing the repetition of information should be a goal of every database designer.

Using a customer number instead of a name means that you can simply add the number to the invoice and save the expense of having redundant data in your database. The customer number on the invoice would be the same as that in the customer database. Using the Paradox for Windows relational database, you can match the customer numbers without entering the data two, three, or more times. The customer number becomes the common element of the two tables.

Guidelines for Designing a Table

You will save yourself a lot of work down the road if you plan your database following these guidelines. Be proactive to your database design, rather than reactive. Even if your design is not ideal, Paradox does allow you to redesign your tables at any time. But, some redesigns are easier than others, and so good up-front thinking will help solve this problem.

Keep the Database Simple

Include as few fields in a table as you can, while keeping all the information you need. Too many fields make a table hard to manage, and more difficult to develop reports from. It is better to link several small tables than manage one large bulky table.

Reduce Redundancy

After you make lists of the main categories of data and information that goes into each category, check to make sure that the same information is not found in each database. It is one thing to find a customer number in each database table. But if name, address, phone number, and zip code are found over and over, you create unnecessary work.

Imagine having customer names and addresses in four separate tables. Then imagine that a customer changes her address. You need to edit four tables, entering the new address in each one. This is redundancy Maximus. If, instead, you have one table with the customer name, address, and customer number, and three other tables with customer number alone, how many times do you have to change the address? Right! Only one time. Change the address field one time, and any reference to that data, from any other table, is automatically changed.

Customize Tables

The paper piles on your desk are a database. You need to incorporate all of that data into an electronic database as similar to your pile of paperwork as you can. All the products you sell have an inventory number. Use that same number on your Paradox invoice. For example, if you keep a list on your desk of the patients you've seen and why, make a table called Patients Seen.

Tie any reference to a patient to that patient's number. Use the patient's number to eliminate redundant information.

NOTE

Use Descriptive Field Names

This guideline is key when people other than yourself will be using the database you design. If you enter **TMI** as a field name that means Total Monthly Income, other people entering data are going to have a tough time knowing what you mean. Paradox for Windows provides space to name fields in a more descriptive way. Paradox allows a field name to be 25 characters in length. That should be plenty to convey what information is in the field.

Types of Table Relationships

As you write down all the information you need to keep in a database, you will find that there are relationships between tables. A customer number or patient number may appear on three separate tables. A product number may appear in an Invoice table, an Inventory table, and a Sales table.

One example of how tables can be related is a lookup table. This is commonly used and very powerful. If you have an inventory of five products with lengthy descriptions, your invoice table might look like that shown in Table 3.1.

Table 3.1 *Typical invoice table*

Customer	Movie/Director	Quantity	Price
Mitch Duncan	The Count of Monte Cristo /Nat Myking	5	39.95
Carol Creamer	Piano/Sidney Blumenthal	1	24.95
Jake Mehoff	The Continuing Adventures of Debbie in Dallas/Fred Boogs	50	13.99

If you are the data entry person, you do not want to type these long movie titles every time you get an order. Because you are working with Paradox for Windows and the tables are relational, the product description is substituted by a product number.

Keep the product number and product description in its own separate database table. You need to access only this table when you add more products or change the movies you offer. The product description table would look similar to that shown in Table 3.2.

Table 3.2 *Typical product description table*

Product Number	Product Description
CMC	Count of Monte Cristo/Nat Myking
PNO	Piano/Sidney Blumenthal
DDD	The Continuing Adventures of Debbie in Dallas/Fred Boogs
ASO	2001, A Spaced Oddity/Rudolph Preminger
BZH	Blazing Horses/Mel Rivers

Combining these two tables results in Table 3.3 with less typing, less time taken to enter the data, and less chance for error. This method also assures that product descriptions remain consistent with different data entry personnel.

Table 3.3 *Combination of two tables*

Customer	Product Code	Quantity	Price
Mitch Duncan	CMC	5	$34.95
Carol Creamer	PNO	1	$24.95
Jake Mehoff	DDD	50	$13.99

For a company with only a handful of products, this may not seem worthwhile, but if a company has many products, the concept is a lifesaver. Paradox for Windows can look up information related to the product number in any table you develop, quickly and accurately.

As you become a more advanced Paradox user, you can add OLE objects in a database and display a graphic of a product, right in a database field.

N O T E

Flexibility is enhanced because any database table can be changed, altered, and redefined. As a business grows and database needs change, Paradox for Windows can adapt to these new needs.

Other types of relationships exist between tables. Paradox is most useful because it allows the splitting of data out of a table that can be brought together at a later date. The result is tables that are smaller, simpler, and easier to understand and navigate.

Table Keys

Table keys indicate special fields in a table that are used to find records. Suppose that you have a database of 10,000 names and you want to find the record with the last name of Wicker. One by one, Paradox searches through the 10,000 names in the last name field until it finds Wicker. Not only could this take a very long time, but if no Wicker were in the file, you would have to wait for the search to conclude.

Paradox can create a special file with key fields of a database table. Paradox then looks up information much more quickly by using its key field files, which act like an index of your data. Like many of the files Paradox creates, you will not directly access that file. Instead, you deal with the tables, reports, forms, and other objects created in Paradox for Windows.

Characteristics of Table Keys

You can set up each table with a unique key that helps prevent you from entering duplicate records in a table. If you try to assign a customer number that has already been used, Paradox stops you from making the entry. Keys help you enter accurate data. Some table links may require a key field. A key field also keeps data in order. You may enter data out of order while editing, but Paradox for windows will put it in the order specified by the key field when you save the file.

Processing speed is enhanced by using key fields. Compare two methods of trying to find the subject of Making Database Graphs, while looking in this book. Without key fields, you would start at the beginning of the book and, page-by-page, look through the book until you found a section on graphs. With key fields, i.e., the index, you turn to the back of the book, look up the subject of graphs and turn to the page indicated.

A Primary Key

A *primary key* identifies unique data for each record in a database table. If your primary key is the social security number, Paradox for Windows will see that each record has a unique number, that there are no duplicates, and if any duplicates that are found, that they are displayed for your correction.

A primary key is used to sort the data in a table. The sort order is determined by the primary key. This is where the index idea comes in. Paradox for Windows uses this sort order to find records in a database. Plus, the table is easier to link with other tables with the same sort order.

If you specify a primary key in·your design, you must then enter data for each record in the primary key field. This ensures that you have a sort order established and that each record is unique.

When to Use Primary Keys

In every table you create, it is recommended that you create a primary key. Keep this in mind when designing tables so that the primary key field is the first field in a table. Without the primary key field, you will have to look for your own duplicate records manually. Paradox will let you change your mind if you assign a field as a primary key and decide that a different field should be the primary key.

The Secondary Index

The *secondary index* is established in a table for alternate sort orders. You can add a secondary index only to a table that has a primary key. A secondary index is used to link tables or display tables in an order other than that of the primary key.

For example, if the customer number is the primary key, and the secondary index is on the last name field, you can sort in two ways. Sort by the primary key, and the records display in numerical order. Sort by the secondary index of last name, and the records display in alphabetical order by last name.

Referential Integrity

Referential integrity is used to link two tables and validate data. For example, in a table with a list of customers where the customer number is the primary key, you want to check the credit limit of a particular customer. Another table lists the customers and their credit limit. In that second table, the customer number is again the primary key. You need to validate the credit limit and verify that the customer can charge that amount. You use referential integrity to validate the data.

With the customer number the primary key in both tables, you define referential integrity. The table with the list of customers will not accept an entry in the credit field unless it matches a value in the credit limit field. You can be sure that the customer has a valid credit limit.

Determining the Default Path for Tables

In *Chapter 2*, you opened the CUST database table, which was located in the EXAMPLES subdirectory under the PDOXWIN directory. To do so, you had to undertake several steps, using the Browser to locate the files. Paradox allows you to designate the path to take every time you start the program to locate the tables with which you want to work. Click on the File/Working Directory menus to set up that path. The Set Working Directory dialog box appears as shown in Figure 3.1.

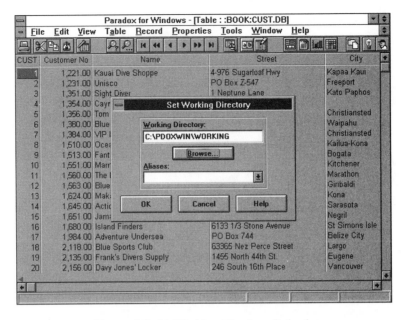

Figure 3.1 *Set Working Directory dialog box*

As you can see, the current working directory is the following path C:\PDOXWIN \WORKING. The CUST table is located in the EXAMPLES subdirectory. There are two ways to change the path.

1. Click on the filed under Working Directory and use the **Backspace** key to delete the word WORKING.

2. Type **EXAMPLES**.

3. Click OK.

Or,

1. Click the Browse button.

2. Click the down arrow in Aliases and select the drive on which Paradox is installed.

3. Click on the directory, PDOXWIN.

4. Click on the subdirectory, EXAMPLES.

5. Click OK. The Set Working Directory dialog box appears.

6. Click OK.

Paradox warns you that all open tables will be closed if you make this change.

7. Click OK.

Or,

1. Click the down arrow in aliases and if you followed the example in *Chapter 2*, you have an alias named BOOK.

2. Click on BOOK.

3. Click OK.

Opening the CUST Table

The previous action closed all open tables, but Paradox automatically opens Project View dialog box, assuming, correctly that you want to open one of the tables in the list. It opens the path as designated by your entry in the Set Working directory dialog box. The Project Viewer dialog box is shown in Figure 3.2.

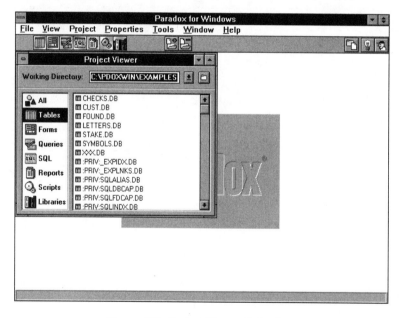

Figure 3.2 *Project Viewer dialog box*

Your list of tables will differ from those listed in Figure 3.2, but the table CUST.DB should be in the list.

N O T E

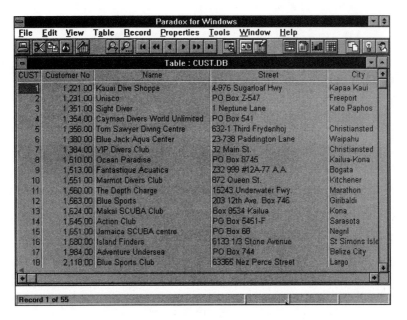

Figure 3.3 CUST.DB opened on the desktop

Examining a Table Structure

All tables in Paradox have the following features. First, Paradox automatically numbers the records and inserts the name of the table in the first column. The names of the each of the fields (which are arranged in columns) are at the top of the table. This CUST.DB table has the record number, headed by the word *CUST*, followed by *Customer No, Name, Street, City,* and so on. The name of the table is displayed in the title bar of the window. When the mouse pointer is in the table, Paradox displays the number of the current record (that record upon which the highlight is located) and the total number of records in the table. These numbers are displayed in the status line and are located in the lower-right corner of the screen. The CUST.DB table has a total of 55 records.

1. Click on the Table menu. It appears as shown in Figure 3.4. There are many options on this menu. At this point, we need to be concerned with the **Restructure** option only.

2. Click on the **Restructure** option. The Restructure dialog box appears as shown in Figure 3.5.

Figure 3.4 The Table menu

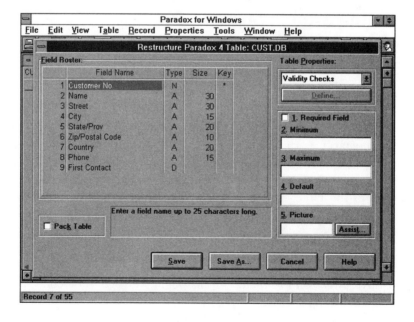

Figure 3.5 The Restructure dialog box

Take a moment to look at the table as it is now presented. This is a simple table with nine fields. To better see how the Restructure dialog box relates to the table itself, move the Restructure window.

3. Click and hold on the title bar in the Restructure window.

4. Drag the window down so that the top of the CUST.DB table is visible, as shown in Figure 3.6.

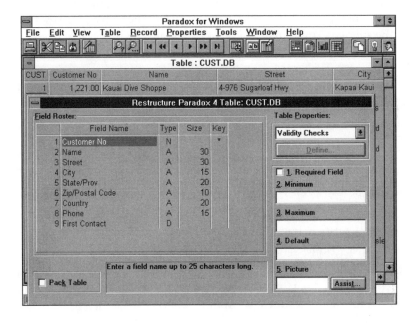

Figure 3.6 *The Restructure window moved down to reveal the top of the CUST.DB table*

Notice that the first field listed in the Field Roster is not the CUST field, but rather the Customer No field. That is because Paradox creates the record number field on its own.

The Field Roster has several headings, which are described below:

▼ **Field Name.** Paradox allows you to create a field name of up to 25 characters in length. You want a field name that reflects the information in the table. With some fields, you may have to abbreviate in order to best convey the information therein.

▼ **Type.** The Type entry is important in that it determines what kind of entry is allowed into the field. The Customer No field has an *N* as its type. The *N* stands for *Number.* A list of each of the types and how they affect table entries is covered in *Chapter 4.*

▼ **Size.** This field determines how long the entry can be in this field. When the **Number** option is selected as the Type, you cannot designate the size of this field.

▼ **Key.** The Customer No field has been designated as the key field. The asterisk in the Key column denotes the field as being the key. The significance of the key field is considerable. The entry in a key field *must* be unique. This makes sense in that you would not want to assign two customer numbers to the same customer. With the key field assigned to Customer No Paradox would not allow you to save the record if you had inadvertently entered a repetitive customer number. The key field must be the first field in the table!

On the right side of the dialog box are several boxes that can be used to further restrict the kinds of data that can be entered into a field. You can specify that an entry in a field is required or that it cannot be smaller than or larger than a specific value. You can even designate a default entry. A default might be the state field, where all of the records you create are going to have the same state.

Click on the cancel button to close the Restructure window.

What you have just seen is the skeleton of all Paradox tables. Each has the same format and options. The only differences among tables is the number of fields and the type of data that can be entered into each. If you understand this concept, the remaining features of Paradox will be easy to grasp.

Using the SpeedBar to Find Records

Before going on to create a table, let's try using some of the other tools available for manipulating records. The SpeedBar has several buttons that can be used to find records. Let's take the navigation buttons out for a spin and then use the locate buttons to find a specific record. Figure 3.7 details the location of the specific buttons.

Locate Buttons

▼ **Locate field value.** This button opens a dialog box that allows you to select the field you want to search and the text or number you want to match. Suppose that you wanted to find the record of a customer that lived in the city of Venice. This option is the one you would use to execute the search. Granted, in a small table such as CUST.DB, you could easily locate a specific record by scrolling the window. But, imagine that your database is 20,000 records. A scrolled search would be practically impossible. Besides, that is what computers are made to do.

▼ **Locate next.** This button continues the search that you specified using the Locate Field Value box dialog box. If the first record that Paradox located was the record you wanted, you can click on this button to search further in the table.

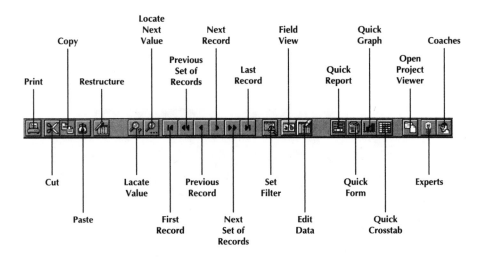

Figure 3.7 *Locate and Navigation buttons*

Navigation Buttons

The *navigation buttons* move the highlight as specified by the button. Each is described below.

▼ **First record.** Click on this button to move the highlight to the first record in the table.

▼ **Previous record set.** Because only a limited number of records can be seen in the Paradox child window, this button scrolls an entire window of records up toward the top of the table.

▼ **Previous record.** This button moves the highlight up toward the top of the table, a single record per click.

▼ **Next record.** This button moves the highlight down toward the bottom of the table, a single record per click.

▼ **Next record set.** Because only a limited number of records can be seen in the Paradox child window, this button scrolls an entire window of records down toward the bottom of the table; it does the opposite of the previous record set button.

Let's see how these buttons work.

1. Click on the first record button. The highlight jumps to the top of the table.

2. Click on the last record button. Figure 3.8 shows the result of clicking on it. Note that the status line reads *Record 55 of 55*, telling you that it is the last record in the table.

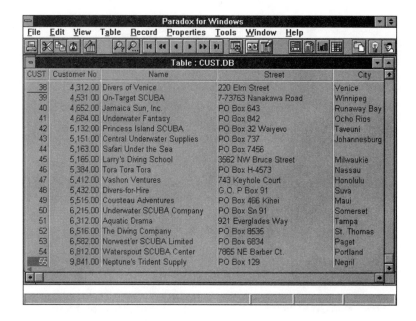

Figure 3.8 *Result of clicking on the last record button*

3. Click on the previous record set button. The result is shown in Figure 3.9.

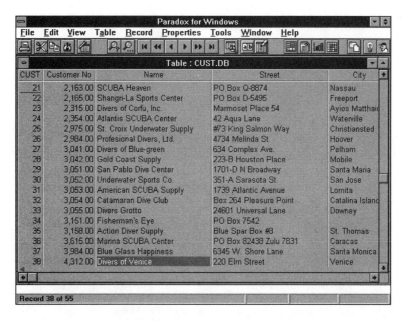

Figure 3.9 *Result of clicking on the previous record set button*

4. Click on the previous record set button again, and you are back to the window where the first record is visible. The highlight is on record 19.

Your screen may differ somewhat in that the video resolution is higher or lower than the screen used to capture these figures. So, don't be surprised if your movement is not identical.

5. Click on the next record button. The highlight moves down to the next record.

6. Click on the previous record button and continue clicking until the highlight is positioned on record 1.

Locating a Specific Record

Paradox can find a specific record by matching the numbers or text you type in the Locate Value dialog box. Of course, this method assumes that you know what you are looking for, which is not always true with a database. Let's try an example of finding a record in the CUST database.

1. Click on the locate field value button. The Locate Value dialog box appears as shown in Figure 3.10.

   The Value field is where you type the number or text that you want Paradox to find. Suppose that you want to find a record by using a specific city as the search value.

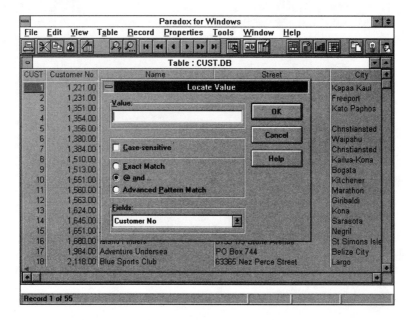

Figure 3.10 *Locate Value dialog box*

2. In the Value field type, **Venice**.

   The other search options are used as follows:

   Case-Sensitive—Click on this option if you want to have Paradox find only those values that are capitalized in the exact same way. For example, *St.Thomas* would not be located by Paradox if you entered **st.thomas** in the Value field and clicked on the **Case-Sensitive** option.

   Exact Match—Paradox can use wildcard characters to find a value. But, if the record you are trying to locate happens to have those characters in the field you are using for the search, click on this option to have Paradox not consider them as wildcards but as legitimate field data.

   @ and . —Check this option to use wildcards. The @ sign will stand in for any single character. If you are uncertain of the spelling of a name, you can use the @ sign to substitute for the letter. The **. .** sign stands for any number of characters (letters or numbers). Entering **B . . B** in the Value field finds matches with *Bob*, *Boob*, or *Blob*. You can also use the @ sign at the end or beginning of a word; **@ee@** locates *deed, seed, need,* and so on. Combine the wildcards as **N@@th..** to locate words such as *north, northern, northwestern.*

Advanced Pattern Match—The Advanced Pattern Match is an extensive and sophisticated means to locate a record. Table 3.4 lists the different operators and the effect on the search.

Table 3.4 *Advanced Pattern Match operators*

Operator	Locates
^	Beginning of the field
$	End of the field
*	Any number of occurrences of the immediately preceding expression, including none
+	One or more occurrences of the immediately preceding expression
?	One or no occurrence of the immediately preceding expression
|	Either the immediately preceding or immediately following character
[]	Any value contained within the brackets
[^]	Any character NOT contained in the bracket
()	Values inside parentheses treated as a group
\	An immediately following wildcard treated literally, not as a wildcard
\r	Carriage return
\n	Line feed
\t	Tab
\f	Form feed

3. Click on the down arrow in the Fields box to identify the field in which to search for the value of Venice. The list of fields appears as shown in Figure 3.11.

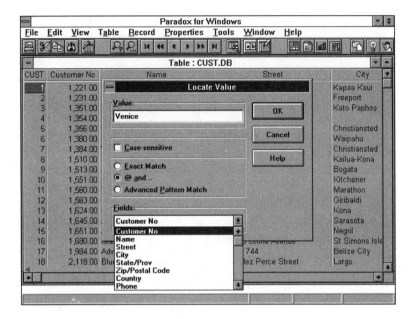

Figure 3.11 *Fields listed from CUST.DB table*

4. Click on the field in which Venice can be found, which is **City**.

Now you have the two settings that you need in order to locate a specific record. You have entered a specific value, **Venice**, and you have directed Paradox to search the City field.

5. Click on OK. The highlight jumps to the first record that has the *Venice* in the **City** field, as shown in Figure 3.12.

The first record found has the business name of Divers of Venice. Notice that Paradox indicates, in the status line, that this record is 38 of 55. If this record is the one you were seeking, this would be the end of the search. Perhaps this is not the correct record. The Locate Next button repeats the search using the same parameters already entered in the Locate Value dialog box.

6. Click on the Locate Next button. Paradox responds with a message in the status line indicating that no other records were located with *Venice* in the City field, as shown in Figure 3.13.

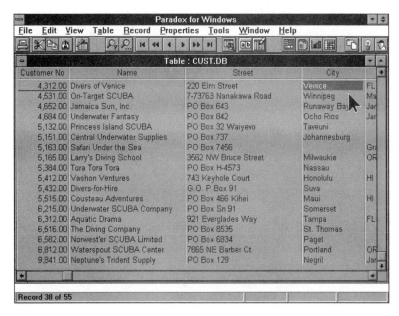

Figure 3.12 *Record located with Venice in the City field*

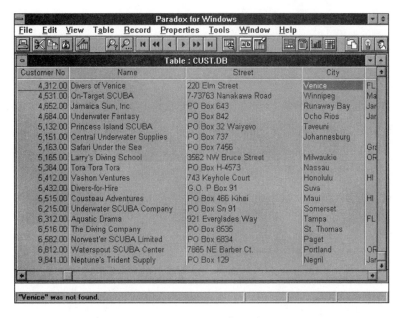

Figure 3.13 *Venice not found message*

Locating a Record by Customer Number

Suppose that a customer calls and asks you to check his mailing address. The customer happens to have his assigned customer number, making it easy for you to locate the record.

1. Click on the Locate Field value button.

2. In the Value field, type in the customer number.

3. Click on **Exact Match** as a search option.

4. Click on the down arrow in the Fields box and click on the Customer Number field.

5. Click on OK.

Paradox would quickly find the record. The speed of the search is increased because in this table, the Customer Number field is the key field.

Object Inspection

Every object in Paradox for Windows has characteristics that affect the way it displays. These characteristics are called *properties* in Paradox terminology. Some examples of properties are how data is justified, the color of the display, and the font.

While in any object, click the *right* mouse button. The Object Inspection menu displays listing the properties that can be adjusted for that object. Figure 3.14 shows a table with the Property Inspection menu displayed for the Customer No field. The Property Inspection menu that displays is determined by the field that is right clicked in the table.

This Object Inspection menu names the field you are inspecting. The filter, data dependency, number format, alignment, color, and font can be changed for this field.

Click on the **Number Format** option, The submenu displays, revealing the options for displaying the numbers in this field, as shown in Figure 3.15.

Because it is the Customer No field, adjust the color so that it displays in a more noticeable color. To do so, click on the **Color** option. A color pallete displays. Click on the desired color and the background display color of that field when it changes to the selected color.

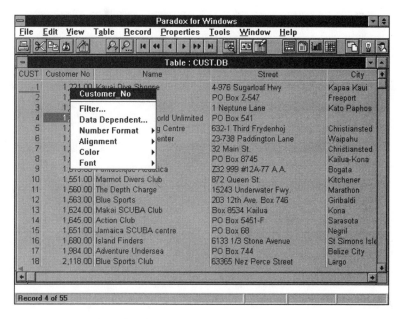

Figure 3.14 *Object Inspection menu for Customer No*

When people are working with this table, their eyes will be attracted to the different color. The Customer No field can easily be spotted. The more complex the object, the more properties it has. A table has different properties for every field. Right-click on the grid line or the header and the properties for those items display in a property menu.

A different menu appears when the right mouse button is clicked with the highlight on a different type of field. The Customer No field is a number field. Let's see what menu appears when you right-click on the First Contact field, which is the field at the far right of the table. Figure 3.16 shows the result.

Printing a Quick Report

Sometimes you just need to print a copy of the data that is displayed in a table. To do that, Paradox includes a quick report button. The quick report button prints the fields names and records on the screen. When you want to create an elaborate, customized report, turn to *Chapter 7* for the details.

While viewing the CUST.DB table, create a report of the table by clicking on the quick report button on the SpeedBar. A dialog box displays, stating that the report is being prepared.

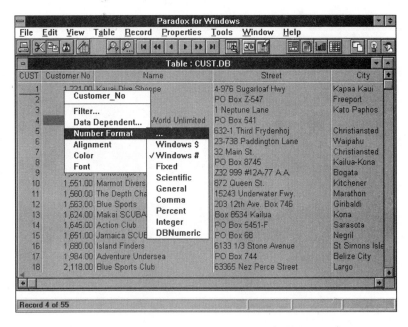

Figure 3.15 *Number Format submenu*

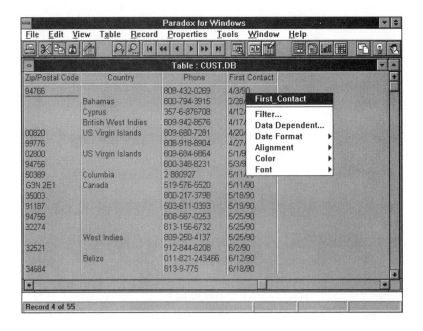

Figure 3.16 *Date field Object Inspection menu*

When preparation is complete, Paradox for Windows sends the table to the screen, creating a neat report of the data you have entered. This report is shown in Figure 3.17. This is the simplest, most basic method of getting a report with Paradox for windows.

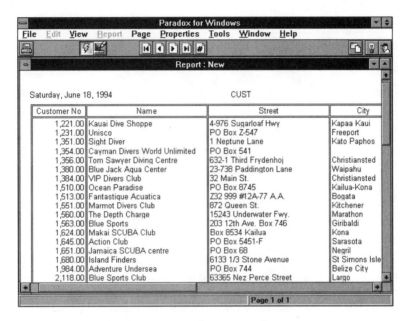

Figure 3.17 Quick report on the screen

To print the report, click on the printer button on the SpeedBar. The Print File dialog box appears, as shown in Figure 3.18. Click on OK.

As you progress through this book, you will learn more sophisticated methods for creating reports. Right now, give yourself a pat on the back for creating and printing your first Paradox for Windows report!

If the report does not print, access the File/Printer Setup options. You may need to modify the printer setup.

Removing the Table Image from the Screen

You have finished working in the table for now. Clear the image of CUST.DB or any other table in which you are working. Click on the window control button for the Table window and then click on **Close**. The table file is closed and removed from the screen. You are back to the Paradox for Windows opening screen. The workspace is blank so that you can create another table or attack another task in Paradox.

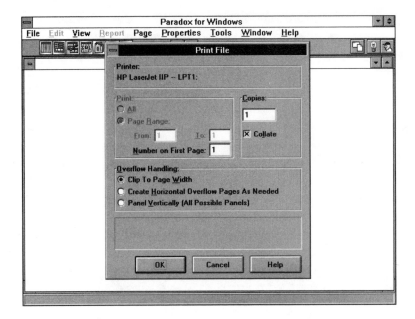

Figure 3.18 Print File dialog box

Using Function Keys

Paradox for Windows is designed to work with a mouse, but if you do not like to use a mouse, you can use the keyboard to perform Paradox functions. For those of you who are working with a keyboard, the Paradox function keys are listed in Table 3.5 along with a brief description of the function they control.

In Table 3.5, you will see **Ctrl+F12** listed as a function key. This convention means that you press the **Ctrl** key and hold it down while pressing the **F12** key. Additional examples are **Ctrl+F3** or **Shift+F6**. The plus sign between keys means hold the first key down and then press the second.

Table 3.5 *Table function keys*

Key	Description
F1	Opens Help window
F2	Field view
Shift+F2	Memo view
Ctrl+F2	Persistent field view
F5	Lock record
Shift+F5	Post record
Ctrl+F5	Post/keep lock
F6	Display Property menu
Shift+F6	Inspect all
F7	Quick form
Shift+F7	Quick report
Ctrl+F7	Quick graph
F9	Enter/exit Edit mode
F10	Menu
F11	Previous record
Shift+F11	Previous set
Ctrl+F11	First record
F12	Next record
Ctrl+F12	Last record

Command Summary

Command:	Mouse Click:	Keyboard Press:
View a Table	Open table button	**Alt+F/O/T**
Quick Report	Quick report button	**Shift+F7**
Remove Table Image	Window control/Close	**Ctrl+F4**

Summary

In this chapter, you learned how to find specific records. In *Chapter 4*, you'll begin constructing your own tables.

Chapter 4

Creating Tables

In the previous chapters, the discussion centered on how a database works, the planning process for a database design, the tools that Paradox brings to the task of using a database, and a look at the structure of an existing database. With all this in mind, you are now ready to apply that knowledge to creating a brand new database. This chapter takes you through that process, using an example political operation.

The key to excellent political operations is information. Paradox is designed to provide any organization fast access to crucial information. A political campaign provides examples of tables that can easily be transferred to any other business or nonprofit organization.

Creating a Table

The table created in the following steps is for a politician's office. The first table is to keep track of those people who donate to the campaign. This table will list the donor number, name, complete address, and donation. The field names look like this:

> Donor Number
>
> Name Address
>
> City
>
> State
>
> Zip
>
> Donation

The Donor Number field is designated as the primary key field. The Donor Number is the field used to link tables so the office staff can link to a second table, Issues.

To create a table, you must begin in the Paradox for Windows desktop.

1. Select File/New/Table from the menus. The Table Type dialog box displays, as shown in Figure 4.1. This will be a Paradox for Windows table. You can also create Paradox 3.5 tables and dBASE IV and dBASE III+ tables.

2. Click on the OK button. The Create Paradox for Windows Table dialog box displays, as shown in Figure 4.2. In this dialog box you enter the field names, the type, the size, and the key.

In *Chapter 3*, you opened the Restructure dialog box, which is identical to this dialog box except that no field names have been entered. The following rules apply for field names:

▼ The name of the field cannot be longer than 25 characters.

▼ Spaces are OK, except at the beginning of the field name.

▼ Each field name must be unique. Capitalization does not make a difference to Paradox.

▼ Any printable character is acceptable, except for the following:

\#   By itself the pound sign will not work. Add it to another set of characters such as Phone \# to use \#.

"   Quotation marks will not work.

{} [] ()   Curly brackets, Square brackets, or parentheses will not work.

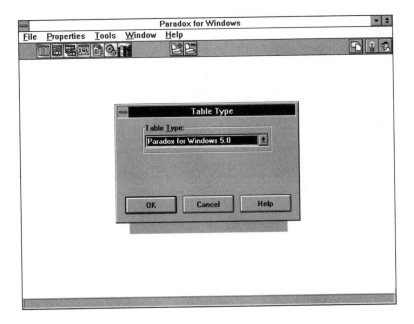

Figure 4.1 *Table Type dialog box*

Entering Field Names and Types

In the Create Paradox for Windows Table dialog box, you will enter the field names, types, size, and how they are to be keyed. It is a good idea to enter as short a name as possible for field names, without making the name too hard to decipher. For example, instead of entering **First Name**, enter **FNAME**. Table 4.1 lists the field types and the results and restrictions of using that type. Remember that with Paradox if you create a table and enter a field type that does not work, you are allowed to change the type afterward.

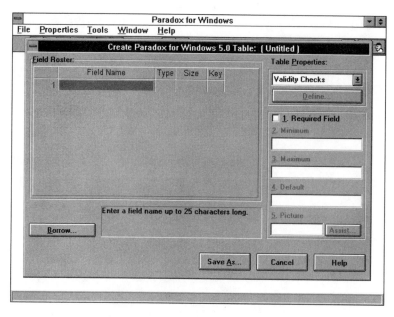

Figure 4.2 *Create Paradox for Windows Table dialog box*

Table 4.1 *Paradox for Windows Field Types*

Field Type	Symbol	Size Allowed	Characteristics
Alphanumeric	A	Maximum of 255	All characters that print. Numbers are treated as text.
Number	N	Virtually unlimited	Any normal numbers are fine, including negative numbers.
Currency	$	Virtually unlimited	The field entries display with a currency symbol and commas.
Date	D	N/A	Paradox checks dates for validity when entered into the table.
Short Number	S	-32,767 to 32,767	Used for specialized applications.

(continued)

Field Type	Symbol	Size Allowed	Characteristics
Memo	M	240 characters	This field type can be used to store longer text entries than 240 characters, but Paradox displays a maximum of 240 characters. In order for the table to work efficiently, text that exceeds the 240 character length is stored in a MB file. When you access the record, Paradox locates the remaining text and then displays it.
Formatted Memo	F	240 Characters	Same as a memo field except that you can add formatting to the text, such as different typefaces, sizes, and colors.
Binary	B	Unlimited	Use this type to store sound files or any other type of file that Paradox cannot interpret.
Graphic	G	Unlimited	Attach a graphic file to a record, such as a photo of a part.
OLE	O	Unlimited	Attach objects which Windows can recognize and that allow Object Linking and Embedding. Objects such as graphs can be attached and manipulated via Paradox.

It is possible to create dBASE tables via Paradox. If you do so, the types of fields available change considerably. Check your documentation for more information.

NOTE

The highlight is in the column called Field Name. To enter the first field name:

1. Type **Donor #** (do not forget the space between **Donor** and **#**) and then press **Enter**. The highlight moves to the Type field. To see the list of field types, right click or press the **Space bar**. The list appears as shown in Figure 4.3.

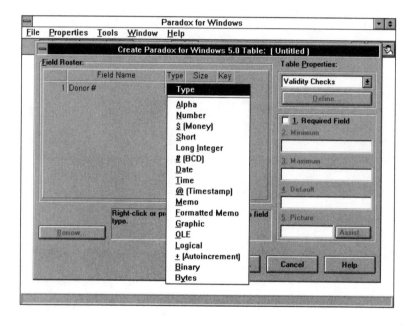

Figure 4.3 Field type list

2. Type **A** for an alphanumeric field and press **Enter**.

3. Type **8** since no donor number will be longer than eight characters. Press **Enter**.

4. Double-click in the Key field. This turns the toggle on for the primary key field.

5. Press **Enter**. The first field is defined as the primary key field. Figure 4.4 shows the dialog box at this time.

Numbers placed in an Alphanumeric field cannot be used in mathematical functions. Use the Number and Currency fields when you want to add, subtract, multiply, or divide numbers.

N O T E

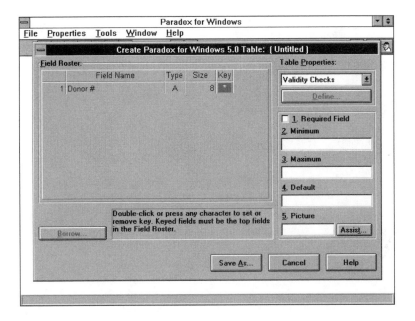

Figure 4.4 *The first field defined*

To complete the table:

1. Type **LName**; then press **Enter**. Type **A** for an alphanumeric field and press **Enter**. Type **12** and press **Enter**.

2. Type **FName**; then press **Enter**. Type **A** for an alphanumeric field and press **Enter**. Type **12** and press **Enter**.

3. Type **Address**; then press **Enter**. Type **A** for an alphanumeric field and press **Enter**. Type **20** and press **Enter**.

4. Type **City**; then press **Enter**. Type **A** for an alphanumeric field and press **Enter**. Type **20** and press **Enter**.

5. Type **St**; then press **Enter**. Type **A** for alphanumeric field and press **Enter**. Type **2** for the Size and press **Enter**.

6. Type **Zip**; then press **Enter**. Type **A** for alphanumeric field and press **Enter**. Type **10** for the Size and press **Enter**.

The Field Roster defines the fields as shown in the dialog box in Figure 4.5.

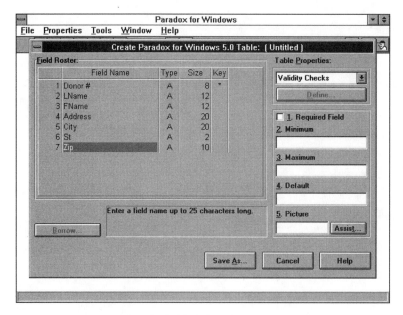

Figure 4.5 *The fields defined in the Field Roster*

Saving the Table Structure

When you save the table structure, it must be named. To save and name the table after the structure is completed:

To save the table:

1. Click on the save as button in the dialog box. The Save Table As dialog box displays, as shown in Figure 4.6.

2. Type the name of the table in the New Table Name text box. For this example type **DONOR**.

There are several other options that you can select when you save the table. You can click on **Display Table**, which cause Paradox to open the new table immediately upon its being saved. Second, if you already have a table with data and want that data to be inserted automatically into this new table, click on **Add Data To New Table**. Paradox displays a list of tables from which you can select the one to insert.

3. Click on the OK button.

This completes the table definition. Now you are ready to view the table and use it.

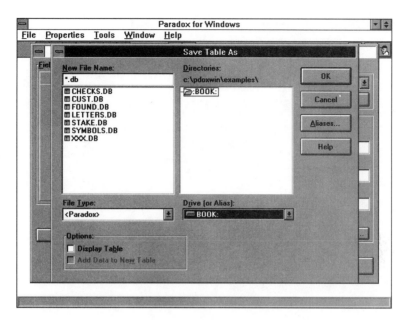

Figure 4.6 *Save Table As dialog box*

Entering Data into the Table

The structure of the table is created. Now you can start to enter data. Start by opening the table.

Opening the Table

Once you have created a table structure and saved that structure, you may open the table. If you have been following the steps as described, the table should have been saved to the PDOXWIN\EXAMPLES subdirectory. If you had changed your working directory using the File menu, it may be elsewhere.

1. Click on the open table button on the SpeedBar. The Open Table dialog box displays. A list of tables appears on the left side of the dialog box, as shown in Figure 4.7.

Your list of tables will differ from those listed in Figure 4.7.

NOTE

2. Select the table you want to view. Click on **DONOR**.

3. Click on the OK button. The table displays.

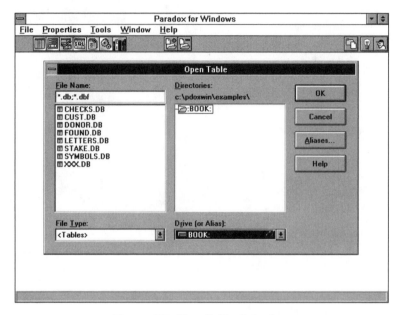

Figure 4.7 *Open Table dialog box*

At this time, no data is entered in the table. The field names, as you have defined them, appear horizontally across the screen. Figure 4.8 shows the table as it looks now. Notice the title bar of the table window. It states that you are in the DONOR file. The file extension.DB is added.

Entering Data into the Table

Now you are ready to enter data into the table, which is called editing the table. Notice that the table is opened as less than a full window. Move the mouse pointer to the edit data button on the SpeedBar. The button appears as if it has a pencil poised over a piece of paper.

To add data to the DONOR table:

1. Click on the Edit Data button on the SpeedBar. The highlight is placed on the first record under the first field, as shown in Figure 4.9. Because the fields take up more space than the screen displays. you will have to scroll to the right to see the entire table.

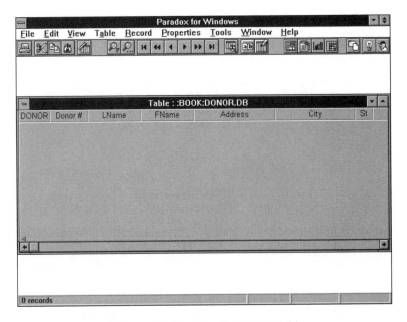

Figure 4.8 *Viewing the DONOR table*

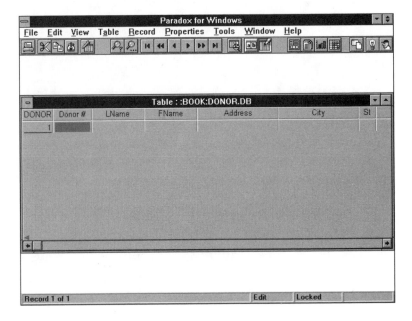

Figure 4.9 *DONOR table in Edit mode*

2. Type **100**. Press **Enter**. The Donor number is entered. When you press **Enter**, the highlight box moves right, to the LName field.

3. Type **Wiley** and press **Enter**.

4. Type **Ann** and press **Enter**.

5. In the Address field, type **123 Elm Street** and press **Enter**.

6. In the City field, type **Los Angeles** and press **Enter**.

7. In the State field, type **CA**.

8. In the Zip field type **93600**.

The first record of data is entered in the DONOR database, as shown in Figure 4.10.

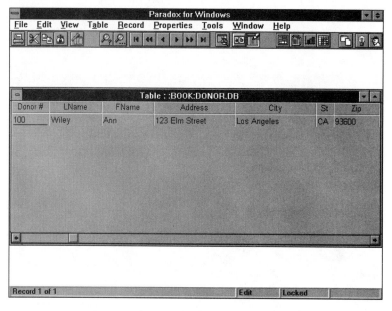

Figure 4.10 *First record added to database*

Repeat steps 2 through 7 to enter four more records.

Donor #	LName	FName	Address	City	State	Zip
101	Pascal	Blaise	456 Maple St	Los Angeles	CA	93599
102	Hegel	Heinrich	1700 P Street	Los Angeles	CA	90067
103	James	William	800 Arch Lane	Los Angeles	CA	92125
104	Spinoza	Baruch	300 Holls Lane	Los Angeles	CA	94500

That's it for the DONOR table. The data is saved to the table as you enter it. The DONOR table with five records is shown in Figure 4.11.

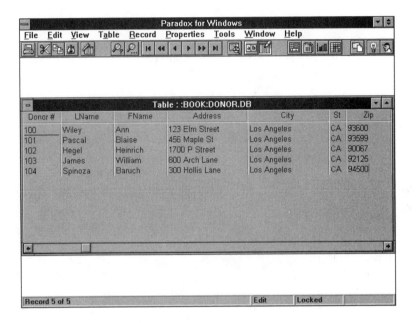

Figure 4.11 *Five records in DONOR table*

Entering data into the table was pretty straightforward. But, one field was not included. The amount that the donor contributed is very important for record keeping, but no field exists for such an entry. To add that field, the table must be restructured.

Restructuring a Table

In the previous sections, you learned how to create a table structure and then to enter data into the Paradox table. But, because the original design failed to include a field for the amount of the donation, you must make a change. This is called *restructuring*. The examples that follow will be in the DONOR table.

Use restructuring when you need to add more spaces to a field; add, delete, change, or rename fields; change field types; or change primary keys.

Displaying a Table Structure

In order to edit the data in a table, you must first be in the Edit mode. When you choose to restructure a table, you have to open the Restructure a Table window. With the table that you want to restructure on-screen, follow these steps to display the Restructure a Table dialog box.

1. Click on the Table menu on the menu bar. The Table menu displays as you see in Figure 4.12. The top two sections of the menu show options that are also available on the SpeedBar. The third section offers the Sort, Restructure, and Info Structure options.

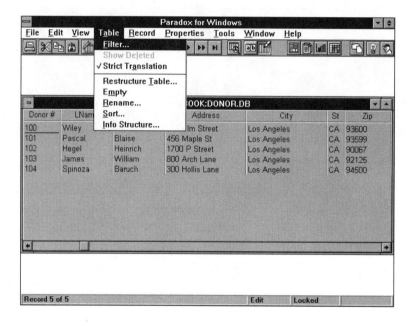

Figure 4.12 *The Table menu*

2. Click on the **Restructure** option. The Restructure Paradox for Windows Table dialog box displays. This window looks very much like the original window in which you created the table structure. All the field names, field types, and sizes are listed in Figure 4.13 just as you entered them.

Changing the Table Structure

The first action to take on restructuring the table is to add a new field for donations. The most logical place for the Amount field is directly after the Donor Number field.

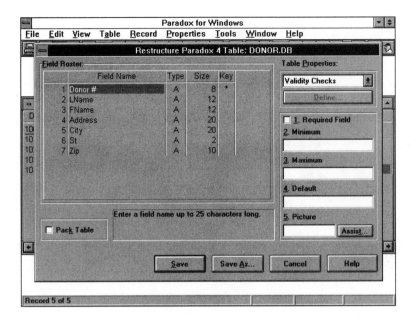

Figure 4.13 *The Restructure Paradox for Windows Table dialog box*

To add a new field:

1. Click on **LName**.

2. Press the **Insert** key. Paradox creates a blank field space between the Donor # and LName fields, as shown in Figure 4.14.

3. Type **Amount**.

4. Press **Tab**. This is an alternative means of moving within the field roster, instead of pressing **Enter**.

5. In the Type field, type **$** which will make the field a Money field.

6. Press **Tab**. The highlight jumps to the Key field.

Paradox does not allow an entry in the Size field because the size is automatically set by the Money attribute. The donation field could be made a key field, but if that was done, only unique entries could be made in the field. For example, if two people donated $100, only one could be entered.

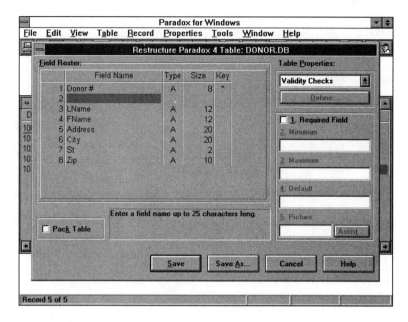

Figure 4.14 *Space inserted in the Restructure dialog box*

Making a Second Change

The Donor # field is too long. Eight characters is a very large number. Let's reduce the size of the field in order to see how Paradox handles this kind of change.

To reduce the size of a field:

1. Click on the **8** in the Donor # field.

2. Type **5**.

3. Press **Enter**.

4. Click on the save button. Paradox responds with a warning dialog box. When you entered the donor numbers, none were longer than four characters. Paradox does not know this. It assumes that there might be data lost because the size of the field has been reduced.

In the Data Loss Warning dialog box, Paradox states that you have possible data loss in the field Donor #. You are asked if you want to trim it. Paradox for Windows is asking if you want to trim the data to fit the new size.

Each action you can take at this point is described as follows:

Choose **Yes** if you want to trim the data (in this example, you know that no data will be lost) so the Donor # fits in the five spaces available. The data is truncated to five spaces.

Choose **No** if there were the possibility that you would lose data. Paradox creates a PROBLEMS table to hold the excess characters from the donor numbers that are longer than five spaces.

Choose **Cancel** if you have made an error and you want to return to the Restructure Paradox for Windows Table dialog box to increase the size of a reduced field.

Choose **Help** if you are not sure how to resolve the trimming issue, and if you need more information.

As you probably have figured out by now, it is best to know before you restructure a table whether any of the data in a particular field will be lost. Check the field before you restructure the table so that you are confident in your decision.

N O T E

5. Click on **Yes** in the Possible data loss... field.

6. Click **OK**. The newly constituted table appears as shown in Figure 4.15.

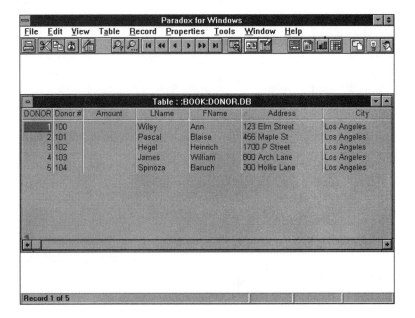

Figure 4.15 *DONOR table with new field*

Effect of Restructuring on Tables

You have seen how Paradox for Windows warns you if you try to shorten an alphanumeric field. The warning encourages you to be sure you want to shorten the field prior to the restructuring action. It also offers you the chance to change the restructuring action by choosing **Cancel** from the Warning dialog box.

There is another restructuring action that produces a warning from Paradox for Windows—the action of deleting a field. Should you try to delete a field that holds data, Paradox for Windows gives you a warning and a chance to change your mind. A warning window displays asking if you are sure you want to delete the selected field and risk the loss of data. Confirm the deletion, and data is removed and lost. Cancel the deletion, and the data remains in the field.

Effect of Restructuring on the Related Objects

Restructure a table, and Paradox automatically goes through any associated objects and adjusts the objects accordingly. For example, if you delete a field in the table restructure, Paradox for Windows deletes the field from the custom form, the custom report, and the associated graph. This effect will become more apparent in later chapters.

Editing the Restructured Table

Let's add some values in the Amount field. Editing records is different from adding records in that the procedure changes.

To make changes to the first record:

1. Click on the edit data button on the SpeedBar. Paradox changes to the Edit mode.
2. Click the mouse pointer on the first record, in the Amount field.
3. Type **100** and then click on the next record below, still in the Amount field. The value is entered as $100 as shown in Figure 4.16.

Finish the rest of the entries in the amount field as follows:

Record 2   50

Record 3   750

Record 4   1000

Record 5   99

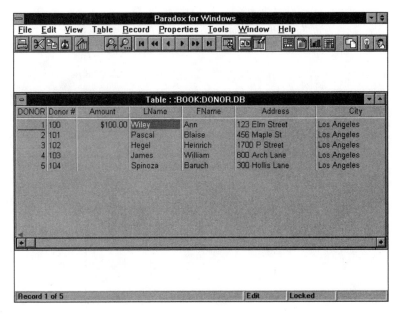

Figure 4.16 $100 entered into Amount field

When editing a series of entries in a single field, (as in this example) pressing the **Down Arrow** key moves the highlight down to the next record and at the same time completes the edit of the current record.

N O T E

The completed table, with the new donation amounts is shown in Figure 4.17.

Editing a table, as opposed to editing a form, is most useful if the table has few fields and records. Few fields means few enough to view on no more than two horizontal screens. That is, if three field columns are visible on one screen, press the **Right Arrow** key and three more fields are visible. This is the maximum amount of jumping around you will want to have to do to edit in the tabular format.

Few records would mean no more than two vertical screens of records. With more fields or records in a table, *Chapter 9* covers editing in a form.

If you find you are jumping around a great deal while editing in list view, switch to form view for easier editing.

N O T E

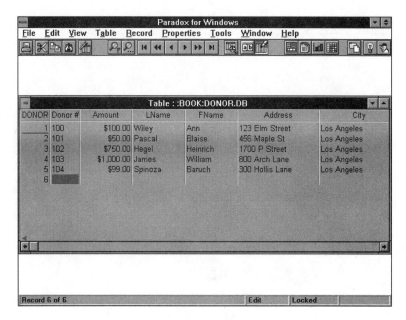

Figure 4.17 *Edited table with new donation amounts*

Looking at Form View

To this point, you have looked at the records in Paradox in tabular form. Let's take a quick look at how Paradox displays the data from the DONOR table in form view. Paradox allows you to design a form, or it will design one for you, with just the click of a button.

To change the layout:

1. With the DONOR table open as the active table, click on the quick form button. A new window opens on the desktop, as shown in Figure 4.18.

A form shows you only a single record at a time. All of the navigation buttons work the same in form view. Click on the next record button, and Paradox responds with the record that follows that current record.

Forms can have a very elaborate design. Paradox creates the quick form for your convenience in editing, or whatever you may have in mind. Because all of the fields of a record are visible, some tasks are much easier.

2. Close the Form window by clicking on the window control button and clicking on the close button. Paradox prompts you as to whether or not you want to save this new object.

3. Click on **No**.

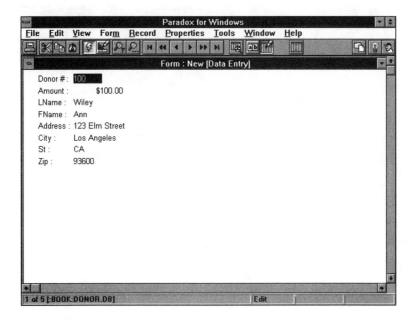

Figure 4.18 *Quick form view*

Editing and Entering Information

This section lists the many ways to add, delete, and change the information entered into a table. You have already learned several. You can edit Paradox records in the table view or the form view. What follows is a list of and definition of the terms used for editing and entering information.

Edit Session. Click on the edit button on the SpeedBar to begin the edit session. During the edit session, you make the desired additions and corrections. If you make mistakes during an edit session, you can correct them before the session ends.

Undo. If you make an edit and then decide you want the original information, using the Undo function cancels the edit. Click on Edit/Undo to cancel and edit. The Edit menu with the **Undo** option is shown in Figure 4.19.

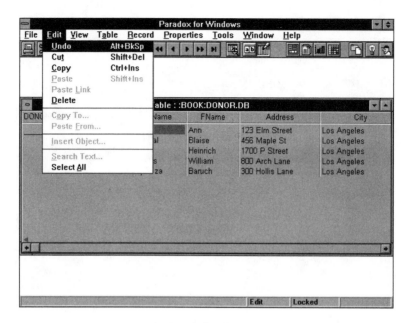

Figure 4.19 *Edit/Undo menu option*

Tabular Edit. A tabular edit is one done in the table view, as opposed to the form view. In a tabular edit, you can change the data as it appears in the table view.

Form Edit. While in form view, an edit is called a *form edit.* You can edit the data in a form, but you can also edit the design, structure, and contents of a form. It is important to distinguish between these two.

Field View. Use the field view to update a field's data by replacing or inserting new information. Click on the field view button on the SpeedBar to begin a field view.

Basic Edit View. This mode of updating fields is used most often. This mode allows you to delete old data and insert new data or add new records to the end of a table. You cannot use this mode to add data to the middle of a field.

Validity Checks. Paradox for Windows checks the data you enter into a field. If you try to enter letters in a number field type, Paradox for Windows will inform you that this is not allowed. Paradox for Windows will also check the range of information you have entered. A validity check also helps you with a lookup.

Lookup. Paradox checks to make sure that what you enter in a field in one table matches an entry in another table. The table you are trying to match is called the *lookup table.*

Multiple Record Entry. You can choose to create and add records as a group. This gives you a concise view of the records you intend to add.

Editing Keys

When the word *Edit* is on the message bar, you are in Edit mode. Press the arrow keys or click with the mouse pointer to move around in the table. The highlighting moves from field to field. Type data in any highlighted field, and the old data is replaced with what you type.

At times, it may make more sense to use the keyboard rather than the mouse to move in the Edit mode. Move around in the table and edit data, using the keys below.

Keyboard Shortcuts

Right Arrow or **Tab.** Moves to the next field, moving from left to right and top to bottom. If you are in the last field of a record, press the right arrow key and you move to the first field of the next record.

Left Arrow or **Shift-Tab.** Moves the highlight to the previous field. If you are in the first field of a record, the **Left Arrow** key moves you to the last field of the previous record.

Up Arrow. Moves to the same field in the previous record.

Down Arrow. Moves to the same field in the next record.

Backspace. When the highlighting is on a field, press the **Backspace** key to delete all the data in the field. When a blinking insertion point is in the field, press the **Backspace** key to delete one character to the left of the blinking insertion point.

Home. Moves the highlight to the leftmost field in the current record.

End. Moves the highlight to the rightmost field in the current record.

Ctrl+Backspace. Deletes all the data in the field.

Ctrl+Right Arrow. Moves the highlight to the rightmost field in the record.

Ctrl+Left Arrow. Moves the highlight to the leftmost field in the record.

Ctrl+Up Arrow. Moves the highlight to the first record in the database, while staying in the same field.

Ctrl+Down Arrow. Moves the highlight to the last record in the database, while staying in the same field.

Ctrl+Home. Moves the highlight to the first field in the first record in the database.

Ctrl+End. Moves the highlight to the last field in the last record in the database.

Adding New Records

Whether you have a list of clients or a list of products in your table, chances are you are going to add new records to the table. If you enter records in a specific order, you can add new records at the beginning or anywhere in the middle of the table. You can also add records to the end of the table.

When adding a record to the top or the middle of a table, you must first move the highlight to the record below the location where you want the new record to appear. In other words, Paradox inserts a new record in the row above the highlight.

To add a new record to the top or middle of a record:

1. Move the highlight to the record after the location of the new record. In this example, move the highlight to any field in the record 100, Wiley.

2. Press **Insert**. The highlight moves to the blank row and the leftmost field. Figure 4.20 shows how the table looks with a blank row added.

3. Enter data in the blank row.

Donor#	Amount	LName	FName	Address	City	State	Zip
99	500	Kant	Imman	400 Dutch Ln	Amster	CA	93005

4. At the end of the entries, press **Enter**. Paradox flashes a message that the new record has been inserted. Figure 4.21 shows how the new record looks in the table.

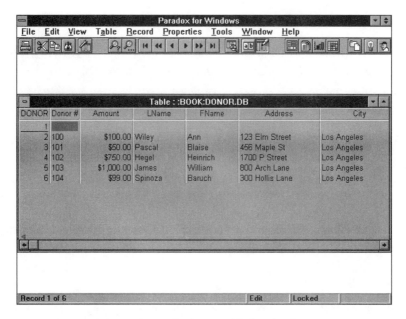

Figure 4.20 *Blank row added to database*

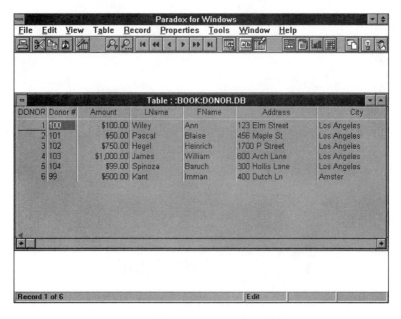

Figure 4.21 *New record in table*

Adding Records to the End of a Table

Add records to the end of a table simply by pressing the **Down Arrow** key beyond the last record. Paradox for Windows opens a new blank row.

In a longer table, click on the last record button on the SpeedBar. Press the **Down Arrow** key now, and the highlight moves to a blank row at the end of the table.

 **Ctrl+End.** Moves the highlight to the end of the table.

When the highlight is at the rightmost field in the last record of the table, press **Enter**. A blank row inserts at the end of the table. The highlight is in the first field of the new blank row.

Deleting a Record

Whether data is entered in a record incorrectly or that record is no longer necessary, there will be times when you want to delete a record.

 Make sure that you want to delete a record before you take this action. You cannot get the record back once it is deleted.

WARNING

To delete a record:

1. Move the highlight to any field in the record you want to delete.

2. Click on Record/Delete.

 Ctrl+Del. Deletes a record from the database.

The record is deleted from the database table.

Changing Existing Records

While in an editing session, you want to change data. You move the highlight to the column or field you want to change and type the new information. The old data is replaced with new data. You have another option, and that is to use the field view to edit data.

Field Editing

The option to replacing text in a field is to use the *field edit*. The field edit is especially useful in a field that holds a great deal of text or complex text you do not want to type over. The field edit option allows you to move a blinking insertion point over text to change it.

For example, if you had a memo field that held lengthy product descriptions and there was an error in the middle of the field, you would not want to delete half the field and then retype it, just to correct the error. Instead, turn on field edit and move the blinking insertion point to the error, correct it, move the insertion point to the end, and then end the field edit.

The field edit saves time because you don't have to retype large amounts of information. Instead, you move directly to the error, and then correct it.

When you enter data in a field edit, characters to the right of the insertion point are moved to the right as you type.

To correct data in a field using a field edit:

1. Move the highlight to the field that holds data you want to change. Do this by clicking the mouse pointer on the field.

2. Click the field view button on the SpeedBar. It has the small letters *ab* on it.

 **F2.** Entering Field View.

The highlight on the field is replaced with a blinking insertion point (vertical line) at the end of the data in the field. In Figure 4.22 the mouse pointer indicates where the insertion point is at the end of a field.

3. Press the **Left Arrow** key, or use the mouse pointer to move the insertion point to the location of the error. Place the insertion point one character to the right of an incorrect letter.

During a field edit, the mouse pointer changes to an insertion point while in the field to be edited. You cannot move the mouse pointer out of this field until the field edit is complete.

N O T E

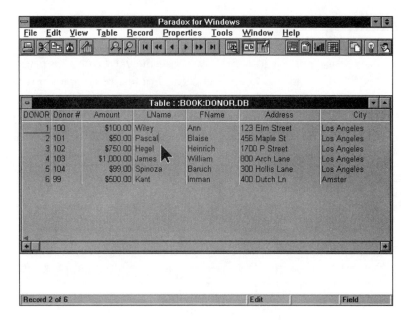

Figure 4.22 *The insertion point in a field edit*

4. Press the **Backspace** key one time for each character you want to delete.

5. Type the character you want to replace the deleted characters. The characters you type in insert in the text at the insertion point. The characters to the right of the new text will move to the right.

6. Click on the field view button on the SpeedBar to end the field edit. The highlight replaces the insertion point in the field in which you have been working.

While you are in the field edit, you will find that the arrow keys and the **Home**, **End**, and **Del** keys work a little differently. Those differences are listed here.

Left Arrow, Right Arrow. Press either key one time, and the insertion point moves one character to the right or left. But the insertion point stays within the field. You cannot move between fields while in the Field Edit mode.

Home, End. Moves to the beginning (**Home**) or end (**End**) of a field.

Del. Deletes the character to the right of the insertion point.

Backspace. Deletes the character to the left of the insertion point.

Ctrl+Backspace. Deletes the characters in the entire field.

Undoing an Edit

Any action you take that is listed on the Edit menu can be undone. Figure 4.23 shows the Edit menu. (You must be in the Edit mode in order to see the menu just as you see in this figure.) The options available are shown in bold, they are Cut, Copy, Delete, and Select All.

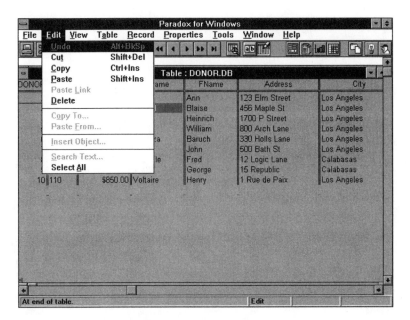

Figure 4.23 *The Edit menu*

While you take an action on any of the options available on the Edit menu, Paradox keeps your last action in memory. With the highlight in a field, you delete the data in the field. But it turns out it was a mistake. Select Edit/Undo to replace the deleted data.

To use the **Undo** option on the Edit menu:

1. Move the highlight to a field that holds data by clicking on the field with the mouse pointer.

2. Select the Edit menu. Select **Delete**. The data in the field is deleted and the Edit menu is removed from the screen. You find that this was the wrong field to delete. Undo the edit.

3. Select the Edit menu. Select **Undo**.

 Alt+Backspace. The deleted data returns to the field.

You must use the Undo command directly after making an editing error. You cannot attempt to correct a mistake made three or four tasks before. In addition, if you use the Table/Empty option, Undo will not work.

N O T E

Ending an Edit

Before you end an editing session, check the data entered to make sure there is nothing you want to undo. With the table edited to perfection, end the editing session by clicking on the edit data button on the SpeedBar. You are back in the View mode.

Reordering Columns in a Table Edit

With one keystroke you can change the order in which columns appear on the screen. Press **Ctrl+R** and the column farthest to the right moves one column to the left. At the same time, the column the highlight is in moves to the far right. A circular motion ensues, with the columns moving around as you continue to press **Ctrl+R**.

This can be illustrated by moving the highlight to the LName field in the DONOR table. You should be in the Edit mode, with the columns in the same order as you have seen in previous figures in this chapter. Click on any record in the LName field and then press **Ctrl+R**. The LName field moves to the far right of the table, while the FName column moves one place to the left, as shown in Figure 4.24. Continue rotating fields by pressing **Ctrl+R** repeatedly.

Rotating the columns for viewing purposes does not change the structure of the table.

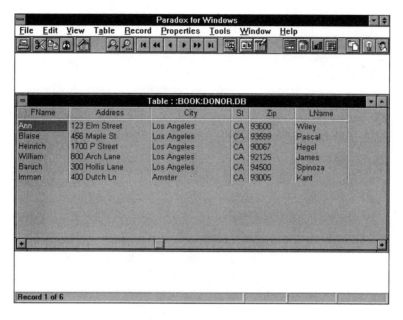

Figure 4.24 *The field columns rotated*

Resizing Table Images

Alt+-/X. Shrink or expand the size of the table image on the screen by using the size buttons in the upper-right corner of the window or by pointing the mouse pointer on the window edges.

With a table in a small window on-screen, click on the maximize button in the upper-right corner of the window. This is the button with one arrow pointing up. The table expands to fill the entire Paradox for Windows workspace.

Alt+-/R. Return the window to the original size by clicking the restore button in the upper-right corner of the window. The restore button for the table window has two arrows, one pointing up, the other pointing down, and is located on the menu bar when the window is maximized.

Alt+-/N. Minimize the table window to an icon by clicking on the minimize button, located next to the maximize button. The minimize button has a single arrow pointing down. Click on the minimize button, and the table window becomes a table window becomes a table icon. This icon is shown in Figure 4.25. The table icon displays with the table file name below the icon.

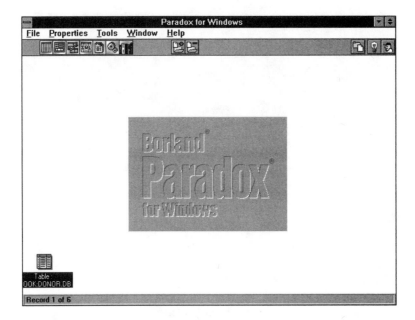

Figure 4.25 *The table icon*

Double-click on the table icon to restore the table to its original size.

Alt+-/S. Use the mouse pointer to make small adjustments in the size of a table on-screen. Move the mouse pointer to the edge of the window. The mouse pointer becomes a white two-headed arrow, as shown in Figure 4.26. Click this arrow on the edge of the window and drag the edge of the window to expand or shrink the window size, then use the arrow keys. Press **Enter**.

With this feature, using Paradox for Windows, you are able to display several tables on-screen at the same time. The table windows can be arranged and sized so that you can view several tables at once. Figure 4.27 shows several tables in the workspace. The tables are tiled, that is they are sized to fit on the screen at the same time, while viewing several tables.

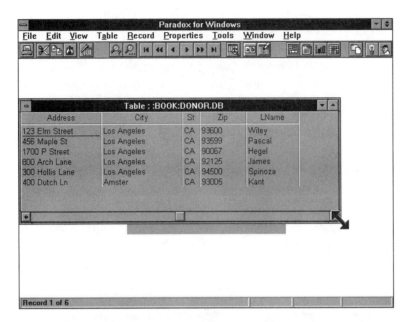

Figure 4.26 *Two-headed resizing arrow*

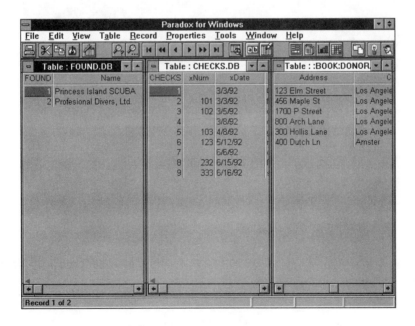

Figure 4.27 *Three tables tiled*

Creating a Quick Graph

Use the instant graph button on the SpeedBar to create a graph on-screen. There are two main elements to any graph, the *y*-axis or vertical axis and the *x*-axis or horizontal axis. In order for a graph to make any sense, the fields used to create the graph must have a relationship. A table has been created especially for this example.

1. Click on the quick graph button on the SpeedBar. A Define Graph dialog box displays. In this box, define the field to display on the x-axis. The file name displays in the large box at the left.

2. Click on the down arrow to the right of the file name. A list of fields in that table displays, as you see in Figure 4.28.

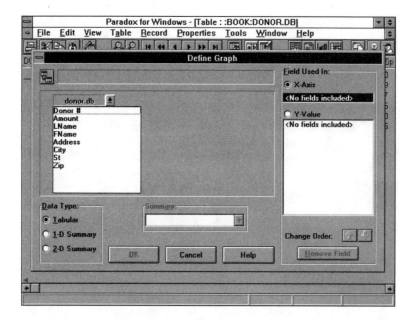

Figure 4.28 *A list of fields to graph*

3. Click on the field you want to graph. In this example, click on **Donor #**. The field inserts under the *x*-axis indicator.

4. Click on the Y-Value.

5. Click on the down arrow to the right of the file name.

6. Click on **Amount**, the only field available for display on the *y*-axis.

7. Click on the OK button.

Figure 4.29 shows the instant graph on-screen. You have graphed one field of data on the x-axis.

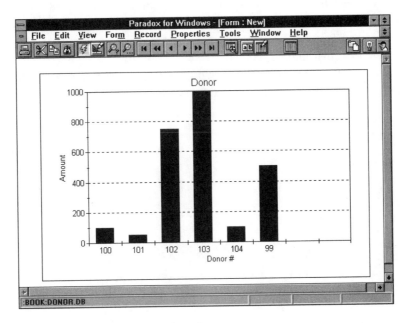

Figure 4.29 *The graph on-screen*

Removing the Graph from the Screen

Admire the graph you have created. You have created an instant picture of the data on the table, but now it is time to return to the table.

1. Click on the window control button for the Graph window. Click on the close button. A dialog box displays. Paradox for Windows prompts you, saying the file is new, do you want to save it?

2. Click on **Yes** to save it. If you choose to save the file that holds the graph, a Save File As dialog box displays. Here you type the name of the graph you want to save; then click on the OK button. The graph is saved as a form. Click on **No** or **Cancel** if you do not want to save it. When you click on No the graph is removed from the screen. Click on **Help** if you need help now.

Saving a New Table

Strange as it may seem, particularly if you have used computers before with other applications, you do not have to do anything to save tables. They are automatically saved when you exit Paradox. If any object, table, form, graph, etc., has not been *named*, when you try to exit Paradox, you are prompted as to whether or not you want to save the object. Do so by adding a name. Every unique object in Paradox has its own extension. Even though you are operating in the Windows environment, you still have to conform to the DOS rules for creating names of files. Every object created in Paradox is saved as a DOS file. Table 4.2 lists Paradox objects with the extensions that describe the kind of object it is.

Table 4.2 *Paradox Object Files Extensions*

Extension	File Type
.db	Paradox table
.cfg	Configuration file
.dbf	dBASE file
.dbt	dBASE memo file
.fam	Paradox list of related files
.fdl	Delivered form created in ObjectPal
.fsl	Saved form
.dtl	Temporary form
.ini	Initialization configuration file
.ldl	Delivered library file from ObjectPal
.lsl	Saved library
.ltl	Temporary library
.mb	Memos for Paradox table longer than 240 characters
.mdx	Maintained index of a dBASE file
.ndx	Nonmaintained index of a dBASE file
.px	Primary index of a Paradox file

.qbe	Saved Paradox query
.rdl	Delivered report
.rsl	Saved report
.rtl	Temporary report
.sdl	Delivered script
.ssl	Saved script
.stl	Temporary script
.tv	Table view settings for a Paradox table
.tvf	Table view settings for a dBASE table
.val	Validity checks and referential integrity for a Paradox table
.xnn	Secondary single-field index for a Paradox table (x00, x01, x03,...)
.ynn	Secondary single-field index for a Paradox table (y00, y01, y03,...)
.xgn	Composite secondary index for a Paradox table
.ygn	Composite secondary index for a Paradox

Command Summary

Command:	Mouse Click:	Keyboard Press:
Create a Table	File/New/Table	**Alt+F/N/T**
Create Primary Key	Double-click key field	**Spacebar**
Save Table Structure	Save As...	**Alt+A**
Begin Edit Session	Edit data button	**F9**
Insert Blank Row		**Insert**
Move One Field Right	On Next Field	**Enter or Tab**

(continued)

Command:	Mouse Click:	Keyboard Press:
Move to End of Table	Last record button	**Ctrl+End**
Delete a Record	Record/Delete	**Ctrl+F12**
Toggle to Field Edit	Field view button	**F2**
Delete Field Data	Edit/Delete	
Undo an Edit	Edit/Undo	**Alt+Backspace**
End an Edit	Edit data button	**F9**
Reorder Field Columns		**Ctrl-R**
Maximize Window	Maximize button	**Alt+-/X**
Minimize Window	Minimize button	**Alt+-/N**
Restore Window	Restore button	**Alt+-/R**
Resize Window	Drag window edge	**Alt+-/S**
Restructure	Table/Restructure	**Alt+T/R**
Move a Field	Field name and drag	

Summary

In this chapter, you learned how to create a basic Paradox table. In *Chapter 5*, you will learn how to add more complex table attributes.

Chapter 5

Table Fine-Tuning

In this chapter the nuances of creating tables will be discussed. For example, if you want to create a table with fields that restrict the values that can be entered, the table must be structured with that restriction included. In the DONOR table created in *Chapter 4*, restrictions were made a part of the structure. In this chapter several restrictions are added, and other ideas for customizing the structures of tables are considered. The topics in this chapter are:

▼ Restructuring with validations
▼ Creating a lookup table
▼ Formatting entries
▼ Formatting dates
▼ Adding a memo field
▼ Changing the view properties of a table

135

Controlling Data Entry

Despite your best efforts, no table that you create is going to be perfect the first time out. As you or other people use the table, you are going to find that you need to make changes in order to maintain integrity in the individual records. That is, you will want to have Paradox stop you or someone else from entering incorrect data. Or, you will want Paradox to enter repetitive data for you. In addition, you can change the manner in which data is displayed in the table, using some of the font attributes available in Windows.

Field Roster

The Field Roster area of the Restructure dialog box gives you access to the controls for data entry. You have already seen the effect of using the **Type** and **Size** options, with which you can designate the kind of data you want entered into a field and the length of the entry. Designating a field as the key field forces an entry for that field.

Table Properties

The Table Properties offers several more control features, including the ability to create Secondary Indexes. This section covers the various types of data entry control features. As you read each one, think of the ways that they may help you in building tables. After the explanation of the various methods, you will restructure the DONOR table adding some of the controls discussed here.

Validity Checks

A *validity check* is what its name implies. Paradox verifies that the data being entered into a particular field is valid for that field, as determined by you. This feature is very powerful in that it captures mistakes before they become part of the table. There are six types of validity checks, and a field can have one or more attached to the entry process.

If an entry is made into a field that does not conform to the restriction set by you, Paradox alerts the data entry person that an error has occurred and does not allow the entry to be made. Depending on the type of error, the data can be entered, but Paradox will not allow the record to be added to the table. Each of the validity checks is discussed later in this chapter.

Required Field

Clicking the Required Field check box in the Restructure dialog box causes Paradox to insist that an entry be made into the particular field. In other words, no record can be created unless an entry is made in this particular field. You select this control when you want the data entry person to always make an entry.

Paradox stops the record from being completed in one of two ways. First, it will not complete the record if you enter data into a different field and try to leave the record without entering data into the required field. Also, if you enter the field and then try to leave it without making an entry; Paradox will not complete the record. This approach is different from the way that Paradox DOS works. If you have used that version, Paradox for Windows will take a little getting used to.

Minimum

Use the Minimum control when you want to specify the smallest number that can be entered into the field. If you specify a minimum, then you must also make an entry in the Maximum field. You can use this type of validity check on an alphanumeric, number, short number, currency, or even date field. In the case of the date field, you can specify the oldest date you want entered.

Maximum

Use the Maximum control in conjunction with the minimum entry specification. You can use this type of validity check on an alphanumeric, number, short number, currency, or even date field. In the case of the date field, you can specify the latest date in the future you want entered.

Default

The default validity check is used in those fields in which you anticipate the entry ahead of the time. For example, if all your clients are living in the state of California, you can enter the abbreviation **CA** in the state field. Now every time you create a new record, Paradox will automatically make the state entry for you. The same is true for area codes for phone numbers, zip codes, etc. When you create the record, you are not restricted from changing the entry in a default field, say from CA to NV. This validity check is strictly to encourage less typing.

Picture

The age of multimedia may be at hand, but the Picture validity check is not a photograph. It is a *template* for data entry. The concept of a template is an outline of the way data should be entered into a field. An example that we can all relate to is the pattern for Social Security numbers. They all have the same structure, NNN-NN-NNNN. So, the *picture* of what an entry should look like in the Social Security field of a record is three numbers followed by a dash, two numbers followed by a dash and then four more numbers. If you type the Social Security numbers without the dashes, Paradox will insert them for you, provided that you had set up the picture. This example is simple. Table 5.1 lists of the types of symbols that can be used to create the picture of an entry.

Table 5.1 *Picture Validity Symbols*

Symbol	Meaning
#	Stands for any number.
?	Stands for any letter, upper- or lowercase.
&	Stands for any letter and converts it to uppercase.
@	Stands for any character, case does not matter.
!	Stands for any printable character and converts it to uppercase.
;	Indicates that the character following is a literal entry, not part of the picture design.
*	Indicates that the next character can be entered any number of times or can be entered a specific number of times. For example, if you entered *&5, up to five characters could be entered.
[ ]	Indicates that characters inside brackets are optional entries. Use this symbol, for example to indicate that an area code is not a required entry in a phone number picture.
{ }	Indicates that characters inside the curly braces are grouped.
,	Characters of alternative values can be entered.

For example, the picture (&&&,##&) means that either three characters are OK for an entry or two numbers followed by a character is also acceptable. Now you should have an idea of the kinds of pictures you can create for data entry into your tables. You can use Paradox to create very complex types of pictures, thereby ensuring the exact entry you desire. The trick is in the design, and that takes some practice. The beauty of Paradox is that you can always go back and restructure your table if the picture does not work.

Adding Validity Checks

In this exercise, you will open the DONOR table and add validity checks. Then, you will save the table and attempt to add a record that violates some of the checks, to see what happens.

WARNING

In this example, the DONOR table has only a few records. If the data in the table were completely destroyed by the restructuring process, it would not be a tragedy. What would be a tragedy, is, if you are restructuring a real table in the future and inadvertently trash the records. Always make a copy of the table so that you have a backup in case the restructure turns out to be an extirpation.

Before proceeding and in light of the foregoing cautionary note, lets make a copy of a table.

Making a Copy of a Table

Copying the table to a floppy disk will work if the table is not too large for the disk capacity. Another option is to copy the table to a different subdirectory on your hard disk.

To make a copy of a table, follow these steps.

1. Click on the **Tools/Utilities** option.

2. From the submenu, click on **Copy**. The Copy dialog box appears as shown in Figure 5.1.

3. Click on the name of the table you want to copy. In Figure 5.1, DONOR was selected, causing Paradox to insert the table name into the From box.

4. Click on the To box.

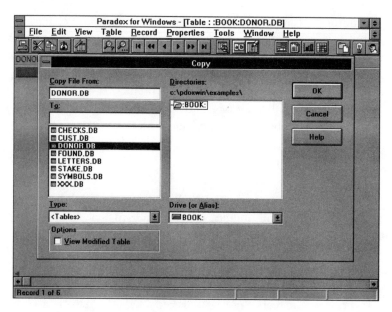

Figure 5.1 *Copy dialog box*

5. Enter a destination for the table. For example, if you want to copy the file to drive B, type the entry as shown in Figure 5.2.

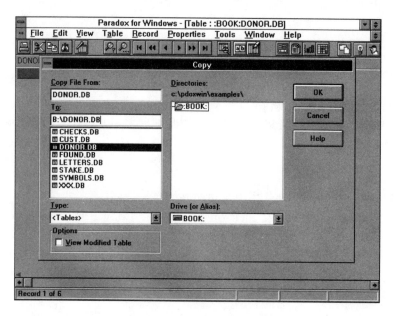

Figure 5.2 *Copying to drive B*

If you do not know exactly where you want to copy the table to, click on the Browse button and navigate as described in *Chapter 3*. Paradox will not enter the path into the To box, but you can see the path, making it easy to type in the parameters.

Changing the DONOR Table

The DONOR table has a few flaws. Let's make some changes to see the effect. First, let's change the Donor # field, even though it is a key field. Paradox will not let a record be created without an entry in the key field. So far, this constraint is the only one; no other specifics are demanded for the entries.

1. With the DONOR table active, click on the **Table/Restructure** options.

2. Click on the Donor # field name.

3. Click on the box in front of Required Field.

4. Click on the Minimum field.

5. Type **100** in the field.

6. Click on the Maximum field.

7. Type **10000**.

8. Click on the Amount field name.

9. Click on the Required Field box.

10. Click on the LName field name.

11. Click on the Required Field box.

12. Click on the FName field name.

13. Click on the Required Field box.

14. Click on the St field name.

15. Click on the Default field.

16. Type **CA**.

17. Click on the ZIP field name.

18. Click on the Picture field.

19. Type **#####-####**.

20. Click on the Assist button. Paradox opens the Picture Assistance dialog box, as shown in Figure 5.3. This dialog box can do as its button indicates, assist you in developing pictures for field entries. When you have created a picture, particularly a complex one, you should save it for future use.

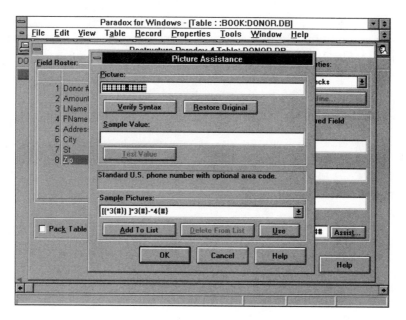

Figure 5.3 *Picture Assistance dialog box*

21. Click on the Add To List button. The Save Picture dialog box appears.

22. In the Description field type **Zip plus Four**.

23. Click on the OK button. The Save Picture dialog box closes.

24. Click on the OK button in the Picture Assistance dialog box.

Before completing the restructure process, let's look at the list of options on the Validity Checks menu.

1. Click the down arrow in the Validity Checks field. The list of menu options appears, as shown in Figure 5.4, which shows the list of other validity checks you can add to a table. At this point, none of them is necessary.

2. Click on the Save Button to finish the restructure. Paradox responds with the Restructure Warning dialog box. The prompt at the top of the dialog box asks if the new validity checks should be enforced on existing data. In other words, should Paradox make changes to existing records, or just those entered after the restructure takes place? In fact, in the Restructure Warning dialog box there are three areas that you can use to specify how Paradox is to apply the changes you have made.

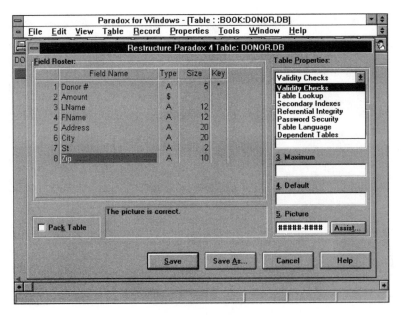

Figure 5.4 *Validity Checks menu*

3. Click on the Yes box at the top of the dialog box.

4. At the bottom of the dialog box, Paradox repeats the question of whether or not the existing data should be affected. Click on the box in front of Validity Checks and then click in the Apply to existing data box. This happens with each validation change made.

5. Click on OK. The restructure process starts.

If the restructuring was perfect (and Paradox was not prompted to change old records), then the DONOR table would reappear by itself. But, it appears, as shown in Figure 5.5, that the restructure creates some problems.

If a problem occurs with old records when a restructure is run, either of two tables will appear. In this instance, the KEYVIOL.DB (key violation) table appears, indicating that entries in the Primary key field were improperly made. The records that contain the violations are transferred to the KEYVIOL.DB table. The other type of table, PROBLEM.DB, performs a different function. If you change the length of a field and excess data is trimmed from existing records, Paradox creates a table to hold that data.

The bottom line is that Paradox gives you a way to rescue data that you may want to keep if you make a change that normally would result in data loss.

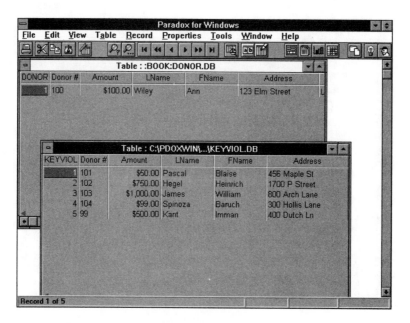

Figure 5.5 *The KEVIOL.DB table and DONOR*

In this example, thanks to the KEYVIOL.DB table, we have not yet lost five of the six records. What happened in the restructuring process?

Fixing a Restructure

To retrieve the records from the KEYVIOL.DB table, you must complete another restructuring. Using little detective work and some logic as to how Paradox works uncovers the answer to the violating records.

1. Click on the DONOR table.

2. Click on the **Table/Restructure** options.

3. Click on the Donor # field, which is the key field.

The type of data allowed in this field is Alphanumeric. This choice is what created the problem. Paradox interpreted the range entry of values, 100 to 10,000 as the only two allowable values in the field, as they were specified as the minimum and the maximum. In other words, Paradox did not consider the numbers 101–9999 to be legitimate entries because of the *type* designation.

4. Click on the Type field for Donor #.

5. Click on the right mouse button. Paradox responds with a list of types. This list is called the *inspection menu.*

6. Click on **Number**.

7. Click on the Save button. Paradox stops you from saving because there is an entry in the Size field.

8. Delete the **5** in Size.

9. Click on the OK button. Paradox prompts you that there may be a data loss.

10. Again, Paradox prompts you that there may be data loss, click **OK** twice in response.

Now the data key violation is corrected, Paradox will accept any number from 100 to 10,000 as being a valid entry. But, how do we get the key violating records back into the DONOR table?

Adding Records to an Existing Table

This example works in many situations where you have records in one table and want to add them to another. It is also the simplest example in that we already know that both tables have identically structured fields. Paradox does allow for the addition of records that have fields that do not match, but that topic is covered later. For now, let's get the key violators back where they belong.

1. Click on the **Tools/Utilities** option.

2. Click on the **Add** option. Paradox opens the Add dialog box as shown in Figure 5.6. The insertion point is in the From box.

3. Click on the File Name box, find the table labeled KEYVIOL.DB, and click on it. The From table is also referred to as the *source table.*

4. Click on the To box. Locate the DONOR.DB file name and click on it. The To table is referred to as the *target table.*

The process is set to add records from the KEYVIOL.DB table to the DONOR table. You must consider a couple more options before Paradox executes this change.

Append—Adds the records from the source (From) table to the target (To) table, even if the target table has an identical record. If the target table is keyed (as in our example), then identical records are not added, but rather placed in a KEYVIOL.DB table, where, if necessary, you can edit the records and then try again to add them to the target. If the target table is not keyed, then Paradox adds the records to the end of the table.

Update—Overwrites matching records in the target table with the records from the source table. Paradox creates a table named CHANGED so that you can identify which records have been overwritten. The target table must be keyed for this option to work.

Append & Update—Adds new records and updates existing records in the target table.

View Modified Table—Displays the newly updated table.

The default setting for the add records process is **Append & Update**.

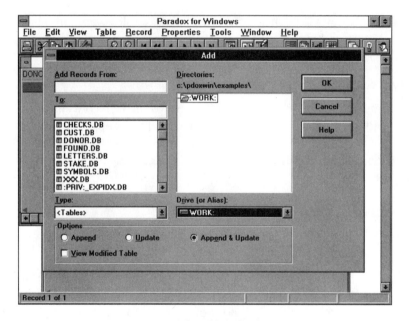

Figure 5.6 *Add dialog box*

5. Click on the **View Modified Table** option. Paradox executes the Append and Update process, but checks with you before making the addition in that the size of the Donor # field has changed.

6. Click on the OK button. Figure 5.7 shows the result.

But wait! One record still has not been added to the DONOR table, and Paradox has created another KEYVIOL.DB table.

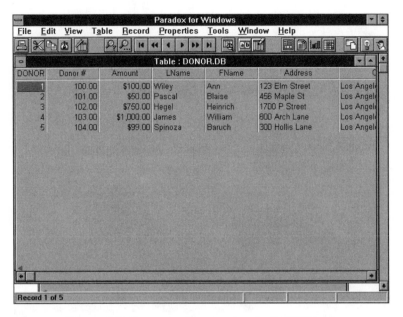

Figure 5.7 *Four records restored to the DONOR table*

N O T E

As you change tables and violations occur, Paradox sequentially numbers the temporary tables holding the records, as KEYVIOL, KEYVIOL1, KEYVIOL2, and so on. Unless you rename the tables, Paradox deletes them when you exit.

The solution to the key violation of this record is much simpler than the previous example. Notice the donor number for Mr. Kant. It is 99, which is less than 100, the value entered in the structure as the minimum allowed. In order to restore the record to the DONOR table, you must edit the donor number to conform to the validity check.

1. Click on the Donor # field in the KEYVIOL1 table.

2. Press the **F9** key to allow the record to be edited.

3. Type **106** in the Donor # field.

4. Press **Enter**.

5. Press **F9** to end the edit and save the modified record.

Let's try to add this record back to DONOR again.

1. Click on the **Tools/Utilities/Add** options.

2. In the From box, insert the KEYVIOL1.DB table name.

3. In the To box, insert DONOR.DB.

4. Click on the OK button. The record is inserted back into the DONOR table. Figure 5.8 shows the restructured table. Notice that the KEYVIOL tables stay on the desktop, too.

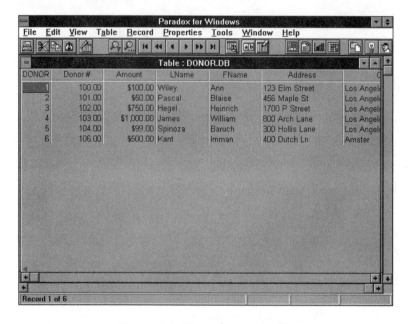

Figure 5.8 *The restructured table*

Adding a New Record

To test the constraints of the new validity checks, add another record to see the effect. You have already seen the effect of specifying an acceptable range of numbers in the Donor # field. The next record includes a nine digit Zip code, testing the picture that was made a part of the structure.

Let's add the new record.

1. Click on the last record in the table.

2. Press **F9**.

3. Press **Enter**.

4. Add the new record as follows:

Donor #	Amount	LName	FName	Address	City	St	Zip
105	**250**	**Locke**	**John**	**500 Bath St**	**Los Angeles**	**CA**	**93006**

As you enter the data, notice that the St entry is made for you—as specified in the restructure, **CA** is entered automatically.

The Zip entry provides another lesson. Namely, Paradox will not allow you to finish the record without a nine digit zip code! This restriction presents a problem. If the donor cannot provide the last four digits, the record cannot be created. Or can it? What if the entry is simply four zeros, 0000?

5. Finish the Zip entry with the values, **0000**.

6. Press **F9**. The new record appears as in Figure 5.9.

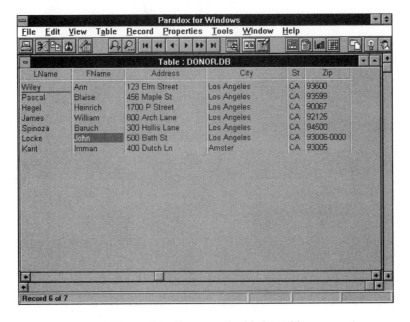

Figure 5.9 *New record added to table*

The record is now added to the table. This example brings up something to think about when creating your own tables in regard to adding pictures to fields. Be certain the burden you place on the person entering the data is not so cumbersome as to be overwhelming. While the purpose of adding validity checks is to ensure clear and accurate records, this process can be overdone. If you find that the validity checks are too onerous and not providing critical functions, use the Table Restructure dialog box to remove the offending validity checks.

Adding a Lookup Table

A lookup table is another form of validity checking. You can use customer numbers, product codes, or any other data that is crucial to correct record creation as the criteria for a field. The process links two tables, one that you are entering data into and a second table that is used as a reference for a specific field.

Suppose Congress passed a law that donations to campaigns could come only from individuals living within the confines of the Congressional District the candidate wishes to represent. A good way for the campaign to be certain that they are in compliance would be to gather the zip codes that are contained within the geographic boundaries of the district. Then, using Paradox, they could create a lookup table (named ZIP) that contained the zip codes. By linking the DONOR table with a ZIP table, the lookup would stop the campaign from creating a record that did not meet the zip criteria. In the following exercise, you will create the ZIP table and then link it to DONOR as a lookup table.

1. Click on the **File/New/Table** options. Paradox suggests that the new table be a Paradox table.

2. Click on the OK button.

3. In the Create Paradox for Windows Table dialog box, enter the field name **ZIP**.

4. In the Type field enter **A** for alphanumeric.

5. In the Size field enter **10** spaces.

6. Make the field the key field by pressing the **Spacebar** under Key. The completed table appears as shown in Figure 5.10.

7. Click on the Save As button. The Save Table As dialog box appears.

8. In the New Table name box, type **ZIP**.

9. In the Options section, click on the box in front of Display Table. The table will be on the desktop when it is created.

10. Click on the OK button.

11. Click on the ZIP table and press **F9** to begin creating new records.

12. Type in each zip code used in the first six records of the DONOR table. The completed table appears as shown in Figure 5.11.

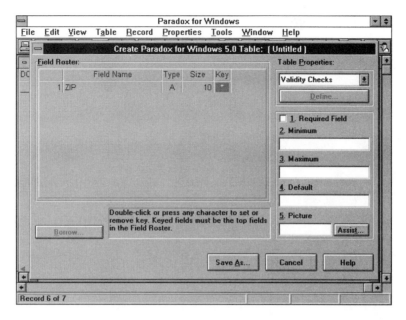

Figure 5.10 *Structure for the ZIP table*

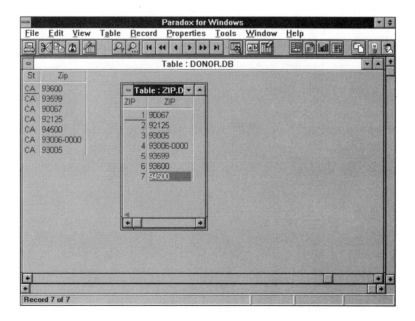

Figure 5.11 *ZIP table with records*

Creating the Lookup Link to ZIP

Creating the Link is an easy step. It is the same procedure used to create other validity checks.

1. Click on the DONOR table.

2. Click on the **Table/Restructure** options. The Restructure Paradox for Windows Table dialog box appears.

3. Click on the Zip field name.

4. Click on the down-pointing arrow next to Validity Checks.

5. From the drop-down list, click on **Table Lookup**. The words Table Lookup now appear under the Table Properties heading.

Although **Table Lookup** is specified, you must define the type of lookup, as shown in the following steps.

1. Click on the Define button. The Table Lookup dialog box appears. Paradox lists the tables available in the working directory, as shown in Figure 5.12.

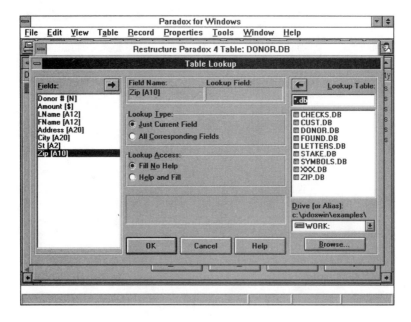

Figure 5.12 *The Table Lookup Definition dialog box*

In the left portion of the dialog box is the list of fields from the table that is being restructured. In the top middle portion, the field that Paradox assumes you want to use for the Lookup link is inserted into the Field Name field. Because the highlight was on Zip when you clicked on the Define button, it appears in the field. In the right portion is the list of tables in the working directory.

2. Click on the **ZIP.DB** table name. Because ZIP is a simple table, Paradox locates the one and only field that will produce a proper link, which is Zip. The field name is inserted into the Lookup field at the top middle of the dialog box. If you click on a different table name, unless there is a matching field in the table, Paradox will give you a warning message that there is no matching field.

NOTE

If the table you wish to link to is not in the working directory, click on the Browse button to find the directory containing the link to table.

Two more options that need explanation are in the middle of the dialog box.

Lookup Type—Paradox can link a single field, as in this example, or many fields in a corresponding table. The fields in each table must match, as in the example of Zip to Zip, Lname to Lname, and so on. An example of how this might work is an invoice. Suppose that you type in the customer number. Paradox then fills in the other fields such as Address and Phone, which reduces the likelihood of keystroke error. If you select the **Help and Fill** option, you can open the linked table, as described next.

Lookup Access—If you select The **Fill No Help** option, Paradox does the comparison to make sure the link is accurate. The **Help and Fill** option goes a step further. If you select it and then press the **Control+ Spacebar** when you enter a value, Paradox opens the lookup table so that you can see the actual records in the linked table. If there is already a valid value in the table in which you are working and you press **Control+Spacebar**, Paradox moves the highlight to that record in the linked table. You can move the highlight to a different value, if necessary. Clicking on the OK button finishes the entry and closes the lookup table.

3. The default settings for Lookup Type and Lookup Access are correct for this example. Click on the OK button to finish the definition. Paradox

responds with the Restructure Paradox for Windows Table dialog box and notes the existence of the Lookup by displaying the link, as shown in Figure 5.13.

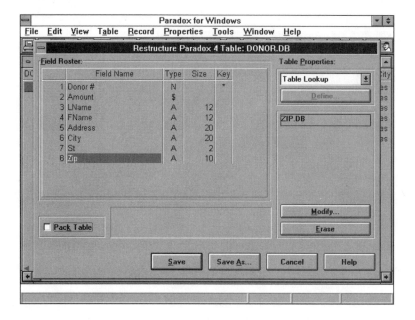

Figure 5.13 *Restructure Paradox for Windows Table dialog box showing lookup link to ZIP*

Notice that two new buttons appear, Modify and Erase. They can be used to change or delete the Lookup relationship.

The reason for creating the Lookup was to guarantee that the donor lived in the congressional district. So, the table had better demand that a zip is entered into every record.

4. Click the down arrow next to Table Lookup. The list appears with Validity Checks as an option. Click Validity Checks.

5. Click on the Zip field and click the box in front of Required Field.

6. Click Save. Paradox prompts you as to whether old data should be subject to the new validity checks. Click Yes.

7. Click OK.

If there was a problem with any of the matching values, Paradox would alert you and create a KEYVIOL table.

Notes on Restructuring Tables

In the preceding example, you completed several restructuring steps that illustrate ideas far beyond simple Paradox tables. It is up to you to apply them to your own tables. You ought to be aware of several more ideas regarding restructuring tables.

▼ You cannot change a table's type. For example, if you have a Paradox table, you cannot change it to a dBASE table.

▼ If you are taking a table created by an earlier version of Paradox, and Paradox must restructure it to a Paradox for Windows table, you are alerted to that change, and you are asked to confirm or deny the conversion.

▼ If you change the primary key or if you add a key to a table that was unkeyed, records that violate the validity of the key are moved into a KEYVIOL table. At that point, you can edit the records that are violating the key and then add them back into the original table.

▼ If you change a field's type, as from Alphanumeric to Number, records that violate the change and cannot be converted by Paradox are moved into a PROBLEMS table.

▼ If you add a default value to a field and existing records have an entry different from the default, Paradox does not overwrite the old entry.

▼ If you add a new field to an existing table, Paradox does not automatically add that field to any forms, reports, or queries associated with the table.

▼ Deleting fields usually results in the loss of data. Paradox warns you about this. Any objects linked to the table that uses the field, must be redesigned or restructured the next time you open the document.

▼ Remember that adding a key to a table means that the field must be the first table in the field. For example, in the DONOR table if you wanted to make Zip the keyed field, then you must move that field to the first position in the Field Roster.

Adding Formatting

The numbers in the Donor # field are formatted according to the Windows # default format, that is, commas and two decimal places. This format may be appropriate for some number fields, but the donor number would be easier to read in a different format. Changing formats is easy, and you can change the format back to the original setting if the results of the change are worse.

1. In the DONOR table, click on a value in the Donor # field.

2. Click the Right mouse button. The Object Inspection menu appears as shown in Figure 5.14.

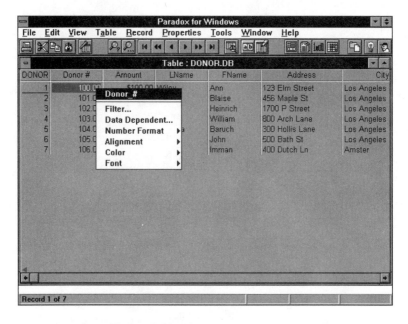

Figure 5.14 *Object Inspection menu*

3. Click on the **Number Format** option. The list of options appears, as shown in Figure 5.15.

4. Click on the **General** option. Paradox reformats all the entries in the Donor # field, as shown in Figure 5.16.

Data Dependent

Suppose that you want to easily identify values in a field that are larger or smaller than are normally expected. The **Data Dependent** option allows you to specify the range of values you want to be displayed in a different font, size, color, or combination of the foregoing. To see an example of such a change, follow these steps.

1. Right click on a value in the Amount field in the DONOR table.

2. Click on the **Data Dependent** option. The Data Dependent Properties dialog box appears, as shown in Figure 5.17.

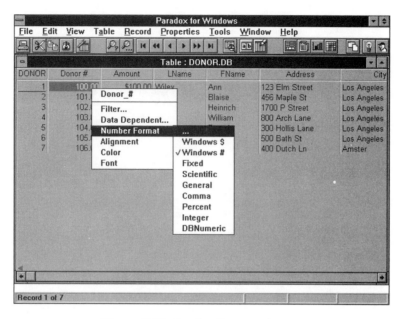

Figure 5.15 *Number Format submenu*

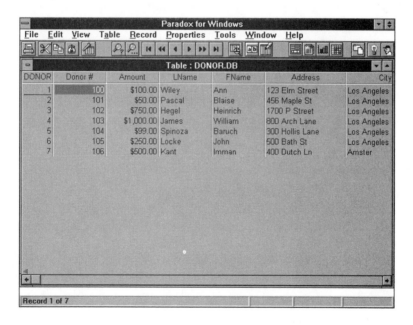

Figure 5.16 *Donor numbers reformatted*

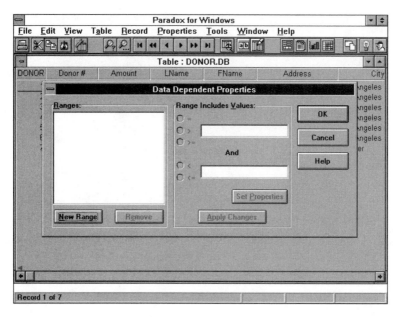

Figure 5.17 *Data Dependent Properties dialog box*

3. Click on the **New Range** button. Paradox inserts a <blank> in the first range field on the right of the dialog box.

4. Click on the field where <blank> has been inserted; delete the <blank> entry, and type **999**.

5. Click on the diamond in front of the greater than (>) sign.

6. Click on the diamond in front of the less than (<) sign.

7. Click on the field below the word And and type **10000**. You have entered a range from 999 to 10,000, as shown in Figure 5.18.

8. Click on the Set Properties button. Two settings are available; you can set a different color or specify a different font for those values that are within the range.

9. Click on **Font**. Four more options appear—**Typeface**, **Size**, **Style**, and **Color**.

10. Click on **Typeface**. The list of typefaces appears, as shown in Figure 5.19.

11. Click on **Roman**. Paradox responds by closing the submenu and displaying a sample of the new typeface.

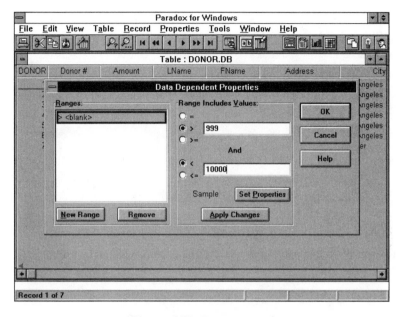

Figure 5.18 *Range entered*

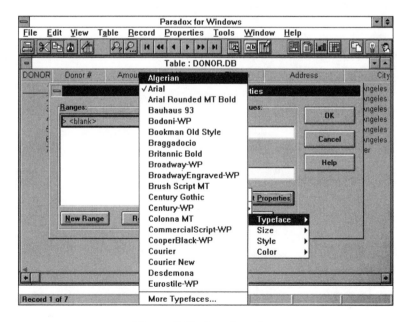

Figure 5.19 *List of typefaces*

12. Click on the Set Properties button and then click on **Font** followed by **Style**. Figure 5.20 shows the submenus.

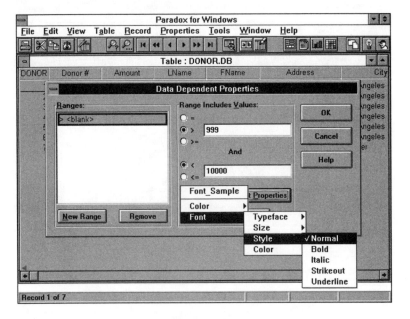

Figure 5.20 *The Data Dependent Properties submenus*

13. Click on the **Italic** option.

14. Click on the **Set Properties/Font/Size** options and then click on the number **14**.

15. Click on the Apply Changes button. Paradox inserts the Range in the Ranges field.

16. Click on the OK button. Any values in the specified range in the Amount field are displayed as 1000, as shown in Figure 5.21.

Use this technique on any field, provided that you use the correct syntax to specify a range of values. For alphanumeric you can use alphabetical order to determine which data is selected.

Customizing Number Formats

The standard choices for numbers formats are listed here. Paradox allows you to customize the way numbers display. After checking the list of standard formats, you can determine what characteristics you might want to incorporate into a customized format.

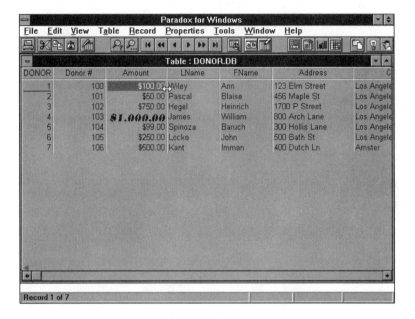

Figure 5.21 *The value 1000 displayed in new format*

▼ **Windows #.** Default format for numbers. It is derived from the format chosen in the Windows control panel. If you have not made a choice, then the numbers are displayed with decimal places.

▼ **Windows $.** Default Windows number format for currency. A $ is included.

▼ **Fixed.** Format that includes two decimal places, including zeros. In the case of a number in the thousands, no commas are included. Negative numbers are displayed with a leading minus sign, for example, **-100**.

▼ **Scientific.** Format that displays numbers in exponential notation, including two decimal places. Negative numbers are displayed with a leading minus sign, for example, **-100**.

In the case where any number, despite your format setting, is too big to fit into the field, Paradox displays the number in scientific format.

N O T E

▼ **General.** Format that displays the number with up to two decimal places, if there is a decimal value. Negative numbers are displayed with a leading minus sign, for example, **-100**.

▼ **Comma.** Format that displays the numbers with two decimal places, no trailing zeros. Any number with thousands has comma separators. Negative numbers are displayed in parentheses.

▼ **Percent.** Format that displays numbers followed by the percent sign (%). If you enter a number as **.3**, the display is **30%**. No thousand separators are used, and negative numbers are preceded by a minus sign.

▼ **Integer.** Format that displays whole numbers only. Decimal numbers are rounded when you convert field data to the integer format. Thousand separators are not used. Negative numbers are displayed with a leading minus sign, for example, **-100**.

When you customize a format, you can pick and choose which attributes to include. To see the Select Number Format dialog box and customize a format, follow these steps.

1. Right click on a number field.

2. Click on **Number Format**.

3. When the list of formats appears, click on the ellipses (. . .) at the top of the list. The Select Number Format dialog box appears, as shown in Figure 5.22.

4. Click on each of the Existing Formats, in the right side of the dialog box to see how the numbers are displayed and details of each format.

5. Begin creating your own format by clicking on the Create button. All the fields in the dialog box are now active.

6. The first step is to name the format you are creating. Type a name in the Name field.

7. Click on the Permanent box, if you want the format to become a permanent selection on the inspection menu. Paradox adds the format to the **PDOXWIN.INI** file, which loads the format when you start Paradox.

The easiest way to design your own format is to select an existing format, make modifications, and then save it under a different name. The options for designing a format follow.

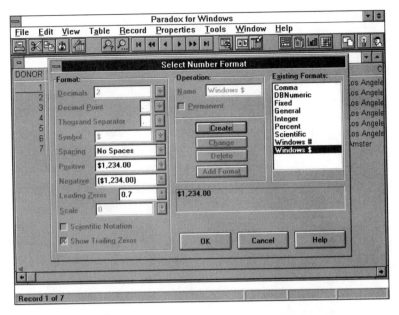

Figure 5.22 *Select Number Format dialog box*

 The name of a custom format does not have to conform to DOS name standards. It can contain spaces or more than eight characters.

N O T E

Decimals—Click on the down arrow to determine the number of decimal places that the format will display. You can have up to 15 decimal places.

Decimal Point—Click on the down arrow to choose between a period or a comma as the symbol for decimal place.

Thousand Separator—Click on the down arrow to choose between the period or comma for this separator symbol.

Symbol—Click on the down arrow to select a symbol for the format such as *inch, lb, DM.* Define your own symbols by entering them into the box. In the next section the table of the IBM extended character set is set out. The extended characters can be used as symbols for your format.

Spacing—Choose **Spacing** if you want spaces between the symbol you have selected in the previous option and the number itself. You must have a symbol selected for this to work.

Positive—Choose **Positive** if you want the number to include a plus (+) sign. The drop-down menu has several options for determining where the sign will appear.

Negative—Choose **Negative** if you want negative numbers to include a minus (-) sign. The drop-down menu includes several options for determining where the sign will appear.

Leading Zeros—Choose **Leading Zeroes** to specify the number of digits before the decimal place you want to display. For example, setting the number of zeros to 5 and entering a number such as 666, Paradox displays it as 00666. The purpose of this format is to ensure that zip codes, which often have leading zeros, are displayed properly.

Scale—Choose **Scale** if you want the number entered to be multiplied by a factor of 10. For example, if you enter **2**, the number is multiplied by 100, i.e, **10*10*number**.

Scientific Notation—Check **Scientific Notation** to display the numbers in scientific notation.

Show Trailing Zeros—Use **Show Trailing Zeros** to display as many decimal numbers as you want. If you want all numbers to have three decimal places showing, even if they are zeros, enter **3** in this field.

8. Click on the Add Format button to add the custom format to the inspection menu. It appears when you right-click on the field.

You can create custom formats for all type of fields in Paradox—number, currency, date, time, timestamp, and logical fields. However, when you name a custom format, it must be unique, even if it is for a different type of field.

Date Formats

Standard date formats are Windows Short, Windows Long, MM/DD/YY, and DBDate. To see how the date formats work, let's open a table with a date field; CHECKS.DB. It is a checkbook register table that calculates the balance in a checkbook account as each check is entered.

1. Open the CHECKS.DB table. It is in the EXAMPLES subdirectory.

2. Right-click on a value in the Date field. The inspection menu appears, as shown in Figure 5.23.

3. Click on the **Date Format** option. The standard date format options are shown in Figure 5.24. The leading checkmark indicates the current format, **Windows Short**.

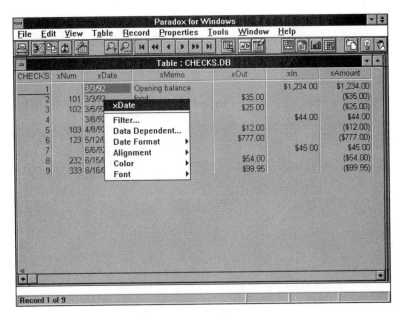

Figure 5.23 *Date inspection menu*

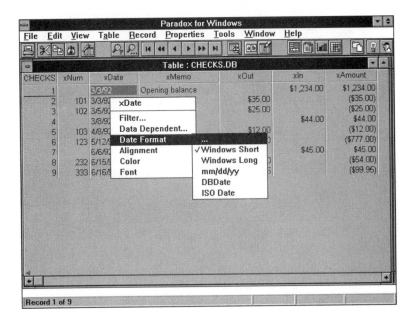

Figure 5.24 *Date Format options*

4. To see the effect of the other standard formats, select them and study the results. The Windows Long format uses a format that includes the day name, the month name, the date, and the year. An example of that format is shown in Figure 5.25.

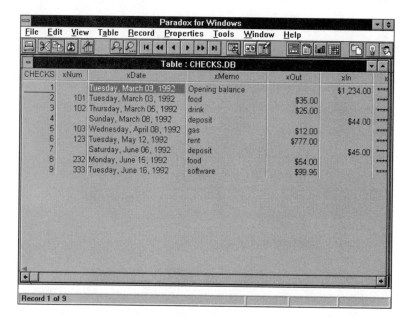

Figure 5.25 *Date in Windows Long format*

The view table properties have been changed in order to see the entire field entry.

NOTE

5. Right-click on the field click on the **Date Format** option, and click on the ellipses (. . .) at the top of the object inspection menu. The Select Date Format dialog box appears, as shown in Figure 5.26.

6. Click on the Create button. The custom date format options follow. To see the details for each format, click on the down arrow.

Weekday—There are two ways to display the day name, as a full name or as an abbreviation.

Day—The day number can be displayed two ways.

Month—The month can be displayed in two number formats, as the full month name, or as an abbreviation.

Year—The year has three display options.

Order—Enter the order in which you want the components of the date to appear. For a military date, you would use **%D**, **%M**, **%Y**. The percent (%) sign stands for the date variable itself.

Case—Select the case in which you want the date displayed—mixed, capitals on the first letter of the word, or all lower- or all uppercase. This option works only if you select the date to be displayed with names instead of numbers.

Name—Type in a unique name for the format.

Permanent—To have the date format become part of the inspection menu, click on this box.

7. Click on the Add Format button to add the name to the list.

8. Click on the OK button.

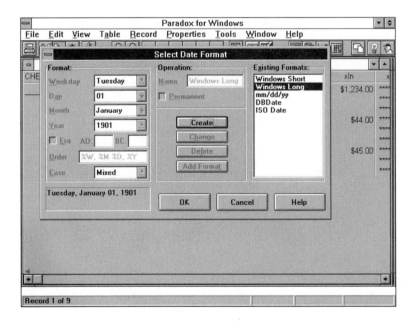

Figure 5.26 *Select Date Format dialog box*

The Extended Character Set

Paradox supports the *IBM extended character set*. The extended character set is a group of characters that are not noted on the keyboard but that can be accessed by pressing of the **Alt** key followed by a series of numbers. The extended character set includes foreign language characters and special symbols such as é, í, and Ä. To insert an extended character into a field, press and hold the **Alt** key and then press the key code numbers in Table 5.2.

N O T E

Do not use the number keys above the letter keys. You must use the separate keypad on the right side of the keyboard. Remember that the **NumLock** key must be active.

The characters are not restricted by the fonts that are applied. You can access them when you are entering data in alphanumeric, memo, and formatted memo fields.

Table 5.2 IBM Extended Characters

Key Code	Symbol
128	Ç
129	ü
130	é
131	â
132	ä
133	à
134	å
135	ç
136	ê
137	ë
138	è
139	ï
140	î
141	ì
142	Ä

(continued)

Key Code	Symbol
143	Å
144	É
145	æ
146	Æ
147	ô
148	ö
149	ò
150	ÿ
151	ù
152	Ÿ
153	Ö
154	Ü
155	¢
156	£
157	¥
158	₨
159	ƒ
160	á
161	í
162	ó
163	ú
164	ñ
165	Ñ
166	ª
167	º
168	¿
171	½
172	¼
173	¡
174	«
175	»

More extended characters are available, but it is not likely that you would need them to enter data into tables.

Borrowing a Table Structure

In the previous examples of building tables, the process was started from scratch. That is, each field was labeled, typed, and sized (if appropriate), and a key field designation was added if necessary. You can also build a table without all the steps concomitant to starting with a blank slate. Borrowing a structure that is close to what you want in the new table is a simple way to begin. Then, you can use the restructure procedure to modify the existing structure if needed.

1. Click on the File menu and the **New/Table** options.

2. Select Paradox for Windows as the table type. Paradox opens the Create Paradox for Windows Table dialog box, as shown in Figure 5.27. In the lower-left corner of the dialog box is a button labeled Borrow.

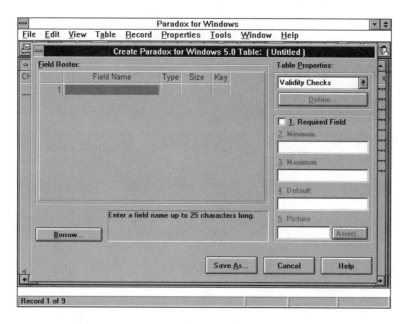

Figure 5.27 *Create Paradox for Windows Table dialog box*

3. Click on the Borrow button. The Borrow Table Structure dialog box appears, as shown in Figure 5.28. Paradox lists the tables that are available in the default directory. If the table from which you want to borrow the structure is not in this directory, click on the Browse button to look at other directories.

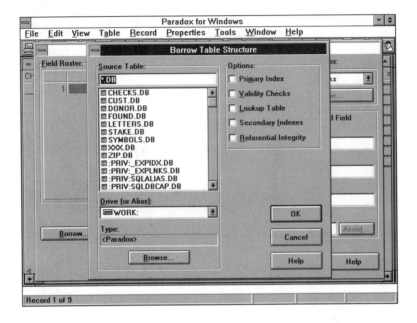

Figure 5.28 *Borrow Table Structure dialog box*

In addition to the basic structure of the borrowed table, you can select other attributes of the table, such as the Primary Index and Validity Checks. Just click on the box in front of the option that you want to include with the borrowing.

4. Click on the table name that has the structure you want to borrow. Paradox returns to the Create window, with the Field Roster filled with the structure you have borrowed.

5. Make any changes you want, just as you would when creating a new table.

6. Click on the Save As button. Paradox opens the Save Table As dialog box, as shown in Figure 5.29. Because you cannot save the newly structured table using the same name as the one from which you borrowed, Paradox opens this dialog box.

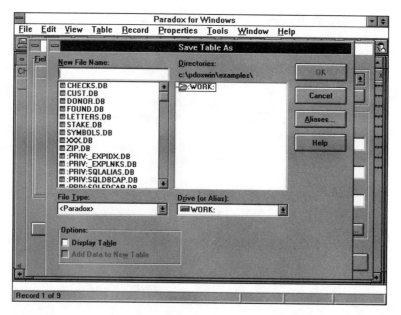

Figure 5.29 *Save Table As dialog box*

7. Type in a new table name.

8. Click on the OK button.

Adding Memo Fields to Records

No matter how well defined your fields are, some kinds of information are not suited to fit neatly into a normal number, alphanumeric, or date field. The information may have elements of all types of data, or the data may be so diverse that it defies easy categorization. What to do? In the example of the political campaign, a field that can contain notes would be very helpful. Paradox has the memo field attribute that can be a part of the structure of a table. In this example, let's add a memo field to the DONOR table and then edit the records to include some notes.

1. Open the DONOR table.

2. Click on the **Table/Restructure** option.

3. Click on the Key column where the Zip field is defined.

4. Press **Enter**. Paradox provides the space for a new field definition.

5. Type the field name **Notes**.

6. Right-click the Type field.

7. From the list of options, click on **Formatted Memo**. The reason for picking **Formatted Memo** is that you can add text formats such as font changes, sizing, and italics.

8. Click on the Size field. Read the notation in the lower-left portion of the dialog box regarding this type of field. As it says, you can specify the maximum amount of text that will be stored directly with the record in the table. Because the memo can be of any length, text that exceeds the value you enter here is stored in a separate file. If you enter a memo that is longer than the value you enter as the field length, only the characters that fit the number you specify are displayed.

9. Type **20** as the number of characters for the memo.

10. Click on the Save button. The newly constituted table appears, as shown in Figure 5.30.

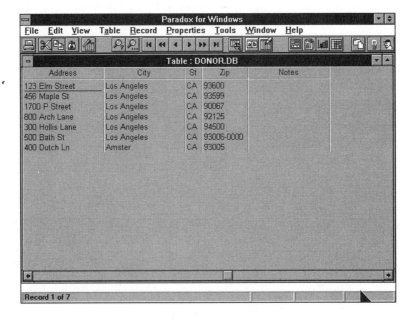

Figure 5.30 *DONOR table with new Notes field*

11. Press the **Shift** key and hold it while you press the **F2** key. This keypress combination allows you to begin an edit of the memo field. Paradox opens a document window as shown in Figure 5.31.

Figure 5.31 *Document window for memos*

12. Press **F9** and type the memo.

13. When you are done typing the memo, press **Shift+F2** again to end the edit. An example of a memo field with an entry is shown in Figure 5.32.

Changing View Properties of a Table

As a table gets longer on the horizontal, determining which record you are working on gets more difficult if you are on the far right side of the table and the names are on the left. In fact, you may not be able see which record goes with what. Paradox allows you to reduce the size of the fields that you see on-screen. This change does not affect the structure of the fields, only the way you see the data on-screen. If you make a change, when you close Paradox, you are prompted as to whether or not to make the change permanent. Remember that this change only affects the view properties, nothing else. To change the view properties, follow these steps.

1. Position the mouse pointer on the line that comes down from the top of the table between the fields Address and City, below where the table makes a T between fields. In Figure 5.33, the mouse pointer is a two-headed arrow.

2. Press and hold the left mouse button, and drag it to the left until the Address field is almost completely obscured. See Figure 5.34.

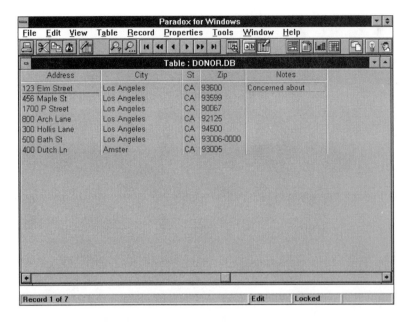

Figure 5.32 *Record with memo attached*

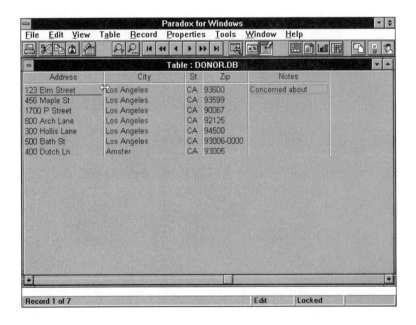

Figure 5.33 *Mouse pointer as two-headed arrow between Address and City*

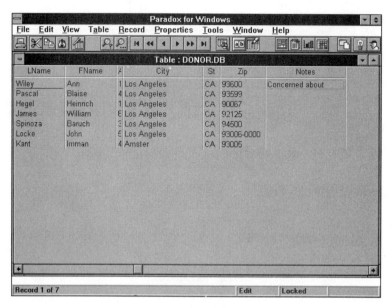

Figure 5.34 *View of the Address field obscured*

3. Repeat the same process with the line between the City and State fields. Figure 5.35 shows the result. With these changes, editing the Notes field is much easier, and you can be certain that the correct records are edited.

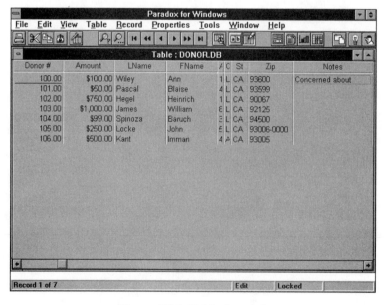

Figure 5.35 *Fields obscured*

4. Click on the **Close** option on the document control menu. Paradox displays the prompt dialog box, as shown in Figure 5.36.

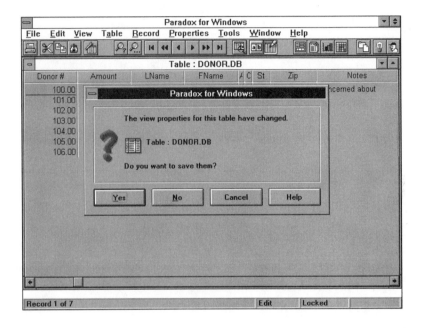

Figure 5.36 *View Properties Prompt*

5. Click on the Yes or No button, depending on what you want. Remember that this change does not affect the way that the data is stored in each record or the way that you add or edit records.

Command Summary

Command:	Mouse Click	Keyboard Press:
Create a Table	**File/New/Table**	**Alt+F/N/T**
Create Primary Key	Double-click on Key field	**Spacebar**
Save Table Structure	Save As. . . button	**Alt+A**
Restructure	**Table/Restructure**	**Alt+T/R**

Summary

In this chapter, you learned how to add complex characters to your tables. In *Chapter 6*, you'll learn how to ask Paradox to find the data you need.

Chapter ▶ 6

Retrieving Information by Query

So far in this book you have created and edited tables. Much of what you have done is not much different from what could be done on paper. In this chapter, you will dive into the real beauty of an electronic database. Not only is it a convenient way to store your data, but you can retrieve that information in useful ways that will help you make better decisions.

The tool used to retrieve information in Paradox for Windows is a *query*. Three types of queries are addressed in this chapter. The first is a single table query, where you look for a record or records meeting one specified condition. The second is still a single table query with two or more specified conditions. Another term for this type of query is a multiple condition query. The third type of query is a query done on multiple tables, where you ask for specific informa-

179

tion about two or more related tables. A new component of Paradox 5.0 is the table filter. A filter is an easy way of locating a series of records in a single table. Earlier in this book, you learned to use the Locate buttons to find a record that met specified criteria. The limitations of this method is that only a single record is identified at a time. The new Filter process allows you to exclude the records that do not meet your filter criteria and work with just those records. The records in the filter are still part of the larger database. The major components of this chapter are:

▼ Creating Filters

▼ Creating a query

▼ Using multiple conditions in queries

▼ Querying multiple tables

▼ Saving queries

Creating Filters

In order to create a filter, you need to have a database open. For this example, open the CUST database that we have used in the past.

1. Click the Open table button and select the CUST table.

2. Click **OK**.

3. With the database open, click the Filter button on the Speedbar. The dialog box opens as in Figure 6.1.

As you can see, the dialog box contains the name of the table and on the right side of the dialog box, the list of fields in the table.

4. Click on the Country field. The CUST table has several records in which the Country is the Bahamas. The Filter allows us to locate just those records in that Province.

5. Type:Bahamas.

6. Click OK.

Paradox responds with the same CUST table but only the records that meet the Filter are displayed as in Figure 6.2.

Any changes you make while in a filtered table are saved with the main table. So, a filter makes it easy to find a series of records that need changing.

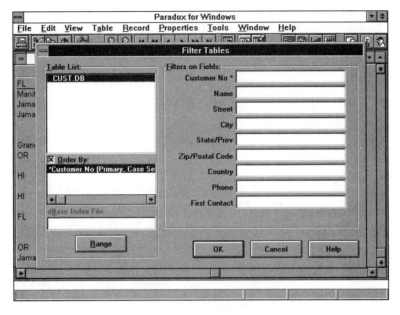

Figure 6.1 *Filter dialog box*

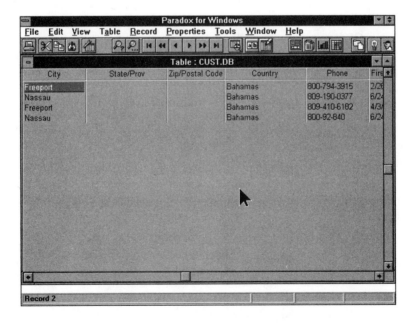

Figure 6.2 *Bahamas records only*

Removing the Filter

To get all the records back, follow these steps:

1. Click the Filter button.

2. Delete the entry in the field that you used for the filter.

3. Click **OK**. All of the records in the table can be seen.

Selecting a Range

In the process of setting a filter, you may wish to further restrict the records that are displayed. You can enter a range of values that correspond to the values in the Primary Field.

1. Click the Filter button and enter the Filter criteria in the field of your choice.

2. Click the Range button. The Set Range for Index dialog box appears.

3. Click the Set Range box.

4. Enter the low value in the top box, and the high value in the box just below.

5. Click **OK**.

6. Click **OK** again. Any records that pass through both filters are displayed in the table.

Object Inspection Filters

Another way to filter a table is to RIGHT click on any field. Form the Object Inspection menu, click **Filter**. Enter the filtering criteria and click **OK**. In order to retrieve all the records again, use the Filter button on the SpeedBar to remove the filter criteria entry.

Creating a Query

A query can help you pull out specific records in a table, examine certain fields from a table, perform calculations in tables, and combine data from several tables into one answer table. While this may sound as if you are doing very complicated activities, you will find that Paradox for Windows is so well designed that these processes can be done simply and clearly.

What Is a Query?

A query is a question that you ask a database table or tables. Paradox scans through the data you have entered and creates an answer table to your question. In other words, a query creates an answer table. The answer table may show that zero, one, or more records that answer the question you ask. You can convert the answer table to a report or graph or use it on-screen to analyze the data you have entered.

 When an answer table is empty, no records meet the conditions you specified in the query.

N O T E

The Query Method

When you query Paradox for Windows, you create an example of what you want the answer to look like. Paradox does all the work by looking through the data tables to find the answer to your question. This is called the *Query By Example* (QBE) method. For example, in querying a single table that includes a student number, name, phone number, and grade, you ask a question about the student's grade. One question might be, which students have a grade greater than 90%? You construct the query, and Paradox for Windows displays an answer table that lists all the student records in the table with a grade greater than 90%.

Looking at the Query Editor

The *query editor* is in a window in which you prepare the query. Before you get to the query editor, clear the screen of all tables. Click on the Window menu and the **Close All** option. If any view changes have been made, or any new tables have been created that have not been named, Paradox prompts you for what action to take.

To create a new query to display the query editor, follow these steps.

1. Click on the **File/New/Query** options. The Select File dialog box displays.

2. Select the file from which you want to display a query.

In the example queries that follow the DONOR table is used, but it now has a total of 20 records which have been added in order demonstrate the queries. You need only to follow the logic of the process to learn how to use queries on your databases.

The Query Editor window displays the query form for the DONOR file. The fields display in the query window in the same order as in the original table. Figure 6.3 shows the Query Editor window with the DONOR query inserted.

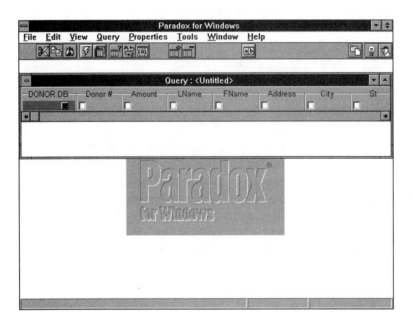

Figure 6.3 *The Query Editor window*

While the Query Editor window displays, you see the menu bar below the title bar. Below the menu bar is a series of buttons specifically for the Query Editor. The buttons on the left side of the Speedbar are Cut to Clipboard, Copy to Clipboard, and Paste from Clipboard. Run Query is the button with the lightning bolt. Toward the middle of the SpeedBar are the buttons for Add Table and Remove Table. Moving to the right, you see the Join Tables button, the Field View and Answer Table Properties button, and on the far right the Open Folder button.

Add or remove a table to a query using the appropriate buttons. When you have prepared the query, click on the Run Query button to execute the query. Click on the Query menu to have access to these same options. The Query menu is shown in Figure 6.4.

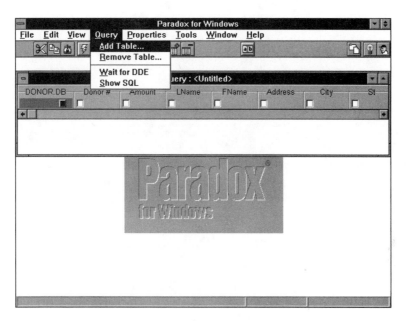

Figure 6.4 *The Query menu*

Notice that the table in the Query Editor window looks similar to a data table. One important difference is that you can type directly into a query form. You do not need to go to the Edit mode first. What you type into a query form is not added to a data table. It is used only to ask a question of that table. Another difference is that the fields expand to accommodate additional information. As you progress through this chapter, you will see many examples of how the Query Editor window works.

Using the Checkmark

Without asking a question of the data, start by using the checkmark to view specific fields in a table. In the DONOR table, you want to view just the LName and Amount fields. To display these two fields, follow these steps.

1. Click and hold the mouse pointer on the small box in the LName field. A list of available check marks displays.

2. Select the standard check, which is first on the list, and release the mouse button.

3. Click on the small box in the Amount field. By just clicking on the box, Paradox assumes that you want to use the standard checkmark. The

LName and Amount fields are both checked. The fields that are checked display in the answer table. The unchecked fields do not display in the answer table. The checked fields look like the ones you see in Figure 6.5.

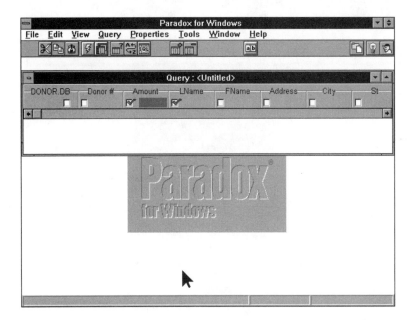

Figure 6.5 *The checked fields*

4. Click the Run Query button on the SpeedBar. An answer table that lists the Name and Amount fields of the table displays. All the records in the table are listed giving you an easy list of names and amount spent. The answer table is shown in Figure 6.6.

Defining the Checkmarks

When you click and hold on the small boxes in the query table, four checkmarks display. At the bottom of the list is a blank box. The four checkmarks are listed and described in this section.

▼ The *Checkmark* indicates a field you want to be included in the answer table. All records with unique values that match the query criteria display in ascending order.

▼ The *Check Plus* displays all the values in a field, including duplicates.

▼ The *Check Descending* displays unique values in descending order, either *Z* to *A* or beginning with the largest number to the smallest.

▼ The *Check Group* is used for advanced queries where records are selected using a SET operation.

▼ The *Blank Box* removes the checkmark from a field. With the checkmark removed, this field no longer appears in the answer table.

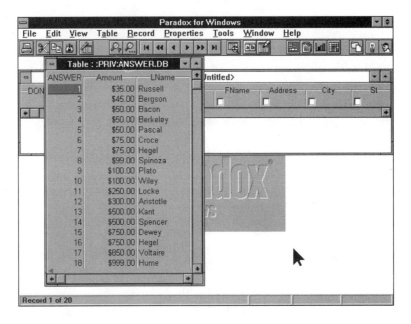

Figure 6.6 *The last name and amount answer table*

A Single Table Query

Suppose that you have a list of more than 200 customers, instead of a database of only 20. You are going to query for all customers from the United States. This is a *single table query*. When using a single table query, you ask questions of only one table. This is the simplest form a query can take. The query will consider only one variable, which also keeps it simple.

An example of a query using two variables would be to ask for all customers from the United States with orders in January.

NOTE

The steps in a single table query follow.

1. Select the fields you want to include in the answer table.
2. Define the records you want to appear in the answer table by specifying the data to be found.
3. Execute the query.

Selecting Fields

Place a checkmark in the fields to be included in the answer table. Determine which of the four types of checkmark you want in a field. In the leftmost column of the table in the Query Editor window, find the name of the file that holds the table. Click on the box in this column, and Paradox adds a checkmark to all the fields in the table. This saves you the trouble of checking each field one at a time.

Closing an Answer Table

Let's take a query one step further. Close the answer table that is currently on the screen and go back to the Query Editor. Click on the Window Control button and select Close.

Defining the Data in Records

In a query you want to look for records that match certain values. You define the conditions for which Paradox for Windows should search the database table. There are four main ways to define the data for which you are searching.

▼ You can look for an *exact match*, for example, all records that match the value **CA** in the St field.

▼ You can look for a *range of values*, for example, all payroll records that have a value greater than $30,000, but less than $50,000 in the Salary field.

▼ You can look for an *inexact match*, for example, all records where the value does not equal 1000 in the Weight field.

▼ You can look for a *pattern*, for example, the Paradox for Windows wildcard operator allows you to search for all records that begin with the letter *T* in the LName field.

For this example, let's query for all the records where a donation was received from a donor in the city of Calabasas. Begin in the Query Editor window with the DONOR query table.

1. Move the highlight to the DONOR.DB field by clicking the mouse pointer on the field.

2. Click on the box, placing a checkmark in the DONOR.DB field.

3. In the City field, type **Calabasas**.

The Query Editor window looks like the one shown in Figure 6.7. Paradox inserts the description Calabasas in the City field.

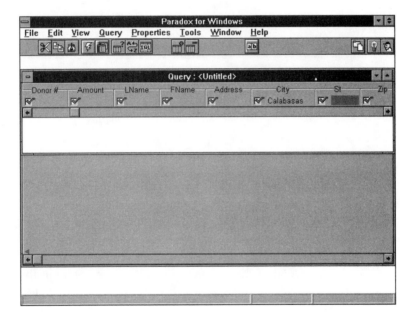

Figures 6.7 *Calabasas in the Query Editor window*

Executing the Query

To direct Paradox for Windows to execute the query, click on the Run Query button. This time the answer table displays the Donor # field and those records in which the donor is from Calabasas. In this answer table, shown in Figure 6.8, three records match the value defined in the query table.

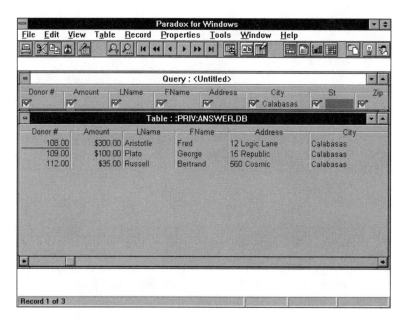

Figure 6.8 *Matching records, city of Calabasas*

Using Query Operators

With Paradox for Windows you can use operators to define query results. There are many kinds of operators which are described in Table 6.1. The category of the operator, the operator, and a brief description and example of each query operator is listed. In the examples that follow, you will not use all these operators but you will use several of them. Practice using the operators in this chapter, and the skills you learn can be translated to work with other operators.

Table 6.1 *Query Operators*

Category	Operator	Description	Example
Arithmetic	+	Addition or alpha-numeric string concatenation	**TODAY+30** lists the date 30 days from now.
	-	Subtraction	**Price-10** takes $10 off the listed price.

(continued)

Category	Operator	Description	Example
	*	Multiplication	**Quant*Price** gives product of the values in the two fields, **Quant** and **Price**.
	/	Division	**TotalCost/Units** gives cost per unit, assuming one field is **TotalCost** and another is Units.
	()	Group operators	**Quant*(TotalCost /Unit)** divides first, and then multiplies.
Comparison	=	Equal to (optional)	**=Poe** lists all records with the last name Poe.
	>	Greater than	**>50** lists all values higher than 50.
	<	Less than	**<10** lists all values less than 10.
	>=	Greater than or equal to	**>=50** lists all values equal to or higher than 50.
	<=	Less than or equal to	**<=10** lists all values 10 or less.
Wildcard	..	Any series of characters	**A..y** lists *anatomy, Anthony, any, allegory,* and so on.
	@	Any single character	**10@** lists *100, 101, 102, 103, 104, 105, 106, 107, 108,* and *109.*
Special	LIKE	Similar to	**LIKE grey** lists *grey, gray,* and *Gray.*
	NOT	Does not match	**NOT Poe** lists all records where Poe is not the last name.

(continued)

Category	Operator	Description	Example
	BLANK	No value	**BLANK** lists all records with no value in that field.
	TODAY	Today's date	**TODAY** inserts today's date.
	OR	Specify OR conditions	**=10 OR =20** lists all records that match 10 OR 20.
	,	Specify AND conditions	**>50,<100** lists all records that are greater than 50 AND less than 100.
	AS	Specify the field name in answer	**AS Income** renames the Salary field to Income.
	!	Display all values in a field	**!** lists all values in a field.
Summary	AVERAGE	Average of values in a field	
	COUNT	Number of values in a field	
	MIN	Minimum value in a field	
	MAX	Maximum value in a field	
	SUM	Total of all values in a field	
	ALL	Calculate summary based on all values in a group	
	UNIQUE	Calculate summary based on unique values in a group	

(continued)

Category	Operator	Description	Example
Set Comparison	ONLY	Display records that match only members of the defined set	**ONLY(15,30,45)** lists only records that match a number in the set.
	NO	Display records that match no members of the defined set	**NO(15,30,45)** lists only records that do not match the numbers in the set.
	EVERY	Display records that match every member of the defined set	**EVERY(15,30,45)** lists only records that match every number in the set.
	EXACTLY	Display records that match all members of the defined set and no others	**EXACTLY(15,30,45)** lists records that match all members of the set and no other numbers.

Planning the Query

The more conditions you want to find in a query, the more complicated the query becomes. Practice writing down exactly what you want to know from a query. This helps you clarify which range operators belong in which field columns. Some examples of queries and how they would be recorded follow.

Example 1:
In a table with a customer number, date of sale, and item number, you want to list all orders with the item number equaling three. In the Item Number field in the query form, you would type **3**. You could type **=3**, but the equal sign is assumed when no operator is included.

Example 2:
In a table with a customer number, customer name, date of sale, and item number, you want to list all orders with the item number equaling 3, and the customer numbers exceeding 13546. In the Item Number field in the query form, you type **3**. In the Customer Number field, you type **>13546**.

Using AND for Record Selection

Part of the ability to select records based on more than one criterion is the ability to use AND options in queries. If a query is to meet two criteria, you must ask a question using AND. Both criteria must be met for a record to be selected. For example, you are looking for all the records that have an item number of 3 AND a customer number greater than 13546. In order for any one record to be selected, it must meet both criteria. Another example is all products with the number A8088 AND that were purchased after December 31, 1993. The selected records will have the specified product number and be purchased after the specified date.

The concept of AND can be extended to three criteria. If you have five fields in a table and you specify that in order for a record to be selected it must equal three criteria, you are asking an additional AND question. For example, all products with the number A8088 AND that were purchased after December 31, 1993 AND that were purchased by customer number 38.

These examples show how selective a query can be. You can get a list of the total number of products ordered by a specific customer in a specific time frame. Let's practice using an AND query by specifying two criteria in the DONOR table. You will ask Paradox to find donors who have given more than $500 and live in the city of Los Angeles.

1. Select the **File/New/Query** options. The Select File dialog box displays.

2. Click on DONOR and then click on the OK button. The DONOR table inserts in the Query Editor window.

3. Click on the box under DONOR.DB to include all fields in the answer table.

4. Move to the Amount field and type **>500**.

5. To add the second criteria, the city designation, move to the City field and type **Los Angeles**. The query looks like the one shown in Figure 6.9. Both fields are checked and defined.

6. Click on the Run Query button on the SpeedBar. The answer table displays on-screen, as shown in Figure 6.10. You have asked the following question: What records show a donation of over 500 dollars and that the donor lives in the city of Los Angeles.

Paradox lists all the records in the DONOR table where the donation is greater than 500 and the donor lives in Los Angeles. Paradox for Windows answers the query with five records displayed in the answer table.

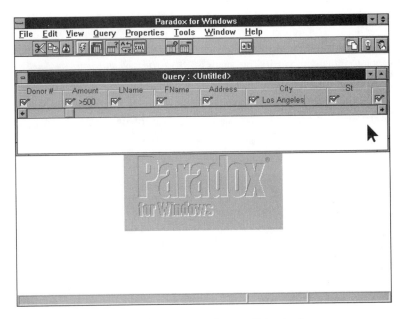

Figure 6.9 *Query with two AND criteria*

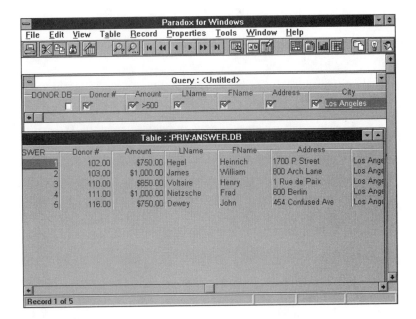

Figure 6.10 *Answer table from AND query*

Closing Answer Tables and Queries

Closing an answer table is the same as closing any child window: Click on the Document Control button in the upper-left corner of the window and from the list of options click on **Close**.

Closing a query is a little different. Paradox expects that you have worked hard to perfect the query criteria, that you will no doubt use it again, and so Paradox prompts you to save the query. Click on the document control button and click on Close from the menu.

Paradox for Windows displays the options when you are closing a query, as shown in Figure 6.11. Select Yes if you want to save the query. Select No if you do not want to save the query. Select Cancel to go back to the Query Editor window. Select Help if you want to see context-sensitive help before you close the query.

Click on the No button. The query is discarded and you are back in a clear workspace.

Using a Wildcard Operator

In this next query example use a wildcard to ask Paradox for Windows to list all the donors with the LName beginning with *H*. Since you have cleared your workspace, begin by opening a new query.

1. Click **File/New/Query**. From the Select File dialog box, click on DONOR and then the OK button.

   The DONOR query form displays in the Query Editor window.

2. Click the box in the LName field to insert a checkmark.

3. Type **H . .**. In a table with hundreds of names, using the **H . .** wildcard will find all records that begin with *H*, including *Hume* and (my personal favorite) *Hegel*. The " . . " operator matches any string of characters in a field.

4. Click the Run Query button on the SpeedBar. Paradox for Windows searches the DONOR database table to find two records where the last name begins with *H*. In Figure 6.12 you can see the Query and Answer table.

Saving the Query

If you decide you may want to use this query on more than one occasion, remove the answer table for this example by clicking on the Window Control button and selecting **Close**. With the answer table removed, save the query.

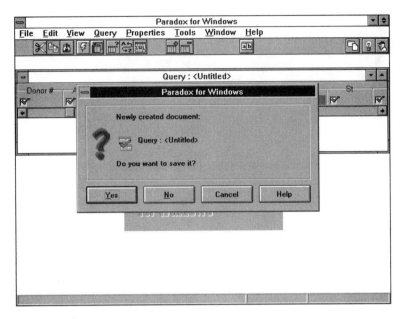

Figure 6.11 *Save Query options*

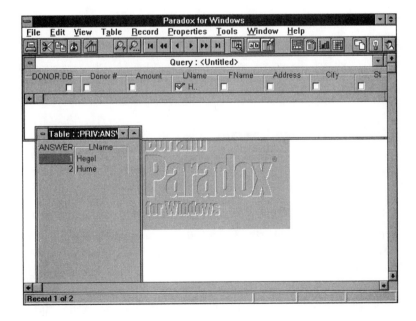

Figure 6.12 *Last names beginning with H query*

If you want to print an answer table, click the Print button. Clicking on the Quick Report button prints the report to the screen.

1. Click on the Query Editor window control button and select **Close**. Four query options display.

2. Click on the Yes button. The Save File As dialog box displays.

3. In the file name text box, type **LNAME**. Click on the OK. button. The query is saved under the name LNAME and then removed from the screen. You are back in a clear Paradox for Windows workspace.

Multiple Conditions in Queries

Earlier you performed an AND query where you asked Paradox for Windows to list records that met two criteria in two separate fields. In the sections that follow, you will practice using AND conditions in the same field and OR conditions in one or more fields.

Using the AND Condition in the Same Field

In this example, you want Paradox for Windows to list all the records in the DONOR table that are above a certain dollar amount AND below another. Both of the specified criteria are defined in the same field. Use a comma to separate the two criteria in the Amount field.

1. Click on the **File/New/Query** options.

2. Click on the DONOR file and then the OK button. The DONOR table displays in the Query Editor window.

3. Click on the box in the Amount field to place a checkmark plus (+) in that field. Click on any other fields you want to display in the answer table.

4. Type; in the amount field, **>300,<700**. You are asking for a list of records where the value in the Amount field is greater than $300.00 AND less than $700.00.

5. Click on the Run Query button on the SpeedBar. The answer table displays as shown in Figure 6.13. Two records meet the AND criteria specified in the query.

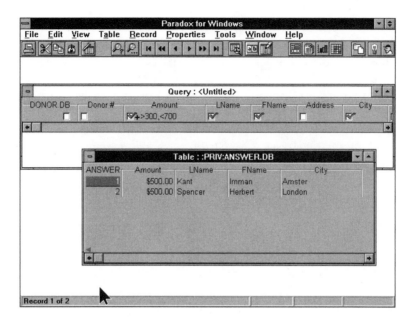

Figure 6.13 *Answer table with two AND conditions in a single field*

Enter as many conditions in a single field as you like. Each AND condition must be separated by a comma. The query field columns will hold the conditions, no matter how many you specify. Not all conditions may display when the columns are the original size.

Viewing All Conditions

When only part of the specified condition displays in the highlighted field space, use one of two methods to display the conditions you cannot see.

With the highlighting on the field with several conditions listed, click on the right side of the highlighting box. The text in the highlighting moves to the left so that you can view more of the conditions specified. If you click on the left side of the highlighting and the text moves back to the right.

Increase the width of the field column to display all the conditions at one time. Move the mouse pointer to the right border of the field column. The mouse pointer becomes a two headed, horizontal, white arrow. Click and drag the white arrow to the right. The column width increases and you can view all the conditions.

Using OR Conditions in a Query

Using the AND condition means you want to include two or more kinds of data. In order for a record to be selected, it must meet both conditions specified. Contrast that with the OR condition. The OR condition selects all the records that meet one of the criteria you specify OR the other criteria. Here is an example. In a Total Invoice field you want to list all the invoices less than $5,000.00 OR more than $10,000. You are going to select the high and low invoices instead of the middle range.

Let's see how the OR condition works in the DONOR table. Select OR criteria where the answer table displays all records where the amount collected was greater than $700.00 or less than $50.00. Clear any other specifications before you begin.

1. Click on the box on the Amount field so that a checkmark plus (+) displays.

2. Type **>700 or <50** in the Amount field. Instead of using a comma as you did to separate the AND conditions, type the word **or** to separate the OR conditions.

3. Click on the Run Query button on the SpeedBar. Figure 6.14 shows the answer table that lists Amount values less than $50.00 but more than $700.00. The Amount field also displays in the answer table, since that field was checked. Eight records meet the OR criteria.

Using OR Conditions in Different Fields

The method for using OR conditions in different fields is a little different than the previous method you used. In the DONOR query form, ask an OR question by specifying the data to be selected in two separate fields. For example, you can query for all records in the DONOR table that show the Amount paid was greater than or equal to $750.00.

Let's use OR conditions in different fields. Start by clearing all previous specifications.

1. Click on the box in the DONOR field column to place a checkmark plus (+) in the box.

2. Type **>=750**. You ask for a list of all records where the donation is equal to or greater than $750.

3. Click on the Run Query button on the SpeedBar. The answer table displays with the six records that meet the specified criteria.

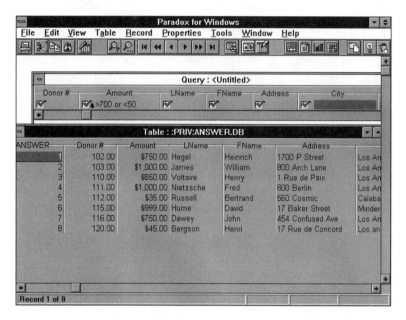

Figure 6.14 *Answer table with OR condition*

Adding the Second OR Condition

Next, add the second criterion. To make this an OR condition, add another line to the query table.

1. Close the answer table by clicking on the Window Control button and selecting Close. You are back in the query window.

2. Press the down arrow. A new row inserts in the query form. You may have to enlarge the query window to see both rows.

3. Click on both boxes in the DONOR field column, so all fields are checked, in both rows.

4. Move the highlight to the second row in the City field column.

5. Type **Minder** to tell Paradox for Windows to list records where the donation was equal to or greater than $750 OR the City is Minder.

6. Click on the Run Query button on the SpeedBar. The answer table displays as shown in Figure 6.15.

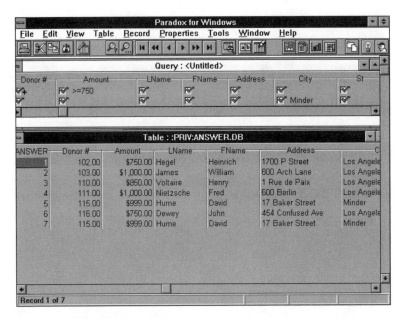

Figure 6.15 *The answer table with OR conditions*

In a query form where you use OR conditions for more than one field, you can have up to 22 lines. This means you can ask 22 OR questions of your data. Paradox for Windows selects records that match any line in the query.

When you enter multiple lines in a query, you must check each line in each column, as well as the same fields in each line. If you do not check the same fields in each line, Paradox for Windows displays a warning screen noting that there is a query syntax error. The query cannot be completed.

Changing the Order of Records in an Answer Table

Any time you have a set of records in an answer table, they are listed in a specific order. If the primary field has numbers, the answer table displays the records in ascending numerical order. The lowest number is at the top of the table, with the numbers getting larger as you move down the list of records.

Paradox for Windows provides a way for you to reverse the order. Check a column to appear in the answer table in descending order. The largest number is at the top of the table, with the numbers getting smaller as you move down the table. When no numbers are involved, this concept works with alphabetical order.

Practice changing the order in any table with a number column to see its effect. Before rearranging the order, remove all checks and data inserted in field columns from the DONOR query form in the Query Editor window.

1. Click on the checkmark box in the Amount column, inserting the down arrow checkmark.

2. Click on the LName field.

3. Click on the Run Query button on the SpeedBar. The answer table lists the Amount field with the smallest value first. The LName field is included in the answer table. Figure 6.16 shows the answer table with records in descending numerical order.

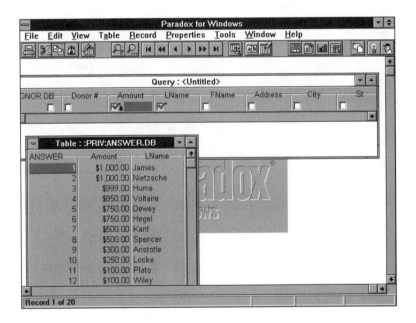

Figure 6.16 *Answer table in descending order*

Removing a Table from the Query Editor Window

You want to continue using the Query Editor window but you do not want to save this particular query. Close the answer table window and then remove the DONOR query table from the Query Editor window.

1. Click on the Window Control button for the answer table, and then click Close. The answer table is removed, and you return to the Query Editor window.

2. Click on the Remove Table button on the SpeedBar. The tables in the Query Editor window list in the Remove Table dialog box.

3. Click on the DONOR file and then click on the OK button. The Query Editor window is cleared. You can add another table at this time to continue querying.

Querying from Multiple Tables

Paradox for Windows is built on the relationship between tables of data. When designing your Paradox for Windows tables you kept your tables simple. Now, you pull together the data you need from related tables. In this section you query multiple tables to pull together related tables. Querying from multiple tables brings together related data from more than one table. The related data appears in one answer table.

Defining the Answer

Two tables have been created for this exercise of querying multiple tables. Both tables are shown in Figure 6.17. Each table has ten records.

The table on the left side of the screen is the Customer Sales table, SALES in this example. The SALES table has two fields. The first field, which is defined as the primary key field, is the Customer #. The second field lists the annual sales for each customer.

The second table is called CUSTID because it contains the customer number and the name and address of each customer. The Customer # field is defined as the primary key in this table, as well.

Create these or similar tables by following the steps in *Chapter 3* on how to create a table.

The sales manager of an organization wants a list of all the customers who purchased more than $1,000.00 worth of products in the previous year. This question alone could be answered by a single table query of the SALES table. However, the sales manager also wants to know the names and addresses of these same customers in order to send them a special promotional mailing.

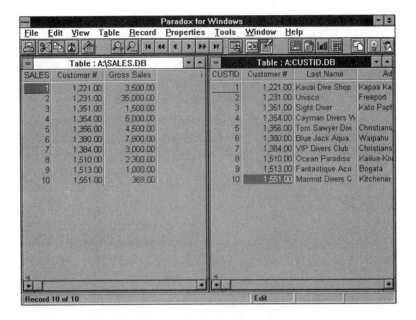

Figure 6.17 *Two tables in query*

When entering customer numbers and values in fields, make sure that they are formatted as you want them. If they are not formatted properly, right-click the mouse button to display field properties. Correct the format using this menu.

The answer table should give the name and address of the customers who purchased more than $1,000.00 worth of products in the previous year. This is accomplished by using the related data in the two tables.

Listing for a Multiple Query

There are four steps to a multiple table query after the tables are created.

1. Display a query form for each table in the Query Editor window.

2. Define the example elements.

3. Check the fields that should appear in the answer table.

4. Execute the query and create the answer table.

Displaying the Tables in the Query Editor Window

In a multiple table query, a query form for each table involved must display in the Query Editor window. In this example, place two table forms on-screen.

1. Click on the **File/New/Query** options.
2. Click on the SALES file and click the OK button. The query table for the SALES file appears in the Query Editor window.
3. Click on the Add Table button on the SpeedBar.
4. Click on the CUSTID file and then click on the OK button. Both query tables are on-screen. The screen looks like the one in Figure 6.18.

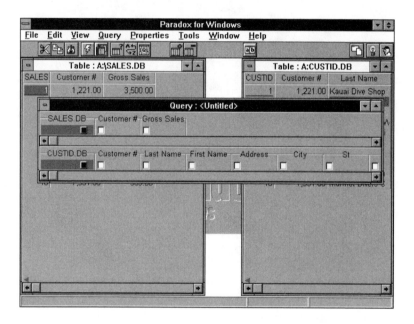

Figure 6.18 *Two query tables in Query Editor window*

Defining Joining Elements

A *Joining element* is a special name you identify to type into a query form. The joining element is placed in the field you want to link to another table. In this example, the field that links the two tables is the Customer # field. The Customer # field in each query form will hold the Joining element.

The field that holds the joining element for each table must have data of the same type, even though the data might not be identical. Joining elements cannot be placed in one field that holds alphanumeric data, while the other holds money data. The fields that hold the joining elements do not have to have the same field name as they do in this example.

Each query form holds a joining element. The joining element in each query form must be identical so that Paradox can match these fields.

Joining elements that you enter yourself are entered in a query form using the **F5** joining key. Paradox for Windows offers automatic joining elements. The automatic joining element is placed with a mouse.

To place the joining elements in the two tables in the Query Editor window, follow these steps:

1. Click on the Join Tables button on the SpeedBar. Two small table icons float with the mouse pointer. (Note the message at the bottom of the screen, **Joining**.)

2. Click on the space below the Customer # field name in the SALES query table. **JOIN1** inserts under the Customer # field name in the SALES query table.

3. Move the mouse pointer to the space below the Customer # field in the CUSTID query table. Click one time to insert the Example. **JOIN1** inserts under the Customer # field name in the CUSTID query table. (If you have a color monitor, the joining elements display in red.)

Figure 6.19 shows the joining elements placed in the two tables.

Checking the Fields to Appear in the Answer Table

In this answer table you want the customer number, customer name, street, city, state, zip, and country. However, you want only those customer with total Sales greater than $1,000.00. The steps in this section include checking the fields to include in the answer table and defining the total Sales greater than $1,000.00.

1. Click on the checkmark box in the CUSTID.DB field. A checkmark appears in each of the following fields: Customer #, Last Name, First Name, Address, City, St, and Zip.

2. Click on the highlight under the Gross Sales field, in the SALES.DB table.

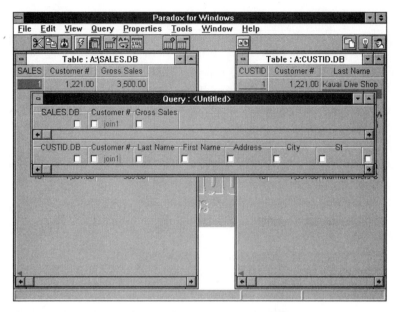

Figure 6.19 *Joining elements linking tables*

3. Type **>1000**. The query is defined. The form appears as shown in Figure 6.20.

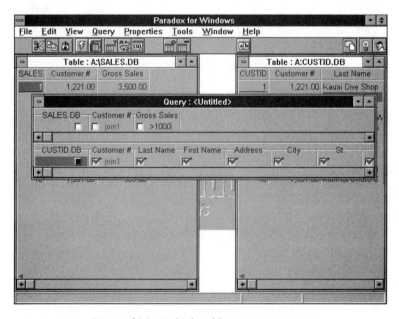

Figure 6.20 *Multiple table query on-screen*

If you check the Customer # field in both table definitions, the Customer # field displays twice in the answer table.

N O T E

The answer table lists only those customers with sales greater than $1,000.00. This field does not have to display in the answer table, however. That is why you have not checked this field.

N O T E

Executing the Query

The final and simplest step is to execute the query. Simply click on the Run Query button on the SpeedBar. Figure 6.21 shows the answer table below the linked query tables. There are eight records where the Annual Sales value is greater than $1,000.00. The names and addresses of these customers are listed in the answer table. Paradox for Windows lists the records in ascending numerical order by Customer number in the answer table.

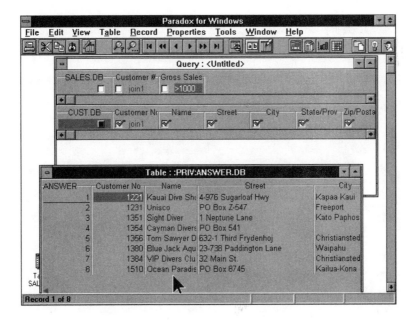

Figure 6.21 *Multiple table query answer table*

To print an instant report of this answer table, click on the Print button on the SpeedBar.

N O T E

Adjusting the Multiple Table Query

You have linked two tables using example elements. You have gotten an answer table with the specific information you requested. That is quite an accomplishment! Now that you know Paradox will do what you tell it to do, try a simple adjustment to the query. The sales manager who defines this query decides that the Total Sales value must appear in the answer table. Follow these steps to adjust the query accordingly.

1. Click on the Window Control button and select Close to close the answer table.
2. Click on the checkmark box in the Gross Sales field. The check is added to the Gross Sales field.
3. Click on the Run Query button on the SpeedBar. Paradox for Windows displays the adjusted answer table, which lists eight records that meet the specified criteria, as shown in Figure 6.22.

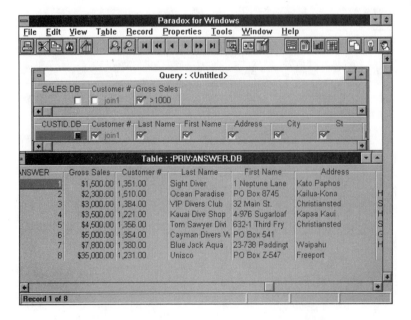

Figure 6.22 *New multiple table query and answer table*

All the elements of a single table query can be used in a multiple table query, including the query operators listed in Table 6.1.

Performing Calculations in a Query

You can use the CALC operator to insert calculations in an answer table. When you use CALC, an additional field is added to the answer table to hold the result of the calculation. For this reason, you can put the calculation in any field in the query table. When you create a new table, you need not add a field to hold calculations; this field is added at the query stage.

Usually arithmetic operators are used with the CALC operator. Use parentheses ( ) to group mathematical operations. In the query table you need not check the field that holds the calculation. Check the field that holds the calculation only when you want that field to display in the answer table.

Suppose you have a PRODUCTS table where you have a field that holds the Sales Price and a field that holds the Cost. Using the calculation features in Paradox for Windows, you can calculate the difference by subtracting the Cost from the Sales Price.

1. Click the **File/New Query** options. In this example, a table named PRODUCTS is used.

2. Click on the space below Sales Price so that the highlight displays in the space. Press **F5**, and type **Sales**. Sales becomes the joining element in this field.

3. Click on the Cost field. Press **F5**, and type **Costs**. The joining element is placed in the Cost field.

On a color screen the joining element displays in red. Combine two words into one word in a joining element for the calculation to work properly.

N O T E

4. With the insertion point after the joining element in the Sales Price field, type **,calc** and press the **Spacebar** one time. Press **F5**, then type **Sales**, and press the **Spacebar** one time. The comma before *calc* separates the joining element from the calculation.

5. Add the arithmetic operator for the calculation. For this example, type a minus sign (-) and then press the **Spacebar** one time. Complete the

equation by pressing **F5**; then type the second joining element of the calculation, **Costs**. The CALC formula is placed in the Sales Price field, as shown in Figure 6.23.

6. Click the checkmark box in the PRODUCTS.DB field. A checkmark is placed in every field in the table. The next step is to execute the query.

7. Click the Run Query button on the SpeedBar. Figure 6.24 shows the result of the query with a calculation in it. Paradox for Windows adds a field that holds the calculated value. The amount in the field is the balance due.

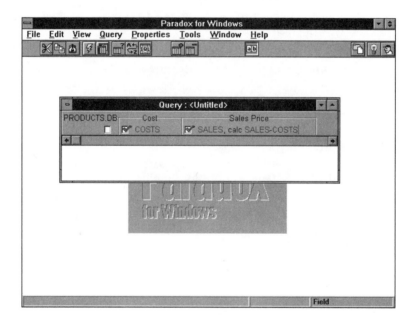

Figure 6.23 *Calc formula*

Saving Queries

Saving queries is important, if, for example, a query gives you a specific month-end report. You don't have to retype the query every time you want to duplicate it. You can simply retrieve the saved query and apply it to the new data at the end of the month.

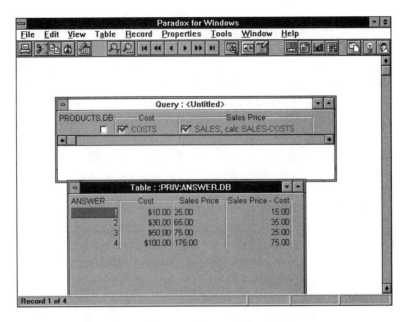

Figure 6.24 *Answer table using the CALC operator*

The steps to saving a query are:

1. Create the query.

2. Execute the query and then verify that Paradox for Windows answers with the correct information.

3. Save the query.

In this chapter you have already completed examples one and two. In fact, you have a query on the screen right now! Let's practice saving this query.

1. With the Query Editor window on-screen with a query defined, click on the Query Editor Window Control button and then click **Close**. A window displays, asking if you want to save the query.

2. Click on **Yes**. The Save File As dialog box displays.

3. Type the name of the query. For the preceding example, type **CALC**.

4. Click on the Save As button. The query definition is saved to be applied again at a later date.

Retrieving a Query

Once you have saved a query and you are ready to see the same query later, follow these steps to retrieve the query.

1. From a clear workspace, select **File/Open/Query**. The Select File dialog box displays.

2. Type the name of the query in the File Name text box or highlight the name of the query in the Files box. Highlight **CALC** and click on **OK**.

The query you saved is on-screen. Notice that the title bar for the Query Editor window now displays the name of the query. The .QBE (Query By Example) file extension is added to all queries. You can modify and/or execute this query. Any changes in data from the previous execution will appear when the new answer table is created.

Command Summary

Command:	Mouse Click:	Keyboard Press:
Create New Query	File/New/Query	Alt/F/N/Q
Add Table	Add Table button	Alt/Q/A
Place Checkmark	Checkmark box	F6
Execute a Query	Run Query button	Alt/Q/D
Close Answer Table	Window Control/Close	Ctrl+F4
Remove Answer Table	Remove Table button	Alt/Q/R
Save the Query	Window Control/Close	Alt/F/S
Instant Report	Quick Report button	
Add Line to Query		Down Arrow
Descending Order	Down arrow checkmark	
Define Joining Element	Join Tables button	F5
Retrieve a Query	File/Open/Query	Alt/F/Q

Chapter 7

Paradox Reports

The Paradox report function goes far beyond the instant reports you have already created. Paradox reports can be customized down to the smallest detail. Whatever your reporting needs are, there is a way to produce them. In this chapter we will examine the many aspects of producing and printing reports:

▼ Instant reports
▼ Custom reports

Paradox for Windows is as friendly and powerful in its ability to create reports as it is in creating tables and queries. As is true of many other topics in this book, you must learn the guidelines for using Paradox tools. This chapter begins with the parameters for creating reports. While these limitations are not rules, they offer a framework for what you can and cannot do with a Paradox report. The limitations listed here increase your understanding of Paradox. As you look at the guidelines, it is easy to see that rarely will you be frustrated.

Paradox for Windows Report Concepts

One important concept in understanding Paradox reports is to know that reports are generated one record at a time. For example, if you were printing a free-form report designed to print invoices, Paradox looks at the first record, prints the corresponding invoice, moves to the next record and prints, and so on. Paradox reads the record, formats the record in the way you have determined in the report definition, and then goes on to the next record. This is how Paradox generates reports. Because the report is an object separate from the table from which it is generated, you can try many report designs without disturbing the original table.

Tabular Reports

One type of report printed by Paradox is the *tabular report*. You have seen this kind of report before in this book. When you have a table on-screen and click on the Quick Report button on the SpeedBar, Paradox generates an instant tabular report. When a tabular report is printed, it looks similar to the way it appears on-screen. The records are listed down the page, with the fields across the top of the page. You can group the records, make subtotals, and keep running totals in a tabular report. The tabular report is almost identical to the Paradox table.

Free-Form Reports

With the *free-form report* you have the freedom to design the printed result. Use this type of report to print mailing labels, create form letters, and invoices, or print checks. Instead of listing data, you can put table fields anywhere on the page. The free-form report is similar to the form view in Paradox.

Report Bands

Report bands are used in Paradox to define and control what is being printed at different locations in the report. Every custom report has four bands. Think of the report as being divided into four separate printing areas, with particular attributes available for each. A description of each band follows:

▼ The *record band* tells Paradox what to do with every record in the table. This band holds the body of the report. You can put comments, field values, and the results of calculations in the record band.

▼ The *group band* (optional) is used to divide records into logical groups. For example, you may want to group a list of campaign donors by the first letter in their last name or to group students according to the scores they received on an exam. Students who got 90% and above would be in one group, students with 80–90% would be in the next group, and so on. You can calculate the sum of values in a report group. This group function allows you to create what is in essence a subgroup of the entire report.

▼ The *page band* includes the information you want to include on the top and bottom of each page of the report. Report titles, page numbers, headers, and footers are some of the things you might want to include in the page band.

▼ The *report band* contains information that is included at the beginning and end of each report. A report header is printed once at the beginning of a report, and a report footer is printed once at the end of a report. A report header and a report footer are placed in the report band. A report footer can hold totals calculated at the end of a report.

Instant Reports

The most basic Paradox report is the *quick report.* With an active window holding a table on-screen, you can create a quick report. A quick report comes in handy when you want to print query results. With any answer table on-screen, click on the quick report button on the SpeedBar. Figure 7.1 shows the printed quick report on screen of one of the answer tables from *Chapter 6.* The quick report holds the date and page number at the top of the page along with the name of the file.

Custom Reports

When a standard report is not enough and you want to add more detail or remove some fields from a report, you must create a *custom report.* Choose the type of report you wish to create, either a tabular report or a free-form report. A tabular report looks similar to the standard report except for some embellishments. The free-form report is more like a form view of a database. The following sections provide information about creating the tabular report.

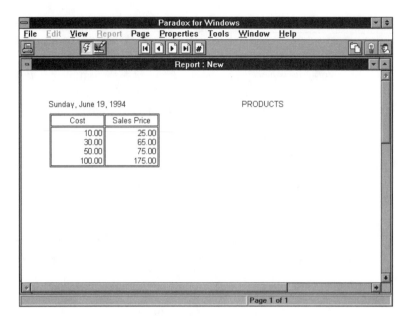

Figure 7.1 *A quick report*

Creating a Tabular Report

Paradox provides you with a design report window in which you place the verbiage in the proper report bands. The process of creating a tabular report starts with getting to the design report window. In this example, you create a report where several columns are removed from the table seen on-screen and column headings are enhanced via the design report window.

Getting to the Design Report Window

Let's start this example by clearing the workspace. If you have other open windows, close all of them beyond the Paradox window.

1. Click on the window control menu and then click on **Close All**. Open windows on-screen are closed. The workspace is clear.

2. Click on the **File/New/Report** from the menus.

The New Report dialog box displays, as shown in Figure 7.2.

3. Click the **Data Model/Layout diagram** option. The Data Model dialog box appears, as in Figure 7.3.

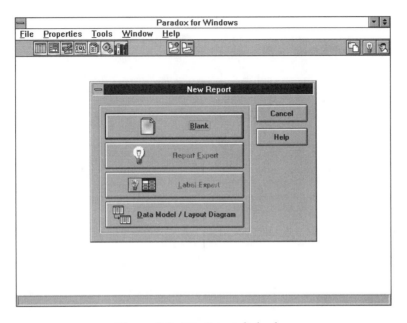

Figure 7.2 *New Report dialog box*

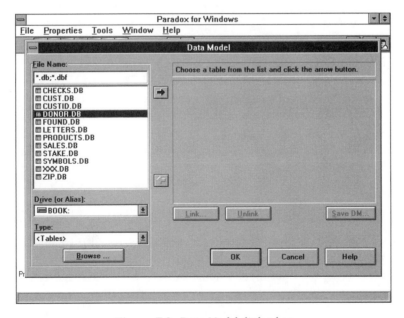

Figure 7.3 *Data Model dialog box*

4. Click the the table file for which you want to create a report. For this example, the selection is the DONOR table. If you prefer, pick any table that you have created with which you would like to work. Click **OK**.

The Design Layout dialog box displays as shown in Figure 7.4. From this dialog box, you can choose the specifications for your report. For this first example, use the default specifications.

5. Click **OK**.

The Report Design New dialog box appears.

6. If the window is not maximized, click on the maximize button for the Report Design window.

Figure 7.5 shows the Report Design window, maximized on-screen.

Describing the Report Design Window

Unlike the query window or the restructuring window, the Report Design window does not start out empty. Paradox assumes many of the design features of the report. The components of the Report Design window are described here.

Look at the Title bar at the top of the screen. Because the window has been maximized, the title bar tells you that you are in the Paradox for Windows—Report Design: New window.

The menu bar is below the title bar. The menu options are File, Edit, View, Report, Design, Properties, Tools, Window, and Help.

The SpeedBar holds a set of buttons that can be used to enhance a report. Eleven buttons are tool buttons just for the Report Design window. Most of these tool buttons are design objects that you can add to a report. Moving to the right on the SpeedBar are more buttons. With these buttons you can add bands, create data models, or create object trees. At the far right is the Open Folder button. At the left of the tool buttons you see one button for viewing the data on-screen and one to print the report. Further to the left are the cut, copy, and paste buttons.

At the top of the report window, you see a horizontal ruler line. A vertical ruler displays along the left side of the window, too. Position the mouse pointer in the workspace. You see lines on the vertical and horizontal rulers. If you were to extend those lines, they would cross at exactly the point at which the mouse pointer is located. The purpose of the rules and lines is to help you place items in the Report Design window in precise locations.

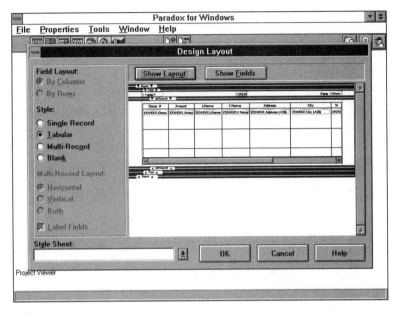

Figure 7.4 *Design Layout dialog box*

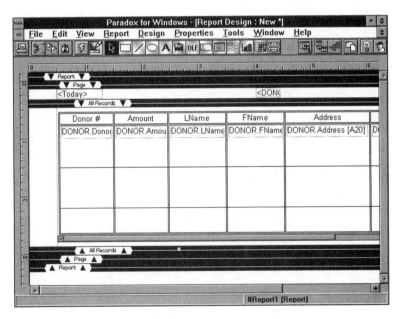

Figure 7.5 *The Report Design window*

Below the horizontal ruler is the top border for the Report band. Just below that is the top border for the Page band. The next band down is the top of the Record band. Each band extends from the top band with the arrow pointing down to the band with the same name with the arrow pointing up. Therefore, the Record band is included in the page band, which is in turn, included in the report band. The report is designed in layers.

In the page header area, you see the symbol <Today>. This is the command that inserts today's date in the report. To the right you see <DONO>. The file name is automatically inserted as the name for the report.

The Records band holds all the fields from the selected table. You will decide whether all these fields should be included in the report.

The report footer and page footer are located at the bottom of the Report Design window. At the very bottom of the screen is the Status line. As you click the mouse pointer in the workspace or move over the buttons on the SpeedBar, notice the indicators on the Status line. They change so that you know the action performed by the button to which the mouse pointer is pointing or what band of the report is being affected.

Removing Fields from the Report

The first thing to do in creating this custom report is to remove some of the fields in the record band. Seven fields now display in the Record band. Only the fields Donor #, Amount, LName, and FName are necessary in the report. Let's start by removing the unwanted fields:

1. Right click on the blank space below the word Address, opening the Object Inspection menu. The Inspection menu is seen in Figure 7.6.

2. Click the Define Table option.

3. Click on the Ellipses at the top of the submenu, opening the Define Table Object dialog box, as shown in Figure 7.7.

4. Click on the field name, Address.

5. Click the Remove Field button.

6. Repeatedly click the Remove Field to remove the City, St, Zip and Notes fields.

7. Click **OK**. The Report Design window reappears as in Figure 7.8.

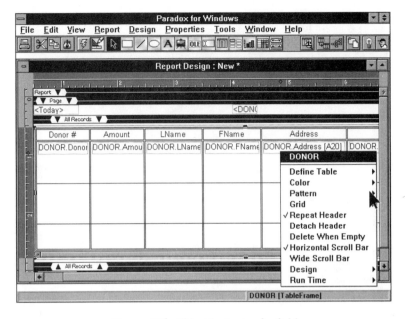

Figure 7.6 *Object Inspector for field*

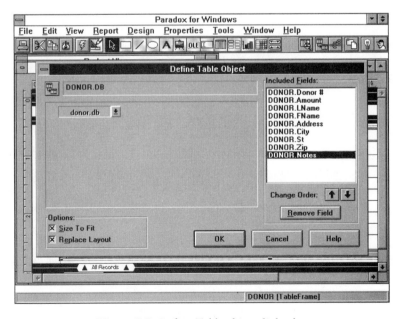

Figure 7.7 *Define Table object dialog box*

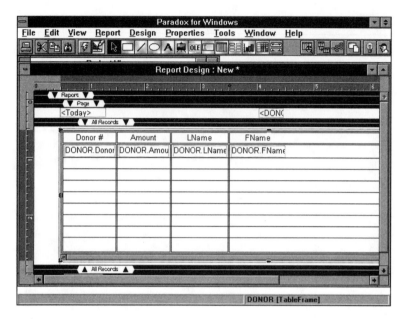

Figure 7.8 *Fields removed from report*

Inserting Literals in a Report

Literals are characters printed in a report, just as you see them on the screen (that is, literally). An example is the report header that you use to alert readers to the contents of the report by inserting **BOSS ONLY**. You might also use a literal to describe a sum. Suppose that you total all the sales per month and then add a literal that labels the sum, such as **Total Monthly Sales**.

Where the literals are printed on the report depends on where you enter them on the design report window. As you move the mouse pointer down the page, the following areas are found. From top to bottom, they are Report header, Page header, Record band, Page footer, and Report footer. When you enter literals in each of these areas, you get a different result on the printed report. The result is described here.

▼ **Report Header.** Literals entered in this area are printed on the first page of the report only.

▼ **Page Header.** Literals entered in this area are printed at the top of each page in the report.

- ▼ **Record Band.** Literals typed above the field names appear above the field names on the printed report. Literals typed below the field names are printed after each record.
- ▼ **Page Footer.** Literals typed in this area are printed at the bottom of each page in the report.
- ▼ **Report Footer.** Literals typed in the area are printed at the end of the report.

Adding a Report Header

The page header has already been added to this report for you. It includes the date (<TODAY>) at the left margin, and the name of the file, centered at the top. In this example, DONOR does not appear in its entirety because of the default size allotted by Paradox for the header. This is easy to changes, as you will see in a moment.

Move the mouse pointer to the report header area to add the report header.

N O T E   You may need to add some space in the report header area. Begin by clicking on the report horizontal line until it highlights. Now, move the mouse pointer to the page band line until the mouse pointer becomes a vertical two-headed white arrow. Click on the page band and drag it down the screen until there is more space for adding text. Figure 7.9 shows the position of the two-headed arrow after the space has been created for the report header.

1. Click on the text tool button on the SpeedBar and then move the mouse pointer to the report header band. The mouse pointer takes the image of the text button. Figure 7.10 shows how the mouse pointer looks now in the report header band.

2. Click on the text pointer at 2 inches and then drag the pointer down and to the right. Release the mouse button at 3 inches. When you click and drag the text pointer, a rectangle whose border is a dotted line is drawn in the report header. When you release the mouse button, an insertion point displays at the left of the rectangle.

3. Type **Key Donor Report**. The literal Key Donor Report appears in the report band. This text will be printed at the top of the first page of the report. The mouse pointer is still an insertion point.

4. Click the mouse pointer outside of the text area. The insertion point is removed from the report band.

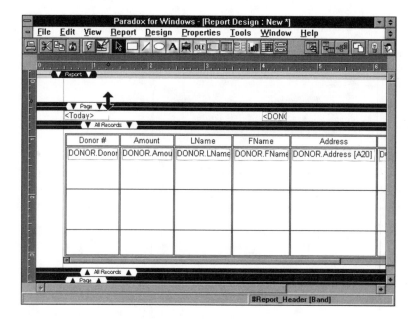

Figure 7.9 *Two-headed arrow creating space*

Adding a Report Footer

Let's add another literal to the report footer, which prints on the last page of the report.

1. Click on the text tool button on the SpeedBar. Move the mouse pointer to the report footer band. Use the vertical scroll button to move the report to where it can be seen.

N O T E

If there is no space to include text in the report footer band, click the *A* (text image) on the word Report. A blank line inserts above the word *Report*.

2. Click the text image at 4 inches in the report footer band.

3. Type **December, 1994**. The text inserts in the report footer band. Figure 7.11 shows the report header on screen.

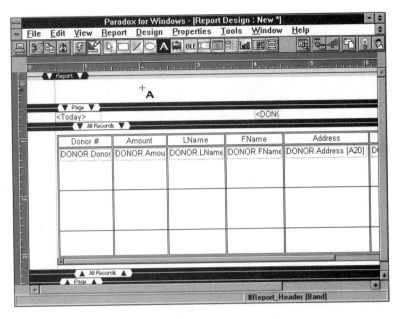

Figure 7.10 *The text button image*

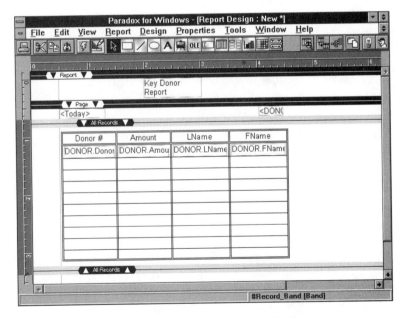

Figure 7.11 *Report header added*

Both methods of inserting literals have been presented to you. In the first method you draw a box and then insert the text. The text fits the size of the box and word wraps at the right margin you establish. With the second method, you click on the text tool button, click in the design area, and begin typing. If you press **Enter** while still in a text area, Paradox adds a new line to the band.

Take the same steps to add page headers and footers. Add text above the bottom page band to add a page footer or below the upper page band to add a page header. The same steps are also used with other tools on the SpeedBar.

N O T E

Grouping Data in a Report

When you are preparing a more sophisticated custom report, you will want to use the grouping data feature. Perhaps you want a list of names and addresses grouped by zip code. You may want data grouped by amount sold or in alphabetical order. Grouping can help make reports more legible.

Let's begin by looking at the Select the Band Group dialog box.

1. Click on the add band button on the SpeedBar. The Define Group dialog box appears, as shown in Figure 7.12.

2. Click on the table name listed in the table box. A list of fields for that table displays in the Field box.

3. Click on the **City** field in the Field box. The field name you select inserts in the Band Label at the top of the dialog box. The Define Group dialog box looks like the one shown in Figure 7.13.

4. Click on the OK button. The group band you have defined appears in the design report window. On the group band it states, "Group on DONOR.DB: City." Notice that handles display around this grouping object you have placed in the report definition, as shown in Figure 7.14.

Previewing the Report

Let's look at how the report appears with the design specifications you have made by clicking on the view data button on the SpeedBar. The report displays on-screen as it would appear printed. If you are happy with the way the report looks, you are ready to print it. Before you print it, save it to disk, so that you do not need to redesign the report. Figure 7.15 shows the first page of the previewed report.

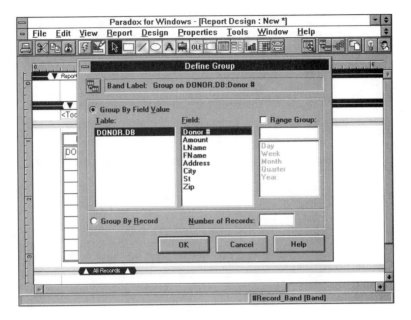

Figure 7.12 *The Define Group dialog box*

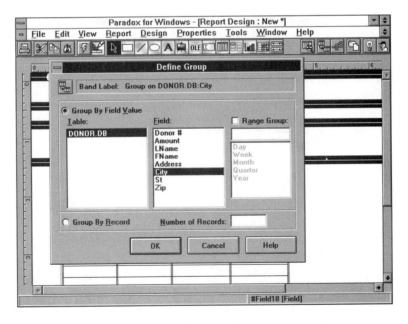

Figure 7.13 *The completed Define Group dialog box*

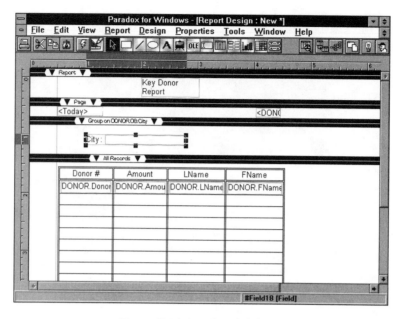

Figure 7.14 *New band defined*

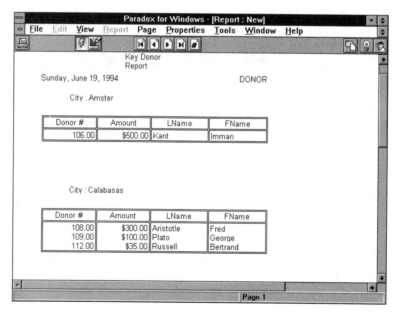

Figure 7.15 *Previewed report*

As you can see, even though the City field was not included as a part of the report, the group was correctly defined. At the top of the report is the literal, Key Donor Report. Paradox inserts the correct date for you.

Before saving the report, return to the design report window. Click on the design button on the SpeedBar.

Saving the Report

While creating a report, it is a good idea to make a few changes, save the report, make more changes, and save the report again. If your work is interrupted, you have a saved product on disk. You do not need to go back and re-create the report. To save the report, follow these steps.

1. Select the **File/Save As** option. The Save File As dialog box displays.

2. Type **DONREP**. The file name inserts in the New File Name box, as shown in Figure 7.16.

3. Click on the OK button. The file is saved to disk. You remain in the design report window where you can continue designing the report.

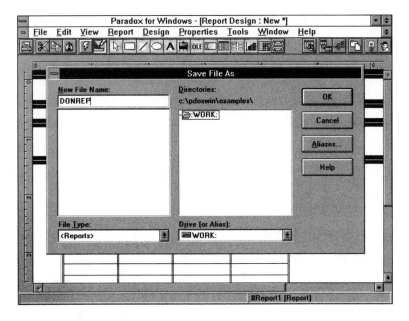

Figure 7.16 *Save File As dialog box*

If you have already saved the report and are saving it the second time, Paradox asks if you want to overwrite the first file. Click on **Yes** to overwrite the old file. Click on **No** to keep the previous file and then create a new name for the redesigned report.

Grouping by More Than One Criterion

In the Paradox design report window you can group by more than one criterion. If you want to group records first alphabetically, then by ten records, and then by the amount sold, you must place several group bands in a report.

The group band that surrounds the other group bands is the primary group. For example, if the group band that surrounds the others says to group by alphabet, then that is the primary group.

The primary grouping is done first. First, all the names are listed alphabetically by the first letter. If the next group band was amount sold and ascending was selected, the names would appear in alphabetical order, but the names would appear in the ascending order of amount sold. In other words, all the *W*s, would be in one group. Within the group of *W*s the records would be listed by amount sold in ascending order.

If the third grouping was to group by ten records, you might see a list like this.

```
Waif      10,000
Wail      11,000
Went      12,000
Weod      13,000
Win       14,000
Wist      15,000
Wivet     16,000
Woes      17,000
Wonton    18,000
Wune      19,000
```

Place more than one group band by repeating the preceding steps in the section entitled "Grouping Data in a Report." Preview the report to the screen to make sure the data is sorting according to your specifications.

With a list of hundreds of names or more, group by the first two letters or first three letters. This gives you smaller groups, which helps make the report more legible.

Changing the Design Report Window

Once you create and save a report design, you can retrieve the report to make changes to it. You may want to add group bands, change headers and footers, add or delete fields, or add design objects.

Retrieving the Report Design

From a clear Paradox workspace, let's retrieve a report design.

1. Click on the Open Report button. The Open Document dialog box displays, as shown in Figure 7.17.

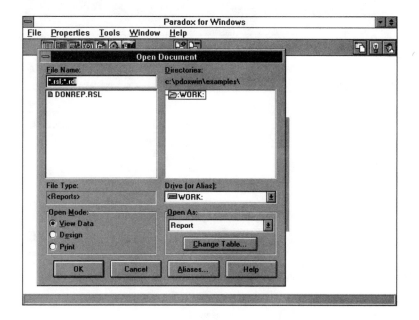

Figure 7.17 *Open Document dialog box*

2. Click on the report name you want to open.

3. In the Open Mode box, there are three choices: **View Data**, **Design**, and **Print**. Click on **Design**.

4. Click on the OK button. The design report window displays for the specified report.

Now you are ready to make any adjustments to the report. Use these steps to design or change a report.

Deleting Design Objects

Earlier in this chapter you placed a design object in the form of text in a report. You can delete the design object by clicking on the object, which causes the object handles to appear. Figure 7.18 shows how design object handles look on-screen. Click on the cut to clipboard button on the SpeedBar to remove that design object from the design report window.

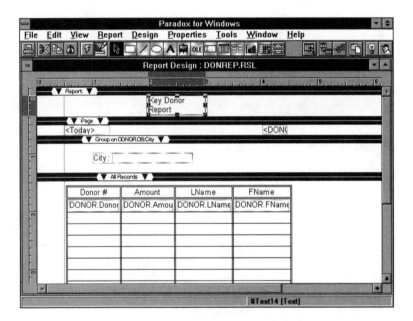

Figure 7.18 *Design object handles*

Moving or Sizing Design Objects

Earlier in this chapter, you saw the name DONOR partially visible in the page band. To change the display of the word *DONOR*, enlarge the box in which it is contained by using the object handles. Follow these steps.

1. Click on the word *DONO*. The object handles appear.

2. Move the mouse pointer to the object handle, at the middle, right border of the box. The arrow points right and left if it is properly positioned.

3. Click and drag the handle to the right. The size changes, allowing the full word *DONOR* to appear, as shown in Figure 7.19.

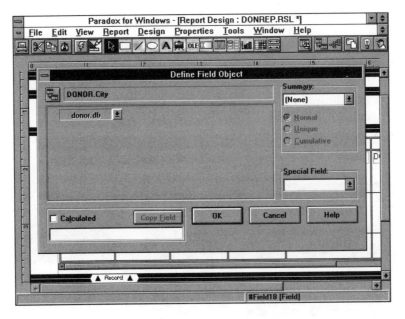

Figure 7.19 *DONOR resized*

Deleting a Band

If you add a group band and decide you want to change it completely or remove it, you can delete the band. These steps work with any band in the design report window. To remove the band from the design report window, highlight the band by clicking on it with the mouse pointer and then click on the cut to clipboard button.

When you use the cut to clipboard button, the object is saved, until you cut another object to the clipboard. If you make a mistake and delete an object, click on the paste from clipboard button to insert it again.

N O T E

Create More Space Between Bands

Suppose that you want to add a paragraph of text to a band or a list of data. Expand the space between bands by moving the mouse pointer to the highlighted band border. (Highlight the band border by clicking on it.) The mouse pointer changes to a double-headed vertical arrow. Click and drag this arrow either up or down to get more room in any band.

Redefining a Band

When a group band is placed in a design report window, you can alter some of the properties of the band. With the mouse pointer on the group band, click the right mouse button for property inspection. The property inspection menu displays, as shown in Figure 7.20. From this menu you can redefine the group, add group headings, adjust the sort order, or change the layout of the group.

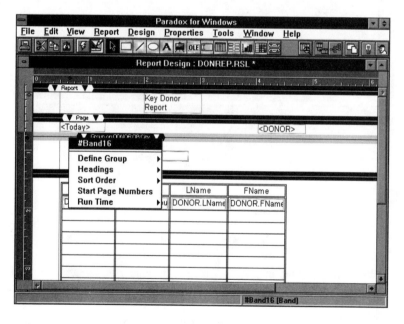

Figure 7.20 *Band property inspection menu*

Select **Define Group** from this menu, and a list of all the fields in the table for which the report is being created displays. Click on a different field to change the field in the group band.

Reformatting Fields

Already, you have controlled the fields that appear in the report, the headers, the footers, and how the records are grouped. You can also control how the fields are formatted. While in the design report window, reformat one of the fields on-screen.

The Amount field displays in the Number format at this time. The [N] following Amount in the field column is the indicator that tells you that the data in this field displays in the Number format. To change the format for the display of numbers in the Amount field column, follow these steps.

1. Click on the word *Amount* twice, so that the object handles display around it. Click the right mouse button. The properties for the field display.

2. Click on **Format** and then on **Number Format**. A window opens up from which you can select different formats for the numbers in the Amount field column. The current format is checked on the menu.

   There is a limit to what formats you can change. You cannot change a numeric format to an alphanumeric format, for example. Only the options available are listed on the property inspection menu.

   N O T E

3. Click on **Windows$**. The properties of the data in this field are reformatted to currency.

Using Aggregators in Reports

There will be times when you want to use *aggregators* when working with Paradox reports. An aggregator gives you a total, an average, a count, a minimum, or a maximum number. These aggregators are especially useful when your data is grouped. For example, a report listing sales, grouped by month, could calculate total sales at the end of each month grouping. The aggregator functions are listed in Table 7.1.

Table 7.1 *The Aggregator Functions*

Aggregator	Function
Aggregator	**Function**
Sum	Shows the total for a group, calculated by adding all the values together.

(continued)

Aggregator	Function
Average	Shows the average for a group, calculated by adding all the values and dividing by the number of values.
Count	Shows the number of records in each group. The Count aggregator does not count records with no value.
Maximum	Shows the highest value found in a group.
Minimum	Shows the lowest value found in a group.
Std	Shows the standard deviation of values in a group.
Var	Shows the statistical variance of values in a group.
First	Shows the value of the field in the first record in the group.
Last	Shows the value of the field in the last record in the group.
Next	Shows the value of the field following the current field.
Prev	Shows the value of the field prior to the current field.

Place an aggregator in the design report window that finds the Sum in the Amount field.

N O T E

The Sum aggregator is used in the following example. You can substitute any aggregator in its place.

Placing Summary Functions in Groups

From the design report window, place an aggregator at the end of every group. You want a total of the amount of each group of donors.

1. Click the mouse pointer on the City group object until handles display around it.

2. Click the right mouse button for property inspection and then select **Define Field**. A list of available fields displays.

3. Click on the ellipses (...) at the top of the list of available fields. The Define Field Object dialog box displays, as shown in Figure 7.21.

4. Click the down arrow next to the DONOR table. Click the field on which you want to place an aggregator. In this example, that field is Amount.

When you click on the down arrow, a list of fields displays. When you make your selection, the field name inserts at the top of the box.

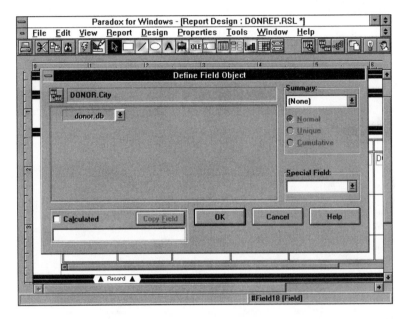

Figure 7.21 *Define Field Object dialog box*

5. Click on the down arrow in the upper-right corner of the dialog box. This is the down arrow near to the word *Summary*. A list of possible aggregators displays.

6. Click on **Sum** (or choose any other aggregator that you want). Sum(DONOR.Amount) displays in the top of the Define Field Object dialog box, as shown in Figure 7.22.

7. Click on the OK button. Where it once said City, it now says Sum (Amount). Paradox calculates the total Amount and inserts that value in the report. Using this method you see a sum of the Amount field after each City group. Figure 7.23 shows an example of such a calculation on the DONOR report.

Saving the Report Design

When you are done creating a complicated customized report, finalize the report and save it to disk. Paradox saves the report format so that you can recall it any time you want. You may want to apply the same report definition to a new set of data or a new time period. Simply select the **File/Save** option. (Select the **File/Save As** option if you have not saved and named this report.) Paradox saves the file to disk.

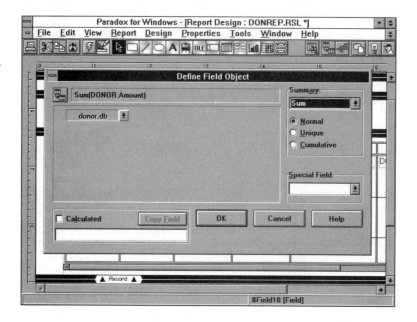

Figure 7.22 *The Define Field Object dialog box*

Printing a Report

Before you print the report, view the report on the screen to make sure that your data displays the way you want it to print. To print the report, follow these steps.

1. Click on the view data button on the SpeedBar. The report you have created displays on-screen, as shown in Figure 7.23. If the report appears the way you like it, print the report.

2. Click on the print button on the SpeedBar. The Print the File dialog box displays. Make decisions here on which pages you want printed, how many copies you would like, etc.

3. Click on the OK button. The report prints to the printer.

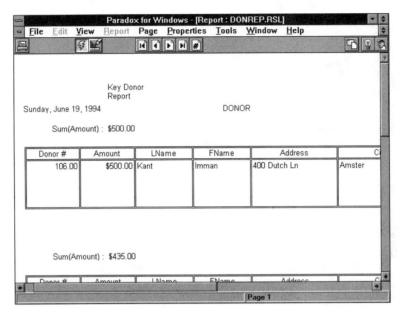

Figure 7.23 *DONOR report with calculation*

If the report does not print, select the **File/Printer Setup** option to make any necessary adjustments in equipment.

Report Options

There are many options in the Report Design window. Most of the tasks you have completed are examples of some of the objects that can be placed in the Report Design window. You have placed text in the report. Placing any design object follows the same steps. You have placed an aggregator. You may place an aggregator combined with text. In the remainder of this section, some of the other options are briefly described as a reference for you.

The Properties Menu

Most of the items on the properties menu are *toggle options.* Select any of the options, and that option is turned on or off. Looking at the menu as it displays in Figure 7.24, the items with the checkmarks are on. Items without a checkmark are turned off.

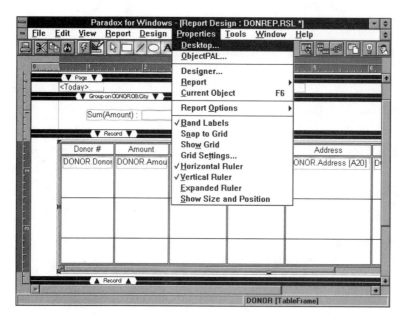

Figure 7.24 *The Design Report Properties menu*

▼ **Desktop.** Use this option set the display properties and options for the Desktop, as described in *Chapter 2*.

▼ **ObjectPAL.** Use this option to set ObjectPAL preferences as described in *Chapter 2*.

▼ **Current Object.** Opens the Object Inspector for the currently selected object in the report.

▼ **Report.** Use this option to save the settings you have in the design window as the defaults.

▼ **Designer.** Use this option to set design preferences such as Outlined/Move and Resize, Frame Objects or not, and Flicker-free draw.

▼ **Band Labels.** When on the band labels are highlighted. When off, only the band text displays.

▼ **Snap to Grid.** Select this option to insert a grid reference for object placement.

▼ **Show Grid.** Shows a detailed Grid on the design report window.

▼ **Grid Settings.** Shows the Grid Settings dialog box. From here you can alter the look of the grid.

▼ **Horizontal Ruler** and **Vertical Ruler.** Select either of these and the ruler either displays or does not display on screen.

▼ **Expanded Ruler.** This turns the expanded ruler on, which, again, assists you in detailed applications.

▼ **Show Size** and **Position.** Causes Paradox to display more information on the ruler in the status bar, right corner.

Command Summary

Command:	Mouse Click:	Keyboard Press:
Instant Report	Quick report button	
Report Design	File/New/Report	Alt+F/N/R
Delete Selected Data	Cut to clipboard button	Shift+Del
Add Text	Text tool button	
Add a Band	Add band button	Alt+R/A
Preview a Report	View data button	Alt+R/V
Save a Report	File/Save As	Alt+F/A
Retrieve a Report	Open report button	Alt+F/O/R
Delete Design Objects	Cut to clipboard button	Shift+Del
Delete a Band	Edit/Delete	Del
Inspect Properties	Right mouse button	
Save a Report Design	File/Save	Alt+F/S
Print a Report	Print button	Alt+F/P

Summary

In this chapter, you begin to see the power of the report design features of Paradox. The next chapter looks at the creation of forms.

Chapter 8

Working with the Form Screen

In this chapter you will explore the form window of Paradox for Windows. A form window displays one record at a time. The concept of a form comes from the world of paper. Every invoice, check, and purchase order is processed one at a time on a piece of paper, that is, as a single record of data. In Paradox the format is to enter data into tables with multitudes of records contained in every table. For many database operations, this view of the records is appropriate. However, many people are more comfortable with a forms view of records, and thus Paradox provides a way to convert records from a table format to a form. This process does not disturb the underlying table of records in any way. The main topics found in this chapter are the following:

▼ The Paradox Form window

▼ Designing custom forms

▼ Using Expert Labels

▼ Designing a Mailing Label

The Paradox Form Window

Instead of just displaying columns of data across the screen, a form can display data in the place you choose. Comments, highlighting, and some graphics may be added to enhance the look of the form. Examples of forms are invoices, customer profiles, and a single student's assignments and grades.

The key advantage of using the form view is being able to see all the data for one record at a time. In table view some of the data might be in fields that are not visible on the screen. In a long text field, the text can be word wrapped to fit on one screen. The table view provides an overall look at the entire table, while the form view allows you to zero in on a specific record or series of records. In addition, you can add comments and short descriptions to items in the Form Window.

With the form window, you have the option of increasing security. You can decide which fields a database user can view and which fields can be modified. If a table holds confidential or sensitive information, you can protect that information.

Viewing the Paradox Form

In the Paradox form view, you specify how you want your table data displayed. Let's look at a standard form from a Paradox table by opening a table. Try this out on a table called ORDERS.DB. This table is shipped with Paradox and is located in the Sample directory, provided that you have installed the sample tables, as shown in the table view in Figure 8.1. Click the quick form button on the Speedbar, and the form window of the ORDERS table displays, as shown in Figure 8.2.

Form Window Components

The form window that displays using the quick form button is a default form. That is, it is a standard form designed by Paradox. The form window opens on top of the table you were viewing when you clicked on the quick form button.

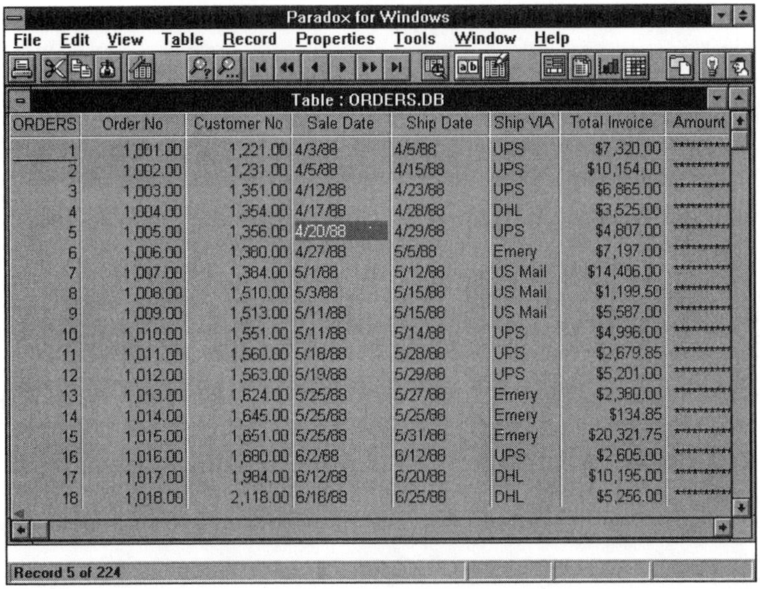

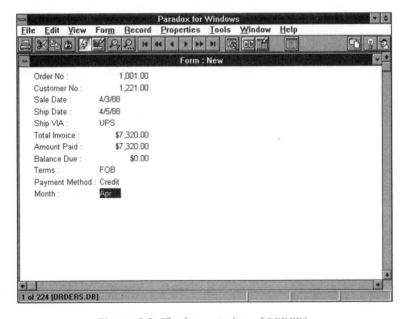

Figure 8.1 *The table view of ORDERS*

Figure 8.2 *The form window of ORDERS*

The form window has not been named, so it is called Form:New at this point. The table menu disappears and is replaced by the forms menu. The SpeedBar also changes as you change from the table view to the form window. On the SpeedBar, the table view button replaces the quick form button. As easily as you switched from the table view to the form view, you can switch back by clicking on the table view button. Or, you can use the **Window/Tile** option to see both windows simultaneously.

Click the mouse pointer on the form window. As you do this, the status line provides information about the data you are viewing. In this form you are viewing record 1 of 224. The table name displays on the status line as well.

The field titles appear on the left side of the form window, with their corresponding values displayed to the right. Click on the next record button on the SpeedBar to see the second record in the table. The form window displays one record at a time, no matter which navigation button you click on. You can also press the **Page Down** or **Page Up** keys to move a single record at a time.

Notice that the field value 1002.00 is about ten spaces from the Order No field name. The Payment Method field has the value right next to the field title. Fields formatted as numbers are displayed farther to the right on the form. Alphanumeric values display closer to the field name, because they are fixed length fields, and Paradox can calculate exactly how much space is needed for the data. Paradox arranges the number fields this way because it has to make some predictions when it places data in a form window. The numeric values do not have specific field sizes. Therefore, Paradox leaves enough room for a very large number when the form window is created.

When you move from the table view to the form window, Paradox places the highlight in the same field and record it was in while in the table view. Go back to the table view, by clicking on the table view button, and the highlight stays in the same field and record you were in, in the form window.

Moving in the Form Screen

While viewing a record in the form window, move from field to field by clicking the mouse pointer on the field you want. Move from record to record using the navigation buttons on the SpeedBar. Figure 8.3 shows the navigation buttons and their function.

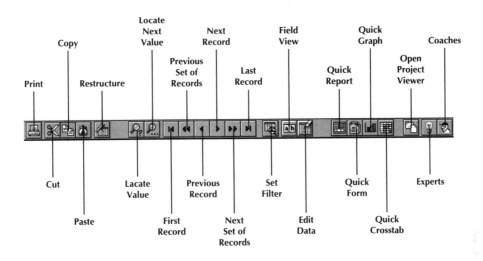

Figure 8.3 *The navigation buttons*

F11. Previous Record

Shift+F11. Previous Set of Records

Ctrl+F11. First Record

F12. Next Record

Shift+F12. Next Set of Records

Ctrl+F12. Last Record

The Form Window SpeedBar

In addition to the Navigation buttons on the SpeedBar, you have additional buttons. On the left side of the SpeedBar are the Print, Cut, Copy, and Paste buttons. The View Data button is next. followed by the Design button. This is the button you use to move fields, add text and graphics, and otherwise embellish the form.

To the right side of the Navigation buttons you see to the Filter button, explained in *Chapter 5*, Field View and Edit Data buttons. These three buttons work in the Form Window just as they do in the Table view. Use these buttons to find a group of records and then correct or make changes to the data in fields.

The Table View button allows you to switch back to the Table view from the Form Window. On the far-right of the SpeedBar is the Open Folder button, followed by the Expert and Coach buttons.

Tiling the Windows

It may be useful to be able to see the records in tabular form as well as form view at the same time. The Window menu includes the Tile option, allowing you to do just that.

1. Click the Window menu.

2. Click **Tile**. The screen appears as in Figure 8.4.

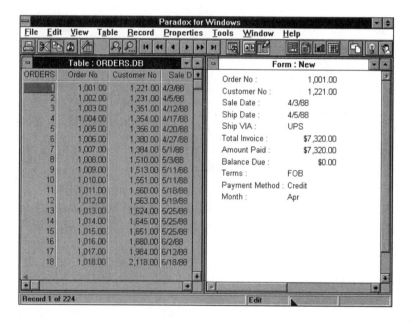

Figure 8.4 *Windows tiled*

When you have both views of the table on screen, they are synchronized unless you want them to be.

In this figure, the Project Viewer has been closed.

N O T E

Depending upon which window is the active window, determines the list of menus and the Speedbar icons. If any other objects were open on the desktop when you clicked Tile, those windows would be included in the workplace display.

Closing the Quick Form Window

You can do anything with the form window that you can do with other Paradox windows. Click on the form window control button to view the Window Control menu. You may restore, move, size, minimize and maximize this window. You may close the window or move to the next window.

1. Click on the window control button and then click on the close button. Paradox notifies you that you have created a new document. You are asked if you want to save it. You may choose to save it or not, cancel the action, or access Help.

2. Click on **No**. Paradox will not save this newly created file and closes the window.

Designing Custom Forms

Getting to and moving around in the Form Window is quite simple. Using the ORDERS table, let's design an invoice form. For this example, use the File menu to create a new form from scratch.

1. Select **File/New/Form**.

   The New Form dialog box appears as in Figure 8.5.

2. Click the Data Model/Layout Diagram.

   The Data Model dialog box displays. From this dialog box, you may select the file for which you want to create a form.

3. Click the ORDERS table. Paradox responds by inserting the name of the table in the space to the right of the list of tables. Figure 8.6 shows the Data Model dialog box with ORDERS as the selected table.

4. Click **OK**.

The Design Layout dialog box displays with the fields from the file you specified. Figure 8.8 shows the Design Layout dialog box.

N O T E

If you have queried a table and want to use the data that the query finds in a form, you may select a saved query file by clicking the down-arrow in the Type box in the Data Model dialog box. Click **Queries** and saved queries displays in the File Name box. Follow the steps above to select one of these files to create a form. Figure 8.7 shows the Data Model dialog box with queries as the selected data model source.

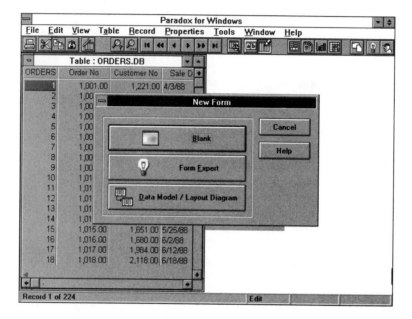

Figure 8.5 New Form dialog box

Understanding the Design Layout Window

By using the Design Layout Window, you can construct the form in any manner you choose. Good form design takes practice and Paradox makes it easy to do. You may want to use a paper form as your design model.

Notice that there are many options in form design.

Field Layout

The default layout used by Paradox when you click the Quick Form button is in the By Columns layout. Click the **By Rows** option and Figure 8.9 shows how the form looks now.

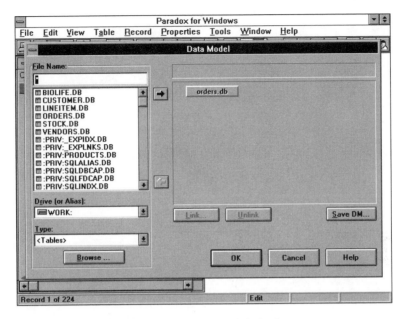

Figure 8.6 *Data Model dialog box*

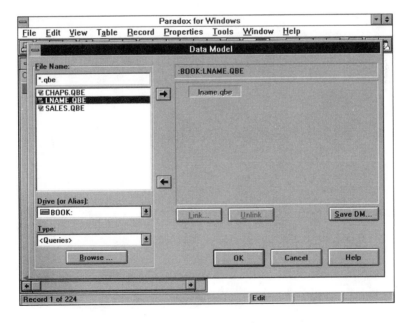

Figure 8.7 *Data Model dialog, queries*

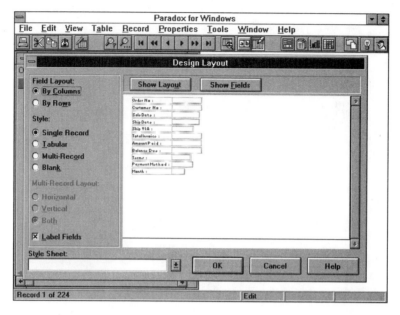

Figure 8.8 *The Design Layout dialog box*

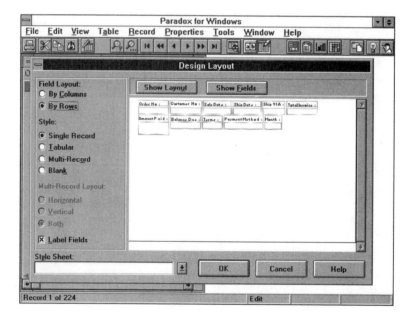

Figure 8.9 *The Design Layout by Rows*

As you can see, Paradox took the table fields and arranged them left to right to the right margin and then wrapped the next field to the second line of the layout.

At the top of the dialog box are two buttons, the Show Layout and the Show Fields buttons. Selecting the Show Layout button displays layout options for the form. The Show Layout button opens a list of the fields in the form. Using the list, you can subtract fields or rearrange the order in which they appear in the form.

Style

Select a different style option than the default types and the example in the Design Layout window changes according to your choice. Figure 8.10 shows an example layout for a Tabular style, while Figure 8.11 shows a Multi record style.

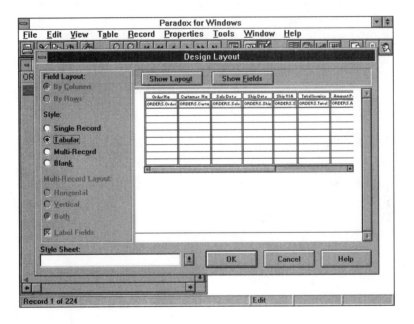

Figure 8.10 *Tabular style*

Multi-Record Layout

The Multi-Record options become available when you select the Multi-Record style. Make selections in this box to choose between displaying records across the page (horizontal), down the page (vertical), or across and down the page (both). If the number of fields that you have included in the form exceeds the space that is allowed in a multi-record form, Paradox alerts you to the problem and tells you which field(s) have been left off.

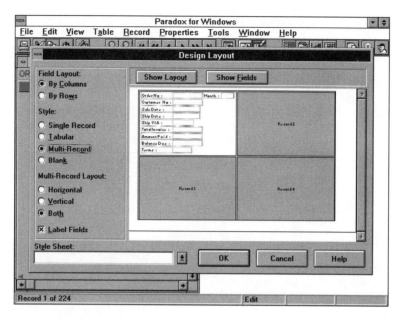

Figure 8.11 A Multi-Record Style

Labeled Fields

Click this box to turn the field labels on and off. With labels off, the field data displays but the labels do not. In most forms, you will want the labels included.

Completing the Design Layout

Once you have selected the general design layout you are ready to design the form.

▼ Click OK in the Design Layout dialog box.

The Form Design: New window displays with the layout you specified.

Viewing the Form Design Window

Your SpeedBar has changed dramatically for the Form Design screen. You have the option of cutting, copying and pasting to the clipboard. Click the View Data button and data from the selected file is placed in the fields on the Form Design. You may print the form.

There are several graphics buttons that allow you to add objects to the Form Design. You may add arrows, boxes, lines, ellipses, text, and graphics to the form. Figure 8.12 shows the unique Form Design buttons.

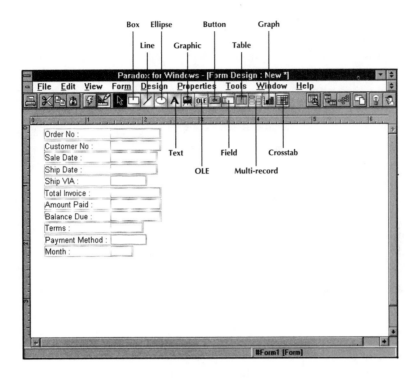

Figure 8.12 *Form Design Buttons*

The menus have also adjusted for the Form Design Window. The Form and Design menu options are specific to this Window.

Selecting Objects in the Form Design Screen

Just as you did when you created a report, you click on objects to select them in the Form Design window. When you select an object, handles appear in the corners and along the edges. Use the handles to move and resize an object.

When you pass the mouse pointer over a handle, arrows that indicate the direction the object size can be changed appear. Change the size of the object by clicking and dragging the handle in the specified direction. This is called *grabbing the handle*.

To select more than one object at a time, press and hold the **Shift** key; then use the mouse pointer to select objects. Use the **Edit/Select All** menu option to select all the objects in the Form Design window.

Designing a New Form

Before you begin, you need to have a good idea of how the form should look. You may want to draw the form on paper, in order to have a blueprint of your form. Because you are designing the form in an electronic medium, you may use the trial-and-error method. You can design, view, and print, and then go back to the drawing board, if the result is not what you wanted.

In the form design steps that follow, many, but not all, options are used. You must learn the general steps of inserting a design element in a form and then use those same steps to insert any design element. Enjoy the experimentation involved in creating your own forms.

Be sure to have the distinction clear in your mind between design elements and data elements. Examples of design elements are boxes, ellipses, and text. Examples of data elements are fields, tables, graphs, or cross-tabs.

Adding a Title to the Form

To add a title to the form, begin by returning to the original window, with the form in single record layout and the columns arranged by columns. Your screen should look like the one shown in Figure 8.13. At the top and center of the form, let's add a title to the form. Begin by moving the fields so that there is room at the top of the form for added text.

Moving the Fields

You could move one field at a time, but follow the steps here to move all the fields at one time.

1. Select the **Edit/Select All** options from the menu. Handles display around all the fields on the Form Design screen.

2. Click on the fields and drag them down the form, so that the top of the Order No field is aligned with the 1-inch mark. If Paradox stops you from moving the fields down as far as you need to move them, click on the handle at the bottom middle of the form window and drag it down. This action increases the size of the form window, allowing you to move the fields down farther. Figure 8.14 shows the fields moved with the handles still active.

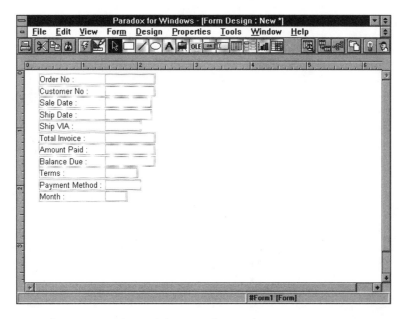

Figure 8.13 *Raw design of ORDER*

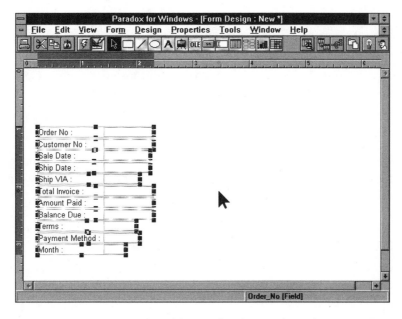

Figure 8.14 *Fields moved to the 1-inch mark*

With **all fields** selected, you can click anywhere on the fields. All the fields will drag at one time.

Adding a Text Object

Now you have space for the form title at the top. To add the text in the newly created space, follow these steps.

1. Click on the Text button on the SpeedBar and move the mouse pointer to the location on the form where you want to insert the text. The mouse pointer becomes a letter A with a crosshair. Use the crosshair to pinpoint the location of the text. Wherever you click the crosshair is where the text you type will insert on the form.

Remember that you don't need to be exact in your placement because you can move the text object after it is inserted in the Form Design screen.

2. Click the mouse pointer at the desired title location. The mouse pointer changes to an insertion point.
3. Type **INVOICE**. The text is inserted at the insertion point. Figure 8.15 shows the form with the fields moved down and the title inserted.

Changing the Text Properties

Accessing the object menus in Paradox is the same here as in previous examples. Follow these steps to change the font and size for the text you just placed on the form.

1. Click on the text object. The mouse pointer changes to the upward pointing arrow, and handles display around the text.
2. Click the right mouse button. The property menu displays, as shown in Figure 8.16.
3. Click on **Font**. From the Font property menu, a font property box displays.

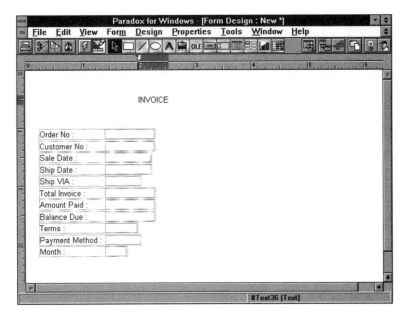

Figure 8.15 *Text added to the form*

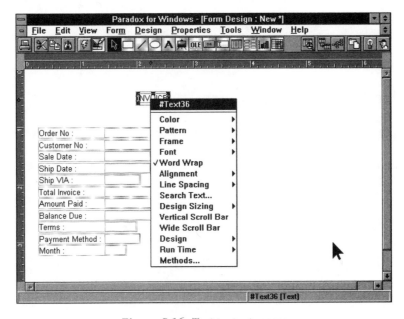

Figure 8.16 *Text property menu*

4. Click on the desired font on the left side and increase the size of the font by clicking a higher point size.

5. Click on the Underline box. This example uses 18-point Bragadoccio, as shown in Figure 8.17.

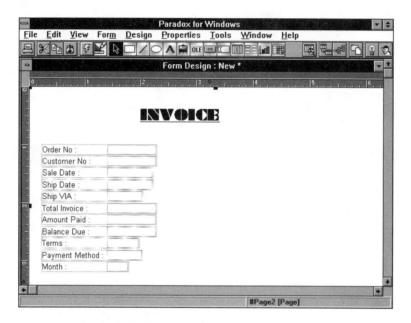

Figure 8.17 *Text changed to 18-point Bragadoccio*

Moving the Fields in the Form

Moving the fields is an easy task. In this example the order number is moved to the upper-left corner, and the Customer number and Sale date appear on a horizontal line. The customer number is placed just below the word *INVOICE*, which had to be moved to the right to make room for the Order No field. See Figure 8.18.

Move the fields by clicking on the field so that handles display. Grab the fields by clicking and dragging them to the new location.

Adding a Grid to the Form Design

When you want to be very precise with the field locations, select the **Properties/Show Grid** options. A grid displays on the Form Design screen as a tool to help you align objects.

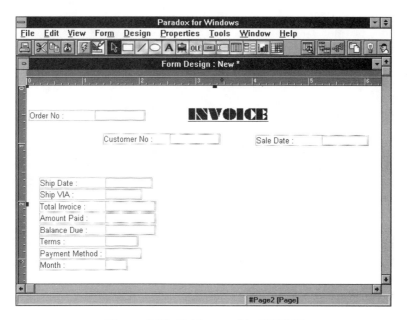

Figure 8.18 *Fields moved in INVOICE*

Adding a Box

For this example, let's add a red box around the customer number, as that is a crucial piece of information in the invoice.

1. Click on the box tool on the SpeedBar. Move the mouse pointer to the Customer No field.

2. Move the crosshair to the upper-left corner of the Customer No field. Click and drag the box object until it surrounds the number.

3. With the handles still on the box, click the right mouse button, and the property inspection menu appears, as shown in Figure 8.19.

4. From the Properties menu, click on **Frame**, **Color**, and then **Red**. The frame of the box is red on the screen (provided you have a color monitor).

Deleting a Field

You are creating a form from a table with many fields. When you do not want all those fields to display in the form, you must delete a field from the Form Design window.

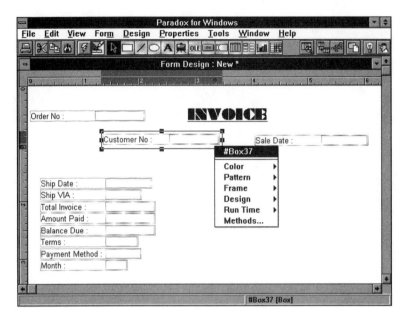

Figure 8.19 *Box property inspection menu*

1. Select the field you want to delete by clicking on the field until the handles appear.

Delete more than one field at a time by first selecting more than one field at a time. Press and hold the **Shift** key; then click on the fields you want to delete.

2. Select the **Edit/Delete** options from the menus. The selected field or fields are removed from the Form Design window.

Saving the Form Design

Paradox does not automatically save the form design you have created. To save the form design, follow these steps.

1. Select the **File/Save As** menu options. The Save File As dialog box displays. The insertion point is in the New File Name box.

2. Type the name of the file.

3. Click on the OK button.

When you are naming a file, you do not need to add an extension. Paradox automatically adds the extension and then saves the file. That file can be accessed by its file type, based on the assigned extension. The .FSL extension is used for forms designed using Paradox.

You may type the name INVOICE in this example, because Paradox assigns a different extension to the file name. The form design would be INVOICE.FSL while the table would be INVOICE.DB. Using this naming convention can help you find related files.

N O T E

Paradox saves the form design. A message indicating that the form has been successfully saved displays on the status line.

If you try to close the Form Design screen without saving it, Paradox opens a window and asks if you want to save it. This also happens if you make changes to the Form Design screen. Paradox asks if you want to save the changes or go back to the original form design.

From the window that asks if you want to save the design, click on **Yes** to save it or **No** if you do not want to save it. When you select **No**, you also lose changes made to a form design. Choose **Cancel** to stop the saving process and go back to the Form Design window. Help is also available from this dialog box.

Viewing Data in the Form

With the form designed and saved, view the data from the table in the new design. Click on the view data button on the SpeedBar. The data from the table inserts in the fields placed in the form. Figure 8.20 shows how one record of data displays in the form created in this chapter. The status line informs you which record is in the form out of the total.

Additional SpeedBar Buttons

You just saw how to use the view data button on the SpeedBar. Two more new buttons—data model and object tree—are found on the SpeedBar in the design form view.

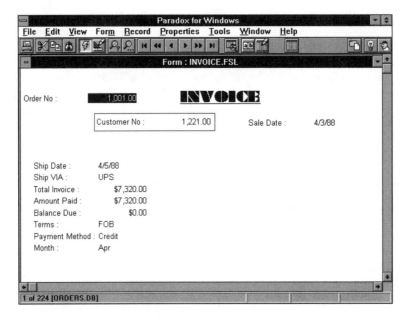

Figure 8.20 *Data inserted in the form design*

Data Model

Click on the data model button, and the Data Model dialog box displays. From this dialog box you may add or remove tables from the design. Use this option to link tables to forms and reports.

Object Tree

Click on the object tree button to see the object tree of all the objects placed in the form design.

Ending the Form Design

Once you have saved the form design and any changes, close the Form Design window to end the session.

1. Click on the form design window control button. The window control button displays.

2. Click on **Close**. The form design session is finished.

Selecting a Form

From a clear Paradox workspace, you may select a form design.

1. Click on the open form button on the SpeedBar. The Open Document dialog box displays. Because you selected the open form button, only files that hold forms are listed in the left box. Note that the form you just created is listed there.

2. Click on the Form file you want to open. Select either the View data mode or the view design mode.

3. Click on the OK button. The Form displays in either view data mode or view design mode as you have selected.

Designing a Mailing Label

In this section, let's design a mailing label. Paradox comes with several pre-design mailing labels for standard Avery 5160, 5161, 5260, 5261 and 5262. To use the prebuilt forms follow these steps:

1. Click the Tools menu and **Experts** option.

2. From the dialog box, select **Mailing Labels**.

3. The Mailing Label Expert dialog box appears as in Figure 8.21.

4. Select the category and type of label you want to print.

5. Click the right arrow button.

6. Select a table from the dialog box, and click the right arrow button.

7. Select a Font for the label, and click the right arrow button.

8. The next dialog box allows you to design the label contents. Click on the field you want and then click Add Field.

9. Click the Add Data button. Paradox designs the label and displays the results in the Form Design window. At this point, you can continue to refine the layout as described in the remaining portions of this chapter.

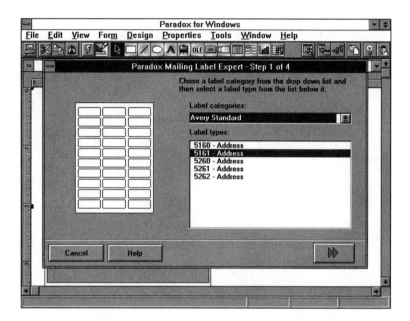

Figure 8.21 *Mailing Experts dialog box*

Opening a New Form File for the Label

Begin by opening a new Form file.

1. Select File/New/Form from the menu.

2. Click **Data Model/Layout Diagram**. The Data Model dialog box displays.

3. Select the File you want to use as the source of your mailing labels from the File Name box. Click on that file and click the right-facing arrow. In this example, the CUSTOMER database is used. Click OK. The Design Layout dialog box appears next. You have several decisions to make on this dialog box. Take a look at some of them.

4. Click the By Rows radio button.

5. You do not want the field labels to display on the mailing labels. So, click the Labeled Fields box. This removes the labels.

6. Click **Multi-Record** as the Style.

7. Click the Show Fields button. The list of fields appears as in Figure 8.22.

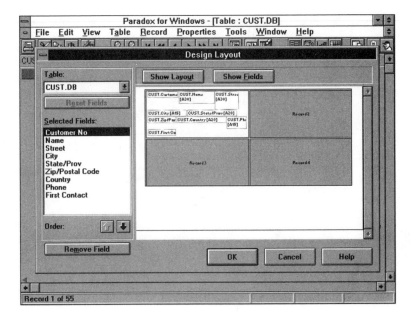

Figure 8.22 *Fields displayed in Design Layout dialog box*

For the purposes of an address label, you do not need all the fields that are listed.

8. Click on **Customer No** and then click the Remove Field button.

9. Remove the Phone, First Contact and Country Fields too.

10. Click OK. The Form Design window opens with a New form as in Figure 8.23.

N O T E

If you are preparing mailing labels that are three across on an 8 1/2 by 11 inch piece of paper, you would select **Both** from the Multi-Record Layout box. The Form Design Window displays. The outline of the specified mailing label appears according to the values you entered on the Page Layout dialog box. So far, there are six horizontal strips down the page, as in Figure 8.23.

Finishing the Mailing Label Form

At this point you can adjust the layout to fit your particular mailing labels. Once you have placed fields, you are able to view data and print the Form document.

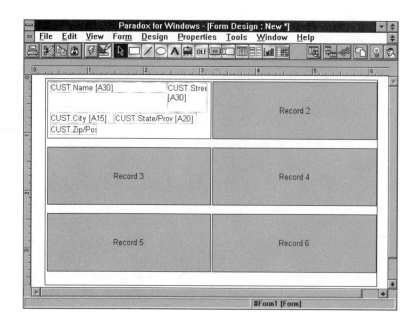

Figure 8.23 *New Form in Form Design window*

Placing the Fields

If you were going to create a letter and insert fields in the letter, you would place a text object, then type the letter in this window, placing the fields where you want them. Because mailing labels are the objective, no text will be added here. Instead, begin by moving the fields to the location for your labels.

In this example, we use three labels down the page.

1. With the mouse pointer pointing to the first label, click the RIGHT mouse button. Select **Record Layout** from the menu.

The Record Layout dialog box opens. From this window select how many labels across and down a single page.

2. Change the entry in the Across box to **1**. Change the entry in the Down box to **3**. Click OK. Three horizontal label bands display down the page. The fields within the label need to be arranged properly.

3. Click several times until the handles show on the CUSTOMER A30 in the upper right corner of the label, which is the Street field. You cannot see the word *Street* because the text box is too small and drag so the field box is flush left on the second line, along with the city, state, and zip code.

4. Stretch the Street text box by clicking on the handle in the right center of the box, until the word Street is completely visible.

5. The Zip field at the bottom of the label needs stretching, too. The completed layout is shown in Figure 8.24.

6. Click the View Data button on the SpeedBar to see if the data inserts where you want it.

If the data does not insert in the correct places, click the design button to return to the Form Design window. Continue clicking and dragging until all of the fields for the mailing label have been moved to the correct location.

Figure 8.24 shows the label layout with data in the field positions.

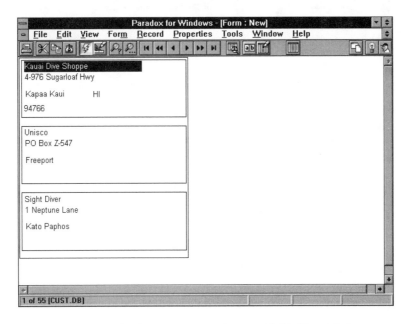

Figure 8.24 *The Form Design Screen with Mailing Labels*

Page Layout

Click the Page Layout button to display the Page Layout dialog box, as shown in Figure 8.25. From this box you may customize the form to the page on which the label will print.

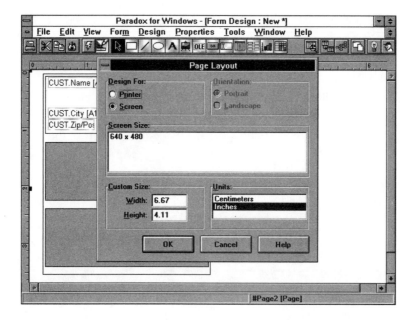

Figure 8.25 *Page Layout dialog box*

Here, you can specify the page size and margins, the orientation of the form, the preferred units of measurement, and you may design the form for the screen or for the printer.

Printing Mailing Labels

With the SpeedBar the task of printing the labels is made easy. While viewing the data, perform the step below to print the labels.

▼ Click the Print button on the SpeedBar.

The Print File dialog box displays. From this box, make any printer selections necessary, then click **OK**. The labels will print to the printer.

Saving the Mailing Label Form

There are many steps to creating a mail merge for mailing labels. Save the product of your labor.

1. Click the Form Design window control button. Click **Close**.

The Paradox dialog box displays asking if you want to save the form design.

2. Click **Yes**.

The Save File As dialog box displays with the insertion point in the New File Name box.

3. Type the name of the file and click **OK**.

The form design is saved for future mailing lists.

Troubleshooting

If you have difficulty printing your results, you may have to check your hardware. Review the manual for the printer and check to make sure that all connections are firmly established.

Review the page layout you have established. Make sure the page size, orientation, and other characteristics match the paper you are using.

Check the printer setup (**File/Printer Setup**). You may need to select a different printer or adjust the printing options.

You can also verify the settings in the Print Manager. Open the Print Manager window on the Main Program Manager. Access the printer setup by selecting the **Options/Printer Setup** option. From this dialog box you can see if you have the correct default printer set up on the correct port. In the Print Manager window you also can see if some queued printing job is preventing the current job from being completed.

Command Summary

Command:	Mouse Click:	Keyboard Press:
Quick Form	Quick form button	**F7**
Move in Form	Navigation buttons	**Arrow keys**
Previous Record	Previous Record	**F11**

(continued)

Command:	Mouse Click:	Keyboard Press:
Previous Set	Previous Set	**Shift+F11**
First Record	First Record	**Ctrl+F11**
Next Record	Next Record	**F12**
Next Set	Next Set	**Shift+F12**
Last Record	Last Record	**Ctrl+F12**
Toggle from Form to Table View	Form button Table button	**F7**
Close a Window	**Window Control/Close**	
Create a New Form	**File/New/Form**	**Alt/F/N/F**
Select All Placed Fields	**Edit/Select All**	**Alt/E/A**
Display Handles	Design object button	
Display Properties	Right mouse button	
Show Grid	**Properties/Show Grid**	**Alt/P/G**
Add an Object	Object button	
Save a Design	**File/Save**	**Alt/F/S**
Viewing Data	View data button	
Open a Form	Open form button	

Summary

In this Chapter, you learned how to design forms. A form can be designed for use in entering data records or for printing labels. In the next Chapter, graphing data in Paradox is explained.

Chapter 9

Creating Graphs

The Paradox for Windows graphing capability allows you to create a visual representation of your table data. Up to this point, you have examined your data, for the most part, as written information. Graphs present a new view of cold numbers and do validate the "worth a thousand words" cliché. In fact, intelligently designed graphs can reveal hidden or unrecognized relationships in your data. The key to intelligent design is making certain that the data you select for graphing has a valid relationship. For example, if your company creates a table of customer invoices that includes a field for date of payments, by graphing the dates of the payments, the graph could reveal when your cash flows are the strongest and the weakest. Or, if your firm divides the country by regions, you can graph the amount of sales from each region. Paradox does not have all the bells and whistles that a true graphing program has, but it has enough capability to allow you to see vital relationships. Like the Report Generator, graphing with

Paradox for Windows is a matter of collecting the data and making the correct menu and object selections. Paradox gives you several graphing options.

▼ Quick graphs

▼ Custom graphs

The Quick graph, which gives you a bar graph of the data, will be covered first. Custom graphs are covered later in the chapter with bar graphs and pie graphs.

Quick Graphs

Getting a picture of data with Paradox for Windows is as easy as pressing one key. Figure 9.1 shows a table with each month listed and a total sales value per month. You may either reproduce this table or use one of your own. To use your own data, assuming that you have a table of invoices or some other records that contain the sales data by date, create a query that sums the amount field and then specify groups by month.

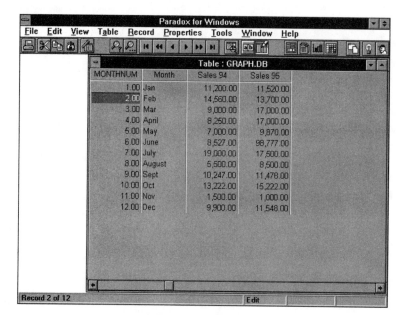

Figure 9.1 *Table on-screen*

Creating a Quick Graph On-Screen

With the mouse pointer on any field or record in the table, create an instant graph.

1. Click the quick graph button on the SpeedBar. The Define Graph dialog box displays, as shown in Figure 9.2.

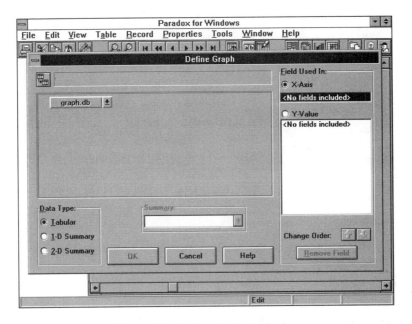

Figure 9.2 *Define Graph dialog box*

2. Click on the **X-Axis** option in the upper-right corner of the dialog box, beneath the words *Fields Used In.*
3. Click on the down arrow to the right of the file name, in this example, the file is named **GRAPH.DB**. A list of fields displays below the file name, as shown in Figure 9.3. From the list, select the field you want to graph on the *X*-axis.
4. Click on the Month field name. The table name and field name display under the *X*-Axis option.
5. Click on the **Y-Value** option, just below the **X-Axis** option. Then click on the down arrow next to the file name. Select the field to display on the *Y*-value. In this example, **Sales 94** was selected.

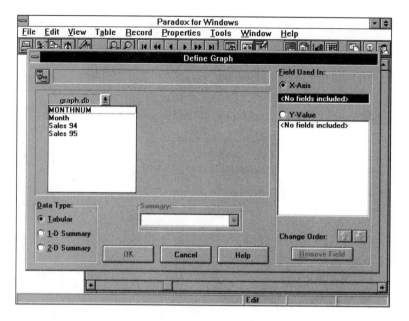

Figure 9.3 *List of field names*

At this point, only three fields are available, because the field Month has already been selected. Paradox prevents you from selecting the same field again.

NOTE

6. In the lower-left corner of the dialog box, select **Tabular** as the Data Type and then click on the OK button. The quick graph displays, with the sales figures listed vertically and the months listed on the X-axis, as shown in Figure 9.4.

Saving the Quick Graph

The quick graph displays in its own window. To remove the graph from the desktop, simply close the window. Let's see what happens if we try to close the window.

1. Click on the window control button and then click on **Close**. A dialog box appears, as shown in Figure 9.5. You are alerted that you have created a new document and closing the window will cause its demise. The options are to click on **Yes** if you want to save the document, **No** if you do not want to save it, or **Cancel** to go back to the graph window. You can also click on **Help** to see the help on saving the graph window.

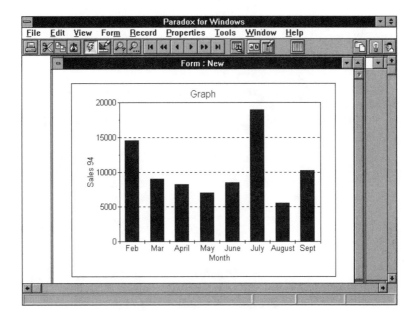

Figure 9.4 *Quick graph with one bar*

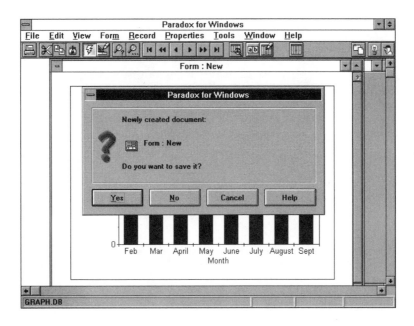

Figure 9.5 *Save dialog box*

2. Click on **Yes** to save the new graph. The Save File As dialog box displays, as shown in Figure 9.6.

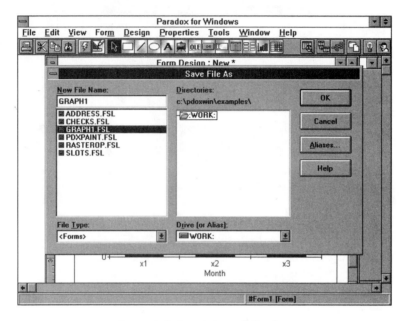

Figure 9.6 *Save File As dialog box*

3. Type in a file name, such as **GRAPH1**, and click on the OK button. The new quick graph is saved, and the window is automatically closed. Paradox assumes that you still want to close the window, even if you took a quick stroll down Save File Lane.

Viewing More Data

Figure 9.4 displays only eight months due to a default setting of Paradox.. But you can see the remaining months, using the navigation buttons on the SpeedBar. Click on the button on the far right, which takes you to the last record, and the remaining months are visible, as shown in Figure 9.7.

Printing the Quick Graph

With the quick graph on-screen, print the graph. Before you do, you may wish to click on the navigation keys at the far left to return the display to the January through August values.

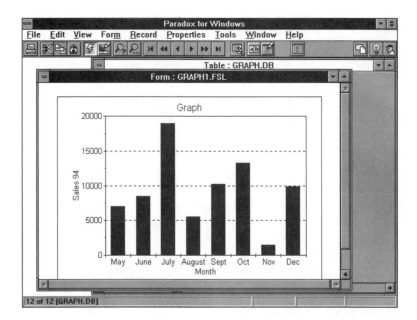

Figure 9.7 *Remaining months in sight*

1. Click on the print button on the SpeedBar. The Print File dialog box displays. Make sure that the printer destination is correct.

2. Click on the OK button. A dialog box displays indicating that the graph has been sent to the print spooler. You may cancel the printing at this time. If you have a fast computer, the Cancel dialog box does not stick around very long. The graph is printed to the specified printer.

If you are printing to a laser printer, the Resolution should be set to 300 dots per inch, or else the graph bars will not print.

N O T E

Custom Graphs

You have created one quick graph on-screen and sent it to the printer. This is a standard tabular graph. As with reports, you can make changes to the graph, making a custom graph.

You cannot add other fields to graph to the original graph. So, if you intend to have several fields included as part of the graph, make sure that you select them all in the Design dialog box.

N O T E

Designing a Graph from the Form Design Window

Although you cannot add fields to a graph once it has been created, you can add many stylistic changes. Use **GRAPH1** for this next example. If you removed it from the screen, select **File/Open/Form** to open the graph. The fact that Paradox stores the graph as a form should give you some insight regarding the type of object a graph is. It is not an interactive object. That is, if you were to change a value in the underlying table that had been part of the graph, the graph will not automatically adjust. You must recreate the graph to capture the new value. Select the graph name (in this case, **GRAPH1**) from the Open Document dialog box and click on the OK button.

With the graph on-screen, the SpeedBar adjusts accordingly. Click on the design button to go into the Form Design mode. The screen looks like the one shown in Figure 9.8. The SpeedBar has features similar to the Report Design screen in *Chapter 7* and the Form Design screen in *Chapter 8*. To get to this screen, you opened a form, so the graph is a form. The window has been maximized in Figure 9.8.

1. Click on the design button on the SpeedBar to open the Form Design screen. The display changes to a generic bar graph, as shown in Figure 9.9.

    Look at what Paradox presents in this screen. Instead of the actual graph, you work in a form screen.

2. Click on the view data button on the SpeedBar to switch back to the GRAPH1 window. (The view data button looks like a bolt of electricity.)

3. Now click on the Window menu, as shown in Figure 9.10. The menu lists only *two* open windows. Not three as you would expect.

The graph displays differently in the Graph design screen. The graph in the design screen represents the design features in the actual graph. The data from the Paradox for Windows table no longer displays. When you click on the view data button, you will see the actual data represented in the graph.

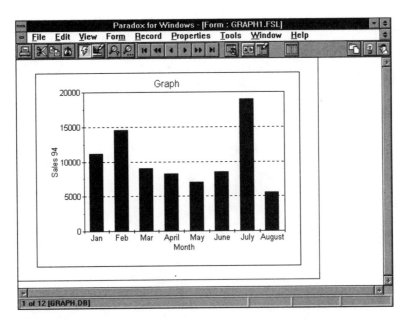

Figure 9.8 *The graph on-screen*

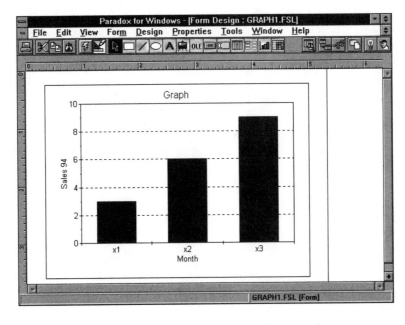

Figure 9.9 *Form Design window for a graph*

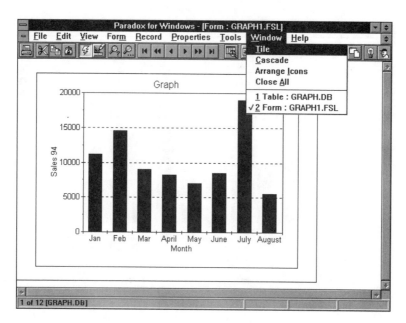

Figure 9.10 *Window menu*

Making Changes in the Design Screen

When making changes to the graph design, use the Paradox property inspection. The procedure for making any changes follows:

1. Move the mouse pointer to the area where you want to make changes.

2. Click the right-mouse button. The property inspection menu appears for that particular component of the graph.

3. Select the option you want to change.

4. Save the file because it is a stand-alone object once it has been created.

Using the property inspection menus, you can adjust the *X*- and *Y*-axis, the title, the color, and the pattern used in the graph, as well as many other design options.

You can also add graphs to reports. Use the same object features to create custom graphs in a report.

N O T E

Changing the Graph Type

In the Graph design screen, adjust the graph type. One of the keys to using graphs is to use the type that best describes the data for your purpose.

1. Click the left mouse button until handles display around the graph. You may need to click several times, because Paradox rotates what is selected, depending on the mouse location, from the largest object to the smallest and then starts over with nothing selected. In Figure 9.11, the handles are correctly selected to change the graph type.

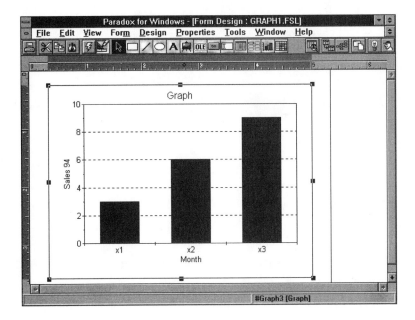

Figure 9.11 *Graph selected*

2. Click the right mouse button. The Graph object inspection menu displays, as shown in Figure 9.12.

N O T E

The object inspection menu varies depending on where the mouse pointer is when you click the mouse button. If you click the right mouse button near the title of the graph, the Title Box property inspection menu displays. If you click the right mouse button near the X-axis, the X-axis property inspection menu displays.

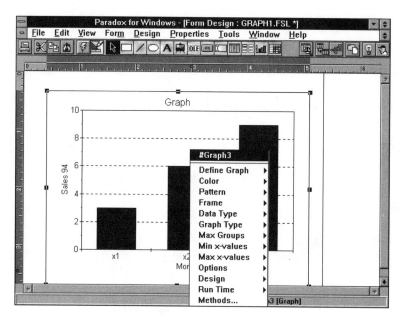

Figure 9.12 *The Graph object inspection menu*

3. Select **Graph Type** from the Graph object inspection menu. The list of available graph types displays, as shown in Figure 9.13. The type that is in use is preceded by a checkmark. In this case it is a **2D Bar** graph.

4. Select the **2D Line** option. The graph in the Graph design screen displays as a two-dimensional line graph. Notice that in Figure 9.14 the graph does not reflect the underlying values from the graph form (**GRAPH1**), it is simply an example of how the data will look.

5. Click on the view data button to see how the real data displays, as shown in Figure 9.15.

Click on the design button to go back to the Graph design screen. The following figures illustrate how data looks with each type of graph. You, too, can select the graph type and then click on the view data button to see how the graph you have selected will display that data.

Click the right mouse button, select the graph type, and view the many different types. Figure 9.16 shows an example of a two-dimensional rotated bar graph. A rotated bar is different from a normal bar graph in one way only, the bars are displayed horizontally instead of vertically.

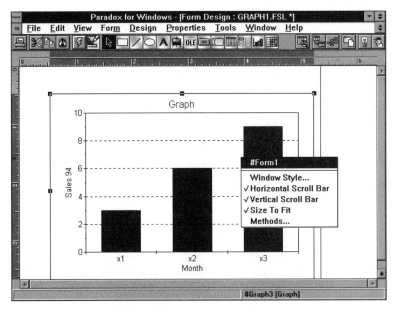

Figure 9.13 Graph types submenu

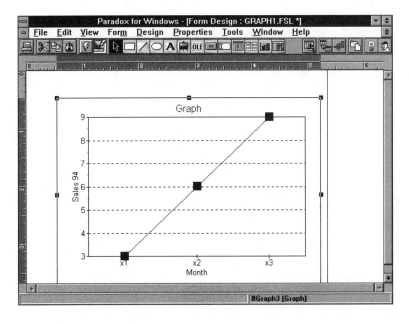

Figure 9.14 Two-dimensional line graph

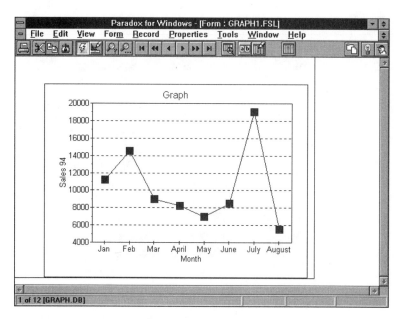

Figure 9.15 *Data in two-dimensional line format*

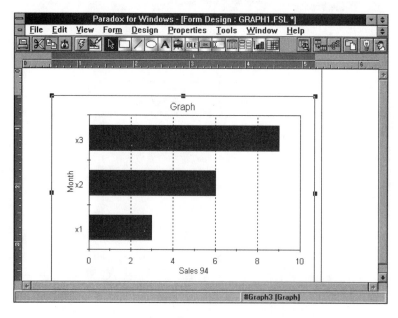

Figure 9.16 *Rotated bar graph*

Figure 9.17 shows the data in a 2D area graph format. An area graph combines the values of the field and makes one large chart. This graph is especially useful for plotting data where you want to see the relationships of each value to the whole. This makes the graph very similar to a pie graph.

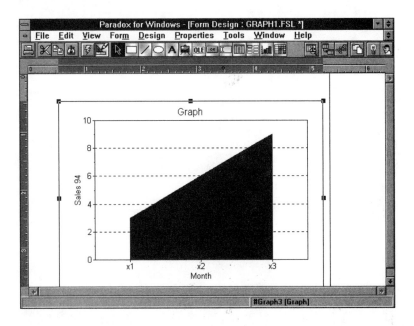

Figure 9.17 *Two-dimensional area graph*

Another way of looking at the data as one whole value is to use the two-dimensional column graph. Each of the values is assigned a percentage as part of the whole. Figure 9.18 shows a two-dimensional column graph.

A pie graph shows each of the values plotted as part of the whole. In Figure 9.19 the month data is plotted, and the labels, in this example the month names, are added to the graph.

Paradox also can display the data with the illusion of depth, thereby adding a three-dimensional effect. Figure 9.20 shows the example chart in three-dimensional bar chart format. A problem arises when the view data button is clicked, as shown in Figure 9.21. As you can see, due to the number of month name labels, they run together at the bottom of the graph. This is not a very effective presentation device. After looking at a few more types of graphs, the way to work around this labeling problem is discussed, later under item entitled "Max-x-values".

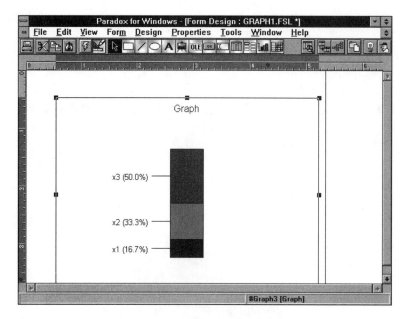

Figure 9.18 *Two-dimensional column graph*

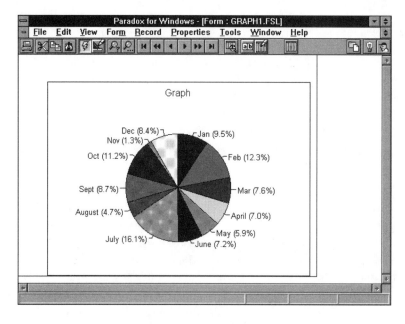

Figure 9.19 *Pie graph of monthly data*

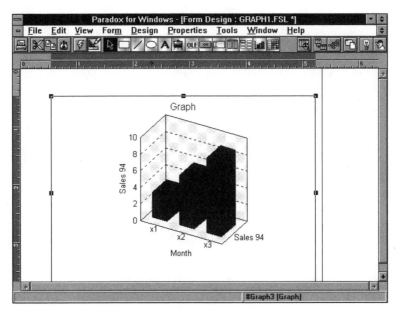

Figure 9.20 *Three-dimensional bar chart*

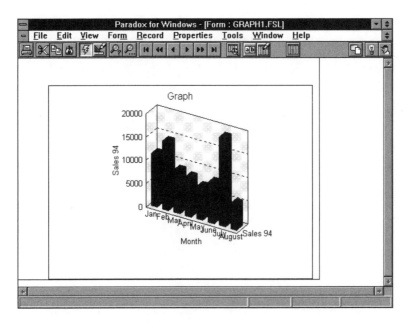

Figure 9.21 *Three-dimensional bar chart with series labels*

There is one more graph example. A ribbon graph represents the data in the same way a line does, except that the line is expanded to look like a strip. Figure 9.22 shows the example ribbon graph.

Using the three-dimensional ribbon graph as an example, let's work on the labeling problem. In Figure 9.23, the view data button has been clicked. The month name labels run together, cluttering the *X*-axis.

Changing the X-Axis Label Display

Any changes made in the display characteristics must be made from the design form screen. In Figure 9.23 the month names ruined the graph.

1. Right click on the graph and, from the menu, click on **Options**. The sub-menu appears, as shown in Figure 9.24. Five new selections appear on this graph. Two are selected by default, the **Show Title** option and the **Show Axes** option.

2. Click on the **Show Axes** option. This action removes the checkmark and closes the menus. To see the effect, switch to the graph of the real data.

3. Click on the view data button. Figure 9.25 shows the results of removing the labels.

4. Click on the design graph button.

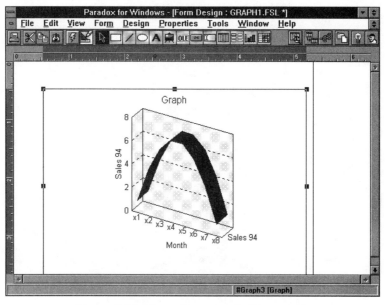

Figure 9.22 *Three-dimensional ribbon graph*

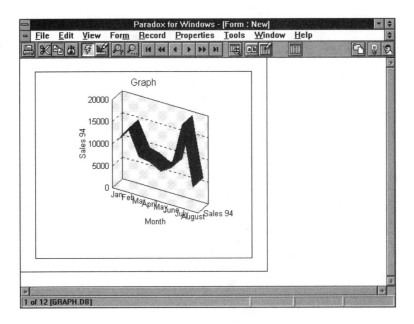

Figure 9.23 *Ribbon graph with too many labels*

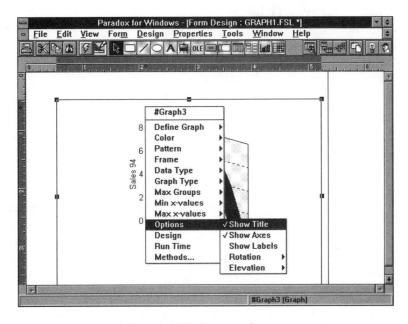

Figure 9.24 *Options submenu*

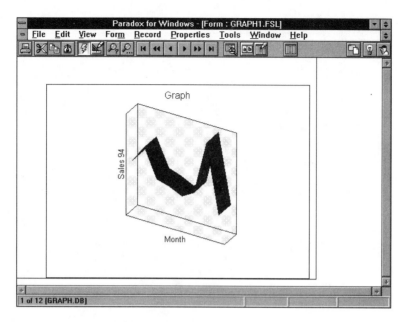

Figure 9.25 *Labels removed from the ribbon graph*

Changing a Graph Title

By default, Paradox uses the table file name as the name at the top of the graph. This default name may or may not be appropriate. Usually, you will want to change the title. To do that, follow these steps.

1. Click once on the graph, so that the object handles appear.

2. Right-click on the word *Graph* at the top of the chart. The object inspection menu appears, as shown in Figure 9.26.

3. Click on the **Title** option. A submenu appears with three options, **Text**, **Font**, and **Use Default**. The **Use Default** option is checked.

4. Click on **Text**. The Enter Title dialog box appears, as shown in Figure 9.27.

5. Type **January to August Sales** The new text appears in the graph, as shown in Figure 9.28.

6. Click on the OK button.

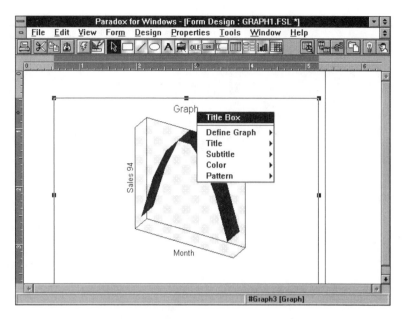

Figure 9.26 *Menu for the title object*

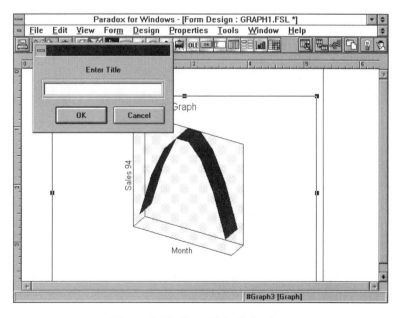

Figure 9.27 *Enter Title dialog box*

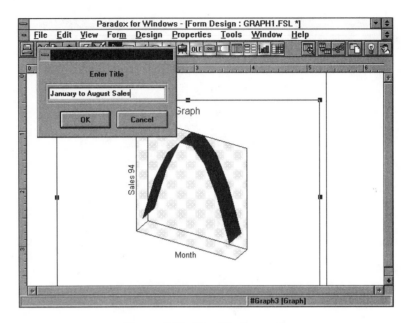

Figure 9.28 *New title for graph*

Let's add a subtitle to the graph.

7. Right-click on the new title to display the object inspection menu.

8. Click on **Subtitle** and type **Record Earnings**! in the Enter Subtitle dialog box.

9. Click on the OK button. Both titles are seen in Figure 9.29.

Other Graph Variables

In addition to the examples that you have already seen, you can make a wide variety of other changes to the graph for the purpose of enhancing the display. Right-clicking on the graph opens the object inspector. From that menu, you have already changed the graph type and modified the display of the *X*-axis. The following options are available on this menu.

▼ **Color.** Click on the **Color** option to open a color palette. Clicking on a particular color fills in the background behind the graph in that color. This is a terrific feature if you are presenting the information on a desktop or have access to a color printer.

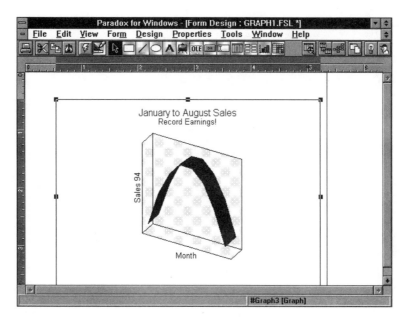

Figure 9.29 *Two titles added to the graph*

▼ **Pattern.** The **Pattern** option causes Paradox to display a submenu with the options of color and style. In Figure 9.30, the Style menu for the background pattern of the graph is shown.

▼ **Frame.** The frame of the graph can be adjusted as to **Style, Color,** and **Thickness**. Make these adjustments carefully in conjunction with the background pattern. A graph that is too busy with stylistic flourishes takes away from the information you are trying to convey in the graph.

▼ **Data Type.** The default setting is **Tabular**. In Figure 9.31 the **2D Summary** option is selected, and the labels have been removed to unclutter the example graph.

▼ **Min x-values. Min x-values** is the minimum number of values represented on the X-axis. In other words, you can select the minimum number of field values that will be presented based on the field you have selected.

▼ **Max x-values.** The **Max x-values** option relates directly to the graph we created earlier, which had 12 values, one for each month of the year, but only 8 months were presented on the graph, as Paradox defaults to 8 as the highest number of values it will plot. To add more values, follow these steps.

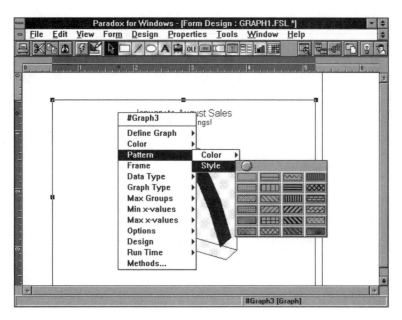

Figure 9.30 *Style palette*

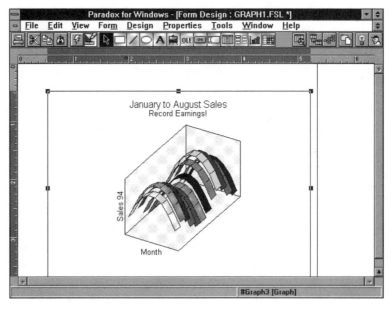

Figure 9.31 *3D Summary example graph*

1. Click on the graph.

2. Right-click to open the object inspector.

3. Click on the **Max x-values** option. The submenu appears.

4. Click on the ellipses at the top of the menu. The dialog box shown in Figure 9.32 appears.

5. In the example of months of the year, type **12** in order to see all the months on one graph.

6. Click on the OK button.

To see the effect of this change, click on the view data button. Now, all 12 months of the year have been included in the graph display. To make the graph accurate, the title must be changed, too. Figure 9.33 shows the graph with all 12 months displayed.

▼ **Options.** Figure 9.34 shows the submenu that appears when the **Options** option is clicked. Each of the options can be turned off and on in order to control the display of the graph. In order to better see the results of using these options, click on the view data button.

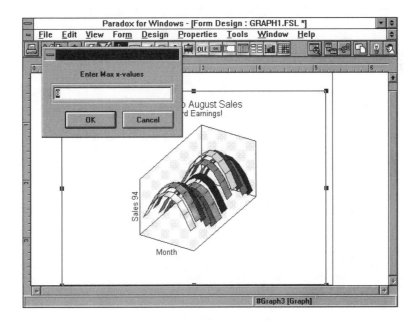

Figure 9.32 *Max x-values dialog box*

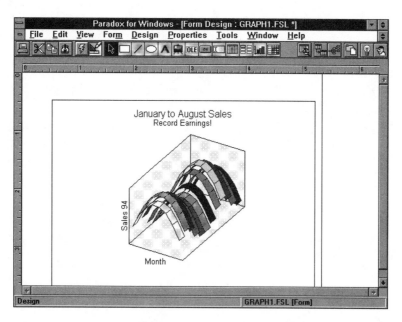

Figure 9.33 *Graph with 12 months displayed*

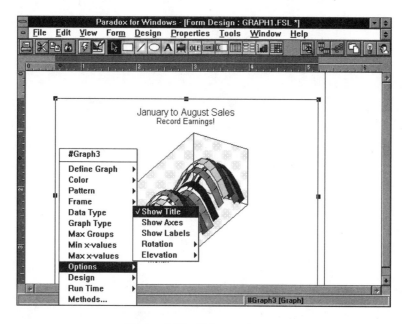

Figure 9.34 *Options submenu*

▼ **Design.** The **Design** option has a submenu, as shown in Figure 9.35. The four options are used to nail down an object within a graph. For example, if you add a boxed title, you may wish to have it remain in a specific location on the graph, despite other design changes you may undertake. So, you can select an object and then use the **Pin Horizontal** or **Pin Vertical** options to anchor the object. The **Contain Objects** option is used when you add two objects to the graph that are related, such as text enclosed in a box. The text is contained with the box. So, this option prevents the text from not moving with the box, if you are redesigning the graph. Last, the **Selectable** option is used to prevent an object in the graph from being changed. Click on the object and then on this option; no change can be made unless you repeat the same steps to turn off the option.

▼ **Run Time and Methods.** The **Run Time** and **Methods** options are used in conjunction with creating an ObjectPAL application. For example, if you create a graph, you can insert a button on the graph, which starts another graph display or prints the graph when clicked.

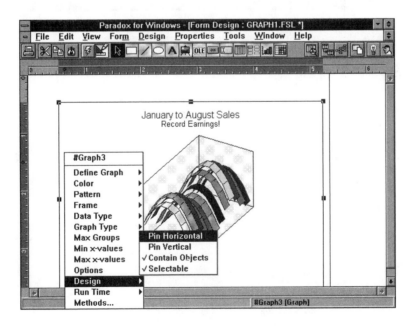

Figure 9.35 *Design submenu*

Changing a Graph Component Using an Object Inspector

In addition to the object inspector for the entire graph, you can right-click on a portion of the graph in order make changes. You must first click on the graph and then click again on the object you want to change. In Figure 9.36, the object inspector is shown. The options are described as follows:

▼ **Define New Y-Value.** Click on this option to select a new field from the underlying table to use as the Y-axis..

▼ **Title.** Click on this option to change the text, or font of the Y-axis title.

▼ **Scale.** The scaling for the Y axis can be auto-scaled by Paradox or if you select Logarithmic, you can enter the range of values to be plotted.

▼ **Ticks.** Select this option to select a font, a number format, a time format or a Timstamp format for the Y-axis.

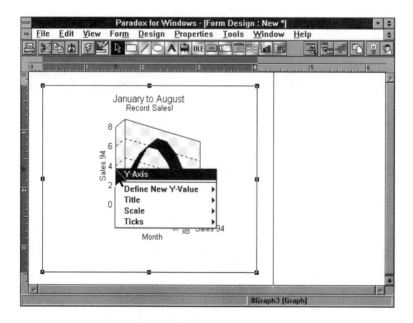

Figure 9.36 *Y-Axis object inspector*

Y-Axis Object Inspector

If you click on the graph where the *Y*-axis title is, the object inspector appears.

Two new options appear on this menu, **Scale** and **Ticks**.

▼ **Scale.** The first **Scale** option is **Auto-Scale**, which Paradox does for you based on the values that are being plotted. In other words, Paradox uses the lowest value and the highest value to determine the number of and the range of the numbers on the *Y*-axis. Click on **Logarithmic** to change the scale to a log of 10. You can also designate the exact low and high values plus the increment between the low and high.

▼ **Ticks.** The **Ticks** option opens a wide range of possibilities for formatting the characters that define the *Y*-values. Figure 9.37 shows the Number Format submenu, which includes all the options you have seen for field values. You can change the Font of the display.

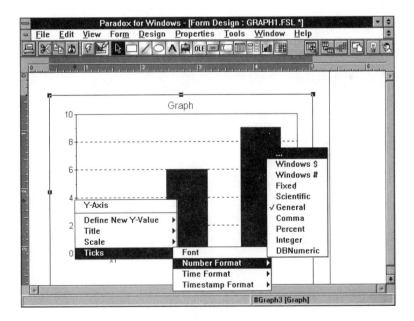

Figure 9.37 *Number Format submenu*

Exploding a Slice of a Pie Graph

Another aspect of graphing is the capability of Paradox to pull one slice out of the whole in order to emphasize that particular value. Follow these steps to explode a pie piece.

1. Move the mouse pointer to the first slice of pie in the design screen.

2. Click on the right mouse button. A property inspection menu displays with three options, **Color**, **Pattern**, and **Explode**. From this menu you can change the color of this piece of pie, after the pattern in which it displays, and explode a piece of pie.

3. Select **Explode**. The selected piece of pie is moved out of the round pie graph. Check how this appears when you view this graph design applied to your data.

4. Click on view data on the SpeedBar. Figure 9.38 shows the graph with 12 months of sales. The piece of pie for the month of January is exploded.

5. Click on the design button on the SpeedBar to return to the design screen.

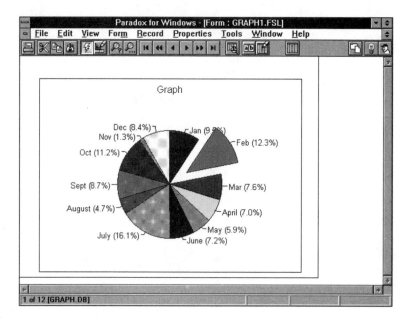

Figure 9.38 *An exploded piece of pie*

Adding a Legend

When more than one field is graphed, add a legend to distinguish the various fields. You must switch the graph type back to a two-dimensional bar graph type to add a legend.

1. Click the right mouse button to get the Graph property inspection menu.

2. Select **Options**.

3. Select **Show Legend**. A legend is inserted at the bottom of the graph design.

Use the property inspection menu to vary the legend. Place the mouse pointer on the legend box or boxes and click the right mouse button. You can then use this menu to adjust the title, color, pattern, and type of information in this legend.

Customizing a Graph Component

When you are graphing more than one field on the *Y*-axis, you will have more than one way to display the data. Another consideration is that, even though you can create your graph on your nice color monitor, if you are able to print only in black and white, you must adjust the patterns so that they appear different when printed.

In the example for this section, we have two fields graphed on the *Y*-axis. You can easily tell the difference between the two fields on the screen. Change the patterns to distinguish the printed version. In this example, a 2D Line graph is used.

1. Point the mouse pointer to one of the boxes that indicates a point on the line graph.

2. Right-click the mouse button. The 1st Series property inspection menu displays. From this menu you can select the *Y*-value, color, pattern, marker, and line characteristics. Because you are adjusting the graph for printing purposes, adjust the marker and the line pattern.

3. Select **Marker**. The Marker options menu displays. From this menu select one marker style.

4. Select **Filled Triangle**.

5. Position the mouse pointer on the 1st Series marker and click the right mouse button.

6. Select **Line** and then **Line Style**. Select a dotted line. The selections you have made display on the Graph design screen.

7. Click on the view data button on the SpeedBar to effect these changes.

Saving a Custom Graph

Return to the design screen by clicking on the design button on the SpeedBar. To save this custom graph, follow these steps.

1. Click on the Design window control button and select **Close**. A dialog box asks you if you want to save the custom graph.

2. Click on **Yes**. The custom graph is saved.

Recalling a Saved Graph

Graphs that are designed in the Form Design screen are recalled through the File menu.

1. Select **File/Open/Form**. The Open Document dialog box displays.

2. Click on the name of the graph file you want to open. Click on the OK button. The graph displays on-screen in a form window.

Summary

Good luck using Paradox for Windows! It is a powerful database management program, with much to offer.

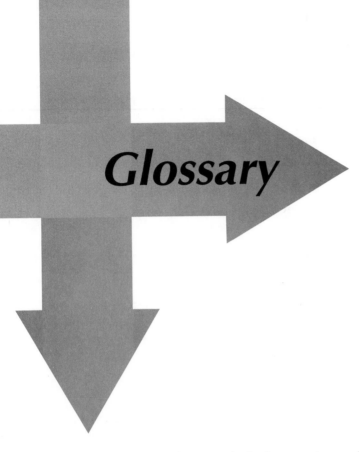

Glossary

Active. The object or window to which the next keystroke or mouse action applies.

Alphanumeric Field. A field type that holds letters and/or numbers.

Answer Table A temporary table that stores the results of a query. It is the answer to the question.

Arithmetic Operators. The operators used to create arithmetic expressions, such as +, -, *, and /. See *Operators*.

Arrow Keys. The keys found on the keyboard that point in four directions. They are used to move the highlight in the direction of the arrow.

Ascending Order. Data sorted from low to high. The alphabet would start with *A* going to *Z*. Numbers start with the lowest number. Dates start with the earliest date.

Axis. Either the horizontal (*X*-axis) or vertical (*Y*-axis) line used to define the range of values plotted on a graph.

Band. Horizontal section found on the report generator that controls the placement of text entered in the band. For example, text entered in the page band is printed on every page of a report.

Binary Field. A field used to store data Paradox is unable to interpret. An example of data held in a binary field is the data that produce sound.

Blank Field. A field that contains no value.

Box. A design object you can place in forms and reports.

Button. The icons represented on the SpeedBar. See *Icon* and *SpeedBar.*

Cancel. Option found in several dialog boxes that stops the action you are doing and returns you to the main workspace.

Cascading Menu. A menu displayed as a result of choosing an option on another menu.

Character. Number, letter, and/or symbol that appears in the workspace.

Check Box. A box you can check or clear to turn an option on or off.

Checkmark. The symbol used in a query table that indicates the fields to be included in the answer table.

Click. To press and release the mouse button.

Clipboard. An area used by Paradox for Windows that temporarily stores information. Use the data stored in the Clipboard to copy and paste from one location to another.

Color Palette. The tool used to apply colors to Paradox objects using property inspection.

Column. The vertical segment of a table that holds the fields of data. A column usually has a name that describes the contents of the field in that column.

Command. A word on a menu or button that you choose to perform an action.

Comparison Operators. The operators used in a query to compare two values, such as <, >, >=, <=, and =.

Copy. To duplicate data or information and save it on the clipboard.

Crosstab. A spreadsheet-like version of three related fields that form the same table. The crosstab is used to create graphs comparing two fields to another field.

Currency Field. A field containing numbers, formatted to display decimal places and a currency symbol.

Cut. To remove information form the workspace, either to discard or to save on the Clipboard.

Data. Information or facts held in fields and records.

Database. An organized collection of information.

Data Integrity. The assurance that the values in a table are protected from corruption.

Data Type. The type of data a field can contain. See *Field Type*.

Date Field. A field that holds dates. A vertical column in a table where the entries are formatted as date data types.

Default Action. The setting used by the computer and printer, unless you specify or select an alternative.

Default Form. The form used by the computer, unless you specify an alternative.

Default Properties. The properties of any object used by the computer, unless you specify an alternative.

Default Value. In validity checks, the value automatically entered in a field if no other value is entered.

Define. To attach a design object to data from a table. For example, you define a field object in a form as a field in a table.

Descending Order. Data sorted from high to low. The alphabet would start with *Z*, going to *A*. Numbers start with the highest number. Dates start with the latest date and go to the earliest.

Design Document. A form or report that you create or modify in a design window.

Design Object. An object you can place in forms and reports. Use the SpeedBar tools to create design objects.

Design Window. The window where you create or modify the design of a form or report.

Desktop. The main window in Paradox.

Dialog Box. A box or window that displays on-screen and that requests or provides information. Often options are displayed. Some dialog boxes display warnings or error messages.

Double-click. To press and release the mouse button two times, very quickly.

Drag. To move an object across the screen by clicking the mouse button, holding it down, and then moving the pointer to the new location.

Drop-down List Box. A single-line text box that opens to display more options when you click a down-pointing arrow. It is often found in dialog boxes.

Edit. To change information contained in tables by altering, correcting, adding, or deleting information.

Edit Mode. A state in Paradox for Windows in which editing can take place.

Example Element. The part of a query that specifies how data from one table should be linked to data from another table.

Exclusive Link. The part of a query that allows you to use an example element to retrieve from one table only those records that match the reports in another table.

Field. A single piece of data in a record found in a vertical column. See also *Column.*

Field Type. The specified kind of information a column (field) can contain. Some field types are alphanumeric, number, and short integer.

Field Value. The data contained in one field of a record.

Field View. An editing mode that allows you to move in a field, character by character.

File. Related information stored under one name on a disk. Many Paradox objects, such as tables and scripts, are held in files.

Font. The typeface in which characters appear. It is the style that determines how characters look.

Font Palette. The display that lists the font options available to you. Use this tool to apply typefaces, font sizes, styles, and colors.

Footer. Text that displays at the bottom of every page of a report. Create footers in the report design screen.

Form. The view of data seen one record at a time. You specify where the fields are located in form view.

Function Keys. The keys labeled **F1** through **F10** or **F12**, depending on your keyboard. These keys are designed to carry out complex actions in one keystroke.

Graphic. A computer picture you place in a graphic field or in a graphic object.

Grid. Horizontal and vertical lines in design windows that aid you in placing objects. You may choose to show or hide the grid.

Group. Records that have certain values in common, placing them in the same set. Groups can be sorted based on similar field values, certain numbers of records, or any other criteria you wish.

Group Band. One of the horizontal areas in the report design screen that controls how records are grouped in a report.

Header. Text that displays at the top of every page in a report. Create headers in the report design screen.

Help. A display of information intended to provide assistance with the task you are trying to complete. Press **F1** to access the Help window at any time.

Highlight. A reverse video shaded area or bolded letters meant to make some words stand out on the workspace.

Icon. A picture or graphic representation of an object in Paradox for Windows.

Insertion Point. The exact location where text inserts when you type. It is indicated by a thin flashing vertical bar.

Insert Mode. The editing mode where characters typed into text push characters that were already there to the right. When in a field edit, you can switch between insert mode and overwrite mode. See *Overwrite Mode.*

Inspect. To view or look at the properties of an object. Right-click the mouse button to view the property menu. From the menu, can see the properties that pertain to that object.

Installation. The process of placing the Paradox for Windows program on a hard disk, preparing it for operation.

Key. Fields established in Paradox that are used to search and locate records. Key fields help prevent duplicate records and help sort and search records more quickly.

Label. Brief explanations found on the axes of graphs to represent the values indicated by the graduated marks on the graph. A label may also indicate what data is found in a field, form, or report.

Legend. Explanations found next to a graph to indicate which line, pattern, or color represents which value on the graph.

Link. The association between tables based on the relational data in the tables. Links are established using Joining elements.

List Box. Areas in a dialog box that holds several items from which you can select an option.

Lock. An option you place in tables that prevents other users from viewing, changing, or locking a table while one user is already working with it.

Logical Operator. One of three types of operators used in queries. The logical operators are AND, OR, or NOT.

Lookup Table. A table that holds information that is referenced by another table. A lookup table is used to make sure values entered in one table are valid, in that they actually exist on the lookup table.

Main Menu. The options displayed across the top of the screen when you open Paradox for Windows.

Message Window. The dialog box that displays to relay some information about your current activity.

Number Field. A field that holds only numbers, and a decimal, or a positive or negative indicator.

Object. Any item on the Desktop. In Paradox, an Object can be a table, a single field, a label, a report text box, or the report itself.

Object Inspector. A feature that lets you view an object's property menu when you right-click on the object. See *Inspect.*

ObjectPAL. The application language used to customize Paradox for Windows.

OLE. The acronym that stands for Object Linking and Embedding. The link that is used to insert files from OLE servers into Paradox tables or OLE objects.

Operator. The indicator that tells which kind of action will take place with numbers or field values. Examples of operators are + (addition), - (subtraction), * (multiplication), / (division), <= (less than or equal to), and = (equal). Operators can be used to create field values or report values or to indicate query selections.

Overwrite Mode. The editing mode where characters are typed and replace characters that already exist. See *Insert Mode.*

Page Band. The section of a report that contains data to be printed at the top and bottom of each page.

PAL. See *ObjectPAL.*

Palette. A visual representation of property choices. Palettes show you the options available to you while inspecting an object.

Point. To position the mouse arrow over an object or area in a screen.

Pointer. The visual marker, usually an arrow, that indicates the mouse location on the screen.

Primary Key. A key field index used to help sort and locate records in a Paradox for Windows table.

Prompt. A message from Paradox for Windows, placed in a dialog box or below the menu line. The prompt usually is set up to accept some typed information from you or to inform you what you are doing at the moment.

Properties. The characteristics of an object. Right-click the mouse button to view or change the properties. Examples of properties are size, color, number format, font, and alignment. See *Inspect.*

QBE. See *Query By Example.*

Query. A question asked about, or a task specified of, the data held in Paradox tables.

Query By Example. A method of designing a query where you provide an example of what you are looking for when you ask a question of the information contained in your database.

Query Statement. A series of commands that define a query. The statement fills out query images in the query window.

Record. One row in a database table that holds a group of related fields. A table is made up of a group of records. See also *Row.*

Record Band. The section in the report design screen that contains the records of the table on which you are reporting.

Record Number. A unique number that identifies each record in a Paradox for Windows table.

Referential Integrity. A method of ensuring that the ties between data in separate tables cannot be broken.

Relational Database. an organized collection of information based on the relational model of information.

Report. Organized information, taken from database tables, that is printed on paper.

Report Band. A section of a report that holds data to be printed at the beginning and end of the report.

Restructure. To move fields, change fields, or adjust the field type in a table.

Right-Click. To press and release the right mouse button.

Row. The horizontal segment of a table that holds a group of related fields.

Scale. The range of values indicated on a graph by tick marks on either the vertical (*Y*) or horizontal (*X*) axis.

Sidebar. The vertical bar found on the left side of the Report Design window. Use the sidebar to insert page breaks.

Sort Order. To arrange records as either ascending or descending.

Special Field. A field placed in a design document that acts as a template to print special information when the document is printed. Examples of special information are Today, Now, and Page Number.

SpeedBar. The set of icon buttons found on the Paradox for Windows screen that are tools for frequently performed tasks. The SpeedBar is located under the menu bar and varies depending on the active window.

String. An expression consisting of alphanumeric characters.

Structure. The organization of a table specifying the order of fields, field types, key fields, and the number of fields in a table.

Summary Field. A field placed in a form or report that displays a computed value in the printed document.

Summary Operator. One of the operators placed in the summary field. Examples of summary operators are average, count, minimum, and maximum.

Table. Categories of information held in rows (records) and columns (fields).

Table Frame. A design object placed in a report or form that represents a table.

Temporary Palette. A palette that displays on-screen only until you make a selection from the palette.

Temporary Table. A table that certain Paradox for Windows operations create. It lasts only until you change your private directory or end the Paradox for Windows session.

Text Object. A design object placed in a form or report used to display text.

Typeface. One characteristic of the font. Various styles are available in Paradox for Windows. The number of typefaces available varies with the ability of your printer to print them.

Undo. A command that reverses any edits or changes made in reverse order.

Validity Check. A check you place on values to determine whether the data can be entered (whether it is valid according to another table). In addition, conditions such as minimum, maximum, picture specifications, and required entry can also be validated.

Wildcard Operators. Characters used in a query to match patterns or strings of characters.

Workspace. An area on the screen where images and characters are placed to be worked on.

Index